Taboo

Taboo looks at the ethnographer and sexuality in anthropological fieldwork and considers the many roles that erotic subjectivity plays in the production of anthropological knowledge and texts.

In this pioneering volume anthropologists discuss their own sexual and erotic experiences in the field, and use those experiences to reflect on problems with the way anthropology is thought about and practiced. How do the gender roles and sexual identities that anthropologists have in their 'home' societies affect the kinds of sexuality they can express in other cultures? How is the anthropologist's sexuality perceived by the people with whom she or he does research? How common is sexual violence and intimidation in the field, and why is its existence virtually unmentioned in anthropology? These are just a few of the questions addressed by the contributions, which will set the agenda for a critical exploration of why and how sexuality and taboos against sex have affected the practice and production of anthropology.

A long-overdue text for all students and lecturers of anthropology and cultural studies, *Taboo* will also appeal to sociologists, feminist scholars and students of queer theory.

Don Kulick is Associate Professor in the Department of Anthropology at Stockholm University, Sweden. **Margaret Willson** is a Lecturer and Research Associate in the Department of Anthropology at Western Washington University, USA.

Taboo

Sex, identity, and erotic subjectivity in anthropological fieldwork

Edited by
Don Kulick and
Margaret Willson

London and New York

First published 1995
by Routledge
11 New Fetter Lane, London EC4P 4EE

Simultaneously published in the USA and Canada
by Routledge
29 West 35th Street, New York, NY 10001

Tyepset in Sabon by
J&L Composition Ltd, Filey, North Yorkshire
Printed and bound in Great Britain by T.J. Press (Padstow) Ltd, Padstow, Cornwall

British Library Cataloguing in Publication Data
A catalogue record for this book is available from the British Library

Library of Congress Cataloguing in Publication Data
A catalogue record for this book has been requested

ISBN 0–415–08818–6 (hbk)
ISBN 0–415–08819–4 (pbk)

For
Jonas Schild Tillberg
and
Elizabeth Willson

Contents

Notes on contributors

Kate Altork is a practicing psychotherapist and cultural anthropologist. She recently completed her Ph.D. thesis, entitled *Land Running Through the Bones: An Ethnography of Place* (Union Institute, 1994). In 1992, she was awarded the Prize for Poetry from the American Anthropological Association's Society for Humanistic Anthropology. In 1993, she was awarded their Prize for Fiction. She is currently working on a series of essays addressing the intersection of person, place, and passionate attachment.

Evelyn Blackwood is assistant professor of women's studies and anthropology at Purdue University, Indiana. Her previous publications include work on Native American female *berdache*/two-spirit people and lesbian relations cross-culturally. She is the editor of the volume *The Many Faces Of Homosexuality: Anthropological Approaches to Homosexual Behavior* (Harrington Park Press, 1986). She is currently working on a monograph about Minangkabau gender, kinship and identity.

Ralph Bolton is professor of anthropology at Pomona College, California, where he teaches courses on human sexuality and AIDS. He is the editor of *The AIDS Pandemic: A Global Emergency* (Gordon and Breach, 1989) and *The Content of Culture* (HRAF Press, 1989). He co-edited the volumes *Rethinking AIDS Prevention: Cultural Approaches* (Gordon and Breach, 1992) and *The Anthropology of AIDS: Syllabi and Other Teaching Resources* (American Anthropological Association, 1992). His most recent articles have appeared in *Human Organization*,

GLQ: a Journal of Lesbian and Gay Studies, and the *Archives of Sexual Behavior*.

Jill Dubisch is professor of anthropology at Northern Arizona University. She has served as Secretary of the Modern Greek Studies Association (1991–93) and President of the Society for the Anthropology of Europe (1992–94). During the past 25 years, she has studied rural–urban migration, gender, and religion in Greece, and is editor of the volume *Gender and Power in Rural Greece* (Princeton University Press, 1986), and author of *In a Different Place: Gender, Politics, and Pilgrimage at a Greek Island Shrine* (Princeton University Press, 1995). Her current research focuses on religion and national identity.

Jean Gearing completed her doctoral dissertation, entitled *The Reproduction of Labor in a Migration Society: Gender, Kinship, and Household in St. Vincent, West Indies*, in 1988, and spent several years after that as a sojourning scholar, holding temporary teaching positions in Alabama, Nevada, and Florida. She is a postdoctoral fellow at the Division of Reproductive Health at the Centers for Disease Control, working with international family planning programmes. She is also an adjunct faculty member at Georgia State University. Jean lives in Atlanta with her son, who is now ten years old. Her former husband, E.C., is also still living in the U.S.

Andrew P. Killick is a doctoral student in ethnomusicology at the University of Washington. His M.A. thesis at the University of Hawaii, 'New Music for Korean Instruments: An Analytical Survey' (1990), is the fruit of the field experiences described in the article in this volume. He is currently in Seoul carrying out research for his doctoral dissertation, '*Ch'angguk*: The Dramatization of Korean *P'ansori* Narratives'.

Don Kulick is associate professor of anthropology at Stockholm University, Sweden. He has edited two volumes in Swedish on cross-cultural approaches to gender, sexuality and emotions: *Från Kön Till Genus* ('*From Sex to Gender*', Carlssons Bokförlag, 1987) and *Att Begå Kärlek* ('*To Commit Love*', Sesam Bokförlag, 1990), and is also the author of *Language Shift and Cultural Reproduction: Socialization, Self and Syncretism in a Papua New Guinean Village* (Cambridge University Press, 1992). He is currently researching language and the practice of gender among transgendered prostitutes in Brazil.

Eva Moreno (a pseudonym) is currently teaching and doing research at a Swedish University.

Helen Morton currently holds a Research Fellowship in the Gender Studies Research Unit in the Department of History, University of Melbourne, Australia. Her doctoral dissertation on child socialization in Tonga is being published by the University of Hawaii Press and is entitled *Becoming Tongan: An Ethnography of Childhood*. Her current research focuses on gender and cultural identity among Tongan migrants in Melbourne.

Margaret Willson is a visiting lecturer at Western Washington University. She conducted her Ph.D. research among Chinese immigrants in Papua New Guinea and has done post-doctoral research in Papua New Guinea and Brazil. She has also worked extensively with ethnographic film, and recently finished directing a film on concepts of vision among the blind. Her current research is on race, class, and gender among Afro-Brazilian players of *capoiera* in northeastern Brazil.

Preface

While the theoretical concerns that underlie the planning and organization of this volume are detailed in our separate introductory and concluding chapters, the original impetus for the book arose, in a perhaps not uncommon way, from much more mundane musings. We first met one another in Port Moresby, the capital city of Papua New Guinea, in a university-owned guest house that functions as a kind of dormitory for visiting scholars. We had both been conducting fieldwork in different parts of the country for many months, and we were back in the capital sorting out bureaucratic problems and having a break. As we began getting to know one another over mugs of wine and sighs of relief about being out of our respective fieldsites for a while, we surprised one another by noticing that one of the topics we were both very keen on discussing was that of sex in the field. Neither of us had had any erotic relationships in the field, and we found ourselves trying to understand why we both felt that we shouldn't, and what might happen if we did. Since we are both attracted to men, all we could really do about sex, between the two of us, was talk about it. And talk about it we did, in a discussion that has extended over many years and several continents, and that has resulted now, finally, in this volume.[1]

As one might imagine, soliciting contributions for the topic addressed in this book was not particularly easy. We quickly discovered that although many anthropologists greatly enjoy gossiping about fieldwork sexual relations (their own, and, especially, those of their colleagues), very few are willing to write about them. One of the many things we learned as we solicited contributions, however, was that received wisdom about who is most willing to discuss sex publicly is inaccurate. In the scanty literature that mentions anthropological sexuality in the field, we discovered a recurring assumption that women, for all their talk about gender, are unwilling to talk about sex. For example, Pat Caplan, in her introduction to a recent anthology on the importance of the anthropologist's gender in fieldwork, finds it 'striking' that while several men in the volume discuss sexuality 'only one woman . . . is courageous enough to discuss it at any length and no woman acknowledges a sexual experience in the field' (1993: 23). Whitehead and Conaway, in another anthology, entitled *Self, Sex and Gender in Cross-Cultural Fieldwork*, summarize their cursory review of previous literature by concluding that '[w]hen males have addressed sex and gender issues in fieldwork they have dealt more with issues of sexual desire or sexual behavior than with the broader issues of the gender [*sic*] self. More recent work by women . . . continues to concentrate only [!] on the field experiences of women' (1986: 4). Even Esther Newton, in her important article on the erotic dimension in fieldwork, implies that female anthropologists are less likely than their male colleagues to write about their erotic experiences in the field (1993: 14).

We disagree. In fact, in preparing this volume and discussing it with colleagues, we experienced exactly the opposite of what the above writers report. Those anthropologists who responded most warmly and enthusiatically to the idea of this book were women (both heterosexual and lesbian) and gay men. The only ones for whom we were repeatedly called on to justify the volume were heterosexual men, many of whom responded with suspicion or even hostility. The only people who actually tried to talk us out of doing the book (usually with the 'think-of-the-damage-this-will-do-to-your-careers' hex) were all heterosexual males. Perhaps because of the way many heterosexual men define both sexuality and their careers, they were also the most elusive as we solicited contributions, and the book nearly went to press without a contribution from a heterosexual male. Our point in relating this is not to wag fingers or stereotype. It is, simply, to note that the resistance to the volume that we have encountered has not been general, but has instead been gendered and sexed. In addition, we make this explicit because we think it is important to counter the idea (which in our experience is completely unfounded) that female anthropologists are squeamish about talking sex.

Having said that, however, we would also reiterate Caplan's important observation that 'for women sexual activity, or, even more so, "confessing" it, still has very different consequences than [for] men' (1993: 23). Because of those different consequences, we think it highly significant that the majority of the contributions in this volume are written by women. We hope that the richness of those contributions will inspire other women to actively contest the sexist and homophobic attitudes and practices within anthropology that continue to make it difficult and risky for them to write about many of the issues, such as sexual violence and sexual agency, that concern them deeply as women and as anthropologists.

The contributions appearing here were solicited in a number of ways. We heard Jill Dubisch give an early version of what later developed into her chapter at the 1991 American Anthropological Association Meetings, and we solicited it on the spot. Two contributions were solicited by directly contacting people we knew were interested in the topic, or who had written about some aspect of sexuality in a way that led us to believe that they might be interested in the topic. In addition, we also placed a call for papers in the cooperation column of the *Anthropology Newsletter.* That call for papers was blocked for several months, because, we were told when we phoned up to enquire why it wasn't appearing, the editors were concerned that our volume would 'encourage people to commit criminal acts'! During the course of a long conversation, it became clear that the editors had not really read what we had written, but had simply assumed that a volume on erotic subjectivity in fieldwork must, by definition, be unethical. We finally managed to convince them to publish the call. In response to that call for papers, we were contacted by a number of people, several of whom we eventually invited to contribute to the volume. The fact that the majority of chapters here are written by scholars whom we did not know prior to working with them on this book has taught us the great value of soliciting cooperation among unknown colleagues, and of not relying solely, as is so often the case with edited volumes, on one's own, necessarily limited, personal network.

Inevitably, there are lacunae, which we hope will compel others to engage critically with the book, and extend and prolong the discussion of the issues raised here. We ourselves feel that the most glaring lacuna is the absence of voices from members of communities in which anthropologists have worked. Of course, this is not a lack particular to this volume – the absence of informant perspectives on the agenda and behavior of anthropologists is a standard and serious flaw with anthropology as an epistemological project. What we have noticed, however, is that the issues raised in this book seem to be singularly effective ones for highlighting precisely that flaw. We have observed that scholars who habitually read anthropological monographs and articles without worrying overly that informants are not given equal time to air their views on the anthropologist suddenly become agitated about this lack of informant perspectives as soon as the topic turns to the erotic subjectivity of the ethnographer. While we would be the first to agree that this is a genuine concern, we believe that much of the agitation we have heard expressed on this point is not so much 'about' concern for informants as it is 'about' unease with the embarrassing issues of hierarchy, boundaries, ethics, anthropological appropriation, and exploitation that surface rapidly as soon as we begin speaking about desire, erotic subjectivity, and sexual violence in the field. As it happens, those are the issues detailed in this book; they are the dimensions that inform the 'sexuality' discussed here; that is what the book is about. Therefore, the volume will succeed to the extent that it provokes debate and reinvigorates discussion about power, privilege and perspective in anthropological fieldwork and writing.

Don Kulick
Margaret Willson
Vashon Island, Washington
13 April 1994

Note

1 Readers who wonder why neither of us has contributed an ethnographically based chapter to this collection should know that our decision not to write about ourselves was influenced by a number of factors. One of our prime ambitions with this book has been to allow contributors the space they need to develop a coherent, theoretically challenging argument. We feel that a general problem with fieldwork anthologies is that they frequently contain too many short, anecdotal papers. We wanted to avoid this here. In addition, we were also given a specific word limit by our publisher. Since we hope that the book will be used by students, we had to be very aware of what it would cost; hence we had to be careful not to exceed that word limit. So, we were faced with a decision: how much of the volume's limited space did we want to take up ourselves?

We both agreed early on that the volume should include an introduction and afterword, which we, as editors, would write. We also agreed that any individual contribution we would write in addition would probably build on many of the same ideas that we wanted to develop in the introduction and the afterword. Therefore, we felt that the volume would be stronger and would exhibit a wider range of perspectives if, instead of authoring two papers each, we invited others to analyze their experiences.

Of course, we could have written the introduction and the afterword in such a way as to include a discussion of our own erotic subjectivity in the field. For a number of largely textual reasons, however, we both found this impossible to do. We regret this, but at the same time, we do not imagine that this book will be the last word on the matter of erotic subjectivity and sex in the field. It is our hope that the issues raised in this volume will provoke extended debate within anthropology and other social sciences. We look forward to continued engagement with that debate, and we anticipate that that engagement will provide us with future opportunities to write about issues, emotions, and experiences that we have been unable to include here.

References

Caplan, Pat (1993) 'Introduction 2: The Volume', in Diane Bell, Pat Caplan, and Wazir Jahan Karim (eds) *Gendered Fields: Women, Men and Ethnography*. London and New York: Routledge.

Newton, Esther (1993) 'My Best Informant's Dress: The Erotic Equation in Fieldwork'. *Cultural Anthropology*. Vol. 8, No. 1, pp. 3–23.

Whitehead, Tony Larry and Mary Ellen Conaway (eds) (1986) 'Introduction', in *Self, Sex and Gender in Cross-Cultural Fieldwork*. Urbana and Chicago: University of Illinois Press.

Introduction

The sexual life of anthropologists: erotic subjectivity and ethnographic work

Don Kulick

> Malinowski was certainly not the only fieldworker troubled by the sex problem
>
> (Hsu 1979: 518)

> Is sex always about 'sex'?
>
> (Goldstein 1991: 205)

> In the field of sex, as I have remarked, it is only to-day that investigation has become possible.
>
> (Havelock Ellis, Preface to Malinowski's *The Sexual Life of Savages*, 1987 [1929]: liv)

This book, which is a collection of papers in which anthropologists discuss desire, erotic relations, and sexual encounters between themselves and members of the communities in which they conducted fieldwork, is a perhaps inevitable consequence of two events: the posthumous publication of Bronislaw Malinowski's *A Diary in the Strict Sense of the Term* in 1967, and the reflexive turn in the discipline that rose to prominence during the 1980s.

Malinowski's *Diary*, which revealed that the legendary Father of Us All 'was not, to put it delicately, an umitigated nice guy' (Geertz 1983: 56), unexpectedly flicked on a light switch in the murky and unacknowledged realm of the anthropologist's sexuality in the field. Rather than remain visible for inspection, however, the issue of whether anthropologists in fact do ever have sex with members of the communities in which they work, and what it might mean if they do, quickly scuttled away again, as anthropologists stood with their backs nervously turned, huffing about the ethics of publishing the *Diary*, and quibbling among themselves about whether Malinowski's licentiousness and colonialist mentality were really relevant to an understanding of his anthropology.

The term 'reflexivity' in anthropology can mean many things, but at its most basic, 'it makes a problem out of what was once unproblematic: the figure of the fieldworker' (Strathern 1991: 8). Problematizing this once self-confident figure has meant subjecting it to scrutiny and criticism: 'What is its basis for "knowing"?', people now ask. 'How does it collect its information? How does it author its accounts? For whom? To what effect?' Questions like these have enriched anthropology by dealing the death blow to the myth of anthropological objectivity, finally putting that out of its misery, and by prodding anthropologists into examining the historical, cultural, and political conditions that must be in place for anthropology to make sense as a field of enquiry and as a methodological and textual practice.

Those unsympathetic to all this attention on the fieldworker charge that reflexive anthropology is only about the 'freedom to engage in mystification and creative self-empowering fabrication unaccountable to any challenge of logic or fact' (Sangren 1988: 414). Ian Jarvie criticizes reflexive anthropologists for 'feigning radicalism', and labels the whole trend 'navel-gazing' (1988: 428). Scholars who agree with Jarvie may have many more belittling things to say about this volume, which brings into purview more than navels. Such people are likely to see the volume as nothing more than the dreaded upshot of a trend that is, by its very nature, they may contend, masturbatory. My co-editor and I have already encountered such reactions during the planning and preparation of the book, and they do not really surprise us, for reasons I will be discussing below. Here I would note what does surprise us – what, in fact, has confounded us for some time, and what led to our interest in this topic; namely, that a critical examination of the anthropologist as a sexual subject has taken such a long time to emerge within the discipline.

Sex is far from new or taboo in anthropology. Quite the opposite: anthropology has always trafficked in the sexuality of the people we study. Early debates about the origins of society and of the evolution of fundamental social forms such as kinship and the family hinged on Euro-American understandings of the sexual relations of 'primitive' peoples – Were they monogamous? Promiscuous? Incestuous? That the second major monograph of one of anthropology's most important figures was titillatingly entitled *The Sexual Life of Savages* (Malinowski 1987 [1929]) is no fluke. (Of course, that Malinowski was later to become remembered more for his own brazen fantasies than for his analysis of the sexuality of the Trobriand islanders is one of the great, and perhaps particularly apt, ironies of anthropology's fixation with both sex and savages.) Nor is it mere fortuity that the best-known American anthropologist initiated her career with a book detailing, among other things, the sexual experiences of adolescent girls in a 'primitive' society (Mead 1949 [1928]).

Sex – their sex, the sex of 'the Other' – has always constituted one of the gawdiest exhibits in the anthropological sideshow. It has provided endless fodder for reflection, speculation, and flourish. In pondering what it is that anthropologists actually do, one can readily agree with Clifford Geertz that much anthropological work (and a great deal of the fun in doing that work) consists of 'keep[ing] the world off balance . . . pulling out rugs, upsetting tea tables, setting off firecrackers' (1984: 275). But to that list of mischief, one might add a time-tested shenanigan that Geertz neglected: peeping through keyholes and broadcasting what we see there. Thus, in addition to Geertz's 'Australopithicenes, Tricksters, Clicks and Megaliths' (1984: 275), anthropologists also peddle polyandry, puberty houses, *baloma* conceptions, subincision, ghost marriage, ritual defloration, chiefly incest, homosexual insemination, and sleep crawling. Merchants of astonishment indeed.

Throughout all the decades of concern with the sex lives of others, anthropologists have remained very tight-lipped about their own sexuality. A main reason for this reticence, of course, has to do with the way that anthropology was constituted as a science dedicated to the objective recording and analysis of the habits and customs of other people. Within this framework, as Kevin Dwyer has pointed out, observation was considered to be 'an objective act that in no way influenced the object's true significance, a significance that existed prior to the act of observing it' (1982: 257). Therefore, the biography and position of the researcher did not matter. Textually, ethnographers achieved this pose of not mattering by making themselves invisible. As Clifford (1988), Geertz (1988), and many others (Marcus and Fischer 1986; articles in Clifford and Marcus 1986 and in Okely and Callaway 1992) have documented, researchers established their authority at the beginning of their accounts with a tumultuous or difficult arrival scene and/or a claim to fluency in a local language, and then they proceeded to vanish from their texts.

Other reasons for the absence of accounts of the erotic subjectivity and experiences of anthropologists are the concomitant disciplinary disdain for personal narratives (which, as Pratt (1986: 31) has noted, 'are often deemed self-indulgent, trivial, or heretical'), and more general cultural taboos about discussing sex – our own sex, anyway. But there is more to it even than this, for if the absence of accounts of the sexuality of anthropologists in the field was simply a corollary of myths of objectivity, modernist textual practices, and Protestant prudery, then one would have expected the revisionist wave of reflexivity to have washed up at least a couple of serious treatments of the topic by now, heretical or no.

This, unfortunately, and very pointedly, has not happened. In her pathbreaking article on 'the erotic equation in fieldwork', Esther Newton has recently suggested a possible reason why. Newton argues that 'the black hole enveloping this nonsubject' (1993: 4) serves the dual purpose of fortifying heterosexual male subjectivity by keeping it beyond the bounds of critical enquiry, and of silencing women and gays, 'for whom matters of sexuality and gender can never be unproblematic' (1993: 8), but who risk their stake in mainstream anthropological debate, their 'respectability', and perhaps even their careers by discussing those problems too publicly. To Newton's observations, one might add that silence about the erotic subjectivity of fieldworkers also works to keep concealed the deeply racist and colonialist conditions that make possible our continuing unidirectional discourse about the sexuality of the people we study.

This disturbing dimension of our discourse about sex is crucial to bear in mind when considering any aspect of Western sexuality, particulary anthropological interest in other people's sex lives. One of the reasons why sex has always been of concern to anthropology is because, in addition to being fetchingly *risqué*, the sexual behavior of other people has been widely understood to be a point of irreconcilable difference between 'us' and 'them'. Mariana Torgovnick (1990) has pointed out that this equation between sex and difference has enriched Western creative possibilities by providing alternative models of gender roles and sexual behavior. But she also stresses the darker side of this equation, which has solid roots in colonial ideologies. And Mercer and Julien (1988: 107–8) have noted that

> [t]raditional notions of sexuality are deeply linked to race and racism because sex is regarded as that thing which par excellence is a threat to the moral order of Western civilisation. Hence, one is civilised at the expense of sexuality, and sexual at the expense of civilisation. If the black, the savage, the nigger, is the absolute Other

of civility, then it must follow that he is endowed with the most monstrous and terrifying sexual proclivity.

The implications of Western discourses about the sexuality of people of color have been explored in a wide variety of contexts by numerous writers (e.g. Davis 1981; Garber 1991, 1992; hooks 1992; Patton 1990; Pieterse 1992; Corbey 1988; Alloula 1986). A point on which these scholars all agree is that racism is implicated in our very concept of sex.

In fact, it is not only racism, but sexism, ageism, and any number of other -isms that one might care to add. Sex is a domain that is perhaps uniquely overdetermined in Western societies. This overdetermined nature of sex, and the attendant possibility for insight that an examination of it might provide, are main reasons behind the production of this volume. Through our own experience as fieldworkers, and in our conversations with other anthropologists, my co-editor and I have come to appreciate that erotic subjectivity in the field is a potentially useful source of insight. This is because erotic subjectivity *does* things. It performs, or, rather, can be made to perform, work. And one of the many types of work it can perform is to draw attention to the conditions of its own production. That is, for many anthropologists, desire experienced in the field seems often to provoke questions that otherwise easily remain unasked, or that only get asked in a rarefied manner once back at home seated comfortably behind one's computer. The questions are basic, quite uncomfortable ones. They are questions about the validity and meaning of the self–other dichotomy, and about the hierarchies on which anthropological work often seems to depend. They are questions about exploitation, racism, and boundaries. They are questions about commitment and about the politics of desire. They are questions, in other words, about issues that lie at the heart of anthropological knowledge.

The main purpose of this volume is to explore some of those questions by submiting the erotic subjectivity of the researcher to critical scrutiny. This means that the volume is not a catalogue of ethnopornography, nor is it a collection of kiss-and-tell tales calculated to tickle the popular fancy – there are already enough of those around; indeed, they seem to be something of a specialty of anthropologists who have worked in the Amazon Basin (e.g. Schneebaum 1969; Donner 1984; Goode 1991). Instead of providing exoticized *frissons*, the chapters here aim to address issues of theoretical and methodological significance. They extend Helen Callaway's question, 'What are the implications of the anthropologist as a gendered knower'? (1992: 30), by asking: 'What are the implications of the anthropologist as a sexually cognizant knower?' Just as a focus on the gender of fieldworkers has been shown to illuminate a wide range of specific questions about the nature and dynamics of fieldwork and writing (questions investigated by the articles in e.g. Golde 1986; Whitehead and Conaway 1986; Bell *et al.* 1993; Okely and Callaway 1992), so does a focus on sexuality draw our attention to specific issues and problems in anthropology, and with anthropology. Particularly now, at a time when anthropologists are finally beginning to examine and even celebrate various dimensions of their subjectivity in their fieldwork and in their writing, it seems both propitious and crucial to place the erotic subjectivity of the anthropologist firmly on the anthropological agenda. More than anything else, it seems pertinent to enquire what we gain by continuing to avoid the topic and *not* examining it.

Sex?

> The time has come to think about sex.
>
> (Rubin 1984: 267)

Before continuing, it is important to be clear on the subject about which we are speaking. What, exactly, is meant by 'sex', and how is the concept used in the contributions that follow?

In addition to Malinowski's *Diary* and the reflexive turn within anthropology, a third event that has made possible the conception and publication of this volume is the exploration of sexuality prompted by the work of Michel Foucault (e.g. 1981, 1986, 1988). Foucault taught us that sex is not a transhistorical, transcultural, natural drive; it is, rather, a social construct with a past. As such, what counts as 'sex' will vary considerably from historically situated group to group. The historian Robert Padgug (1979: 16) has summarized this idea in his explanation that:

> what we consider 'sexuality' was, in the pre-bourgeois world, a group of acts and institutions not necessarily linked to one another, or, if they were linked, combined in ways very different than our own. Intercourse, kinship, and the family, and gender, did not form anything like a 'field' of sexuality. Rather, each group of sexual acts was connected directly or indirectly – that is, formed part of – institutions and thought patterns which we tend to view as political, economic, or social in nature, and the connections cut

> across our idea of sexuality as a thing, detachable from other things, and as a separate sphere of private existence.

Because of its historically and culturally contingent nature, what is meant by 'sex' is impossible to delimit in a general way. Indeed, part of the research problem for anthropologists examining sex in non-Western societies is first of all deciding whether it even exists as a culturally salient domain, and then investigating links between the various understandings and practices that constitute it.

On the level of individual interactions, especially those occurring between people unfamiliar with one another's cultural and social backgrounds, differences in the meanings and practices understood as sexual can generate significant tension. Deborah Elliston (1993) relates such an encounter:

> I met a man on a ferry boat who, after only a short conversation about Tahitian culture . . . asked me to sleep with him, even to come and live with him. I said no: I'm here to learn about Tahitian culture. He said that's nice, then reiterated his desires for me. Perplexed about how to reframe our interaction, I told him I had a fiancé. His response was to point out that my fiancé was not there with me, but he was. Where was the locus of our radical miscommunication that made it impossible for him to hear my disinterest and impossible for me to get out of his interpretive framework?

Elliston's encounter on the ferry boat probably resonates with the experience of most women who have ever lived, let alone done anthropological fieldwork. In fieldwork, however, these kinds of encounters take on a special urgency, because the impulse to respond to them as one might at home can conflict with the anthropologically instilled awareness that one is dealing with culturally grounded interactional forms that one may not fully understand, and with the fear that, therefore, any reaction might be interpreted as a socially destructive *over*-reaction. The fact that individuals, in certain circumstances, sometimes encourage uncertainty and exploit doubt only makes matters worse. Eva Moreno's chapter in this volume illustrates the way in which anthropological uncertainty and a field assistant's manipulation of that uncertainty can have devastating consequences in the field.

Because we can never know in advance what will 'count' as sexual in another culture, and because what counts as sexual varies widely, in any case, between individuals in any culture, we as editors have not imposed any definition of 'sex' on the contributors to this volume.

Instead, we have given them free reign to discuss any aspect of their fieldwork that they consider to be relevant to the topic; hence the purposely nebulous 'erotic subjectivity' of the volume's subtitle. The chapters that have emerged from a consideration of sexuality and erotic subjectivity cover a truly broad spectrum. Jill Dubisch opens the volume with an analysis of the theoretical and practical issues that have arisen as a result of a range of erotic relationships in which she has been involved, both as actor and object, during the course of her extensive fieldwork in Greece. Evelyn Blackwood confronts issues of sameness and otherness that were raised during her fieldwork in Indonesia and as a result of her romantic involvement with a woman in the field. Andrew P. Killick reviews his erotic involvements with a number of Korean-American women in the light of a narrative analysis that sees 'the field' itself as sexually constructed. Kate Altork's essay on the erotic dimension of fieldwork among firefighters in the northwestern United States explores the role that sensuality can be made to play in anthropological perception and writing. Ralph Bolton discusses the ethics of using private sexual encounters as anthropological data, in his account of his fieldwork among gay men in Brussels. Helen Morton reflects on why she chose to become pregnant before beginning fieldwork on the Pacific island of Tonga. Jean Gearing discusses the complex interplay between desire and sexual violence that forms a backdrop to heterosexual relationships in the Caribbean island of St. Vincent, and she analyzes the implications of and responses to her marriage to her main informant during the course of fieldwork. And finally, Eva Moreno writes about the cycle of events that led to her being raped at gunpoint by her field assistant in Ethiopia. Taken together, the chapters in this volume thus document and analyze sexuality in both its most invigorating and its most abusive and violent manifestations. They examine sex both as as 'a domain of exploration, pleasure and agency' and as 'a domain of restriction, repression, and danger' (Vance 1984: 1).

Erotic subjectivity in fieldwork

> Really, I felt asexual in my inclination. I just lost my sexuality. I was nothing.
>
> ('Sue' in Wengle 1988: 91)

> How colonial of me, I later thought: I want into their lives, but only as a voyeur.
>
> (Elliston 1993)

One of the few scholars to have addressed the issue of sexuality among anthropologists in the field at any length is John Wengle, in his book *Ethnographers in the Field: The Psychology of Research* (1988). Wengle's book is a psychoanalytically grounded analysis of the fieldwork accounts of several graduate students and one more senior anthropologist, as well as of Malinowski's *Diary* and Manda Cesara's (1982) book *Reflections of a Woman Anthropologist*. Writing about 'the problem of sexuality for the fieldworker', Wengle tells us that 'the vast majority of anthropologists remain celibate while in the field' (1988: 25). He suggests that there is a powerful reason for this; namely, the need to maintain one's sense of identity:

> An anthropologist's self imposed celibacy can help him preserve his sense of identity by forcing him to direct his probably acute sexual needs and fantasies outside of the field environment and back home to his culture. By doing this, the anthropologist creates a 'strong and ever present link' with his home culture and his sense of identity. . . The celibate anthropologist is, if nothing else, secure in his sense of identity. (1988: 25; the quotation is from Forge 1967: 224, who presents a similar argument)

I will return shortly to some of the problems that I find in Wengle's preoccupation with making sure that the anthropological self remains secure and whole. For now, I want to note that while his explanation of celibacy in the field may make some intuitive psychological and symbolic sense, it strikes me as a rather weak rationalization. One easy way to call it into question is to point out, as Morton does in her contribution (Chapter 6, p. 179), that focusing one's sexual needs and fantasies on someone back home may actually function (particularly when the mail gets interrupted or when letters are misconstrued) to severely *debilitate* one's sense of identity. One can also show, as Blackwood does in her chapter, how a sexual relationship in the field can infinitely *strengthen* precisely one's link with one's home culture, and one's sense of identity.

More interesting than Wengle's attempt at explanation are the questions raised by his statement that most anthropologists remain celibate in the field. My conversations with colleagues give me no reason to dispute this, so what one might wonder is this: What is it about the discipline of anthropology that spawns hordes of celibate fieldworkers? That at any given moment the vast majority of those fieldworkers are also likely to be single graduate students in their twenties (a group hardly renowned for their sexual abstinence at home) makes the fact that most of them spend a year or more of their lives existing as chastely as Mother Teresa a truly curious, if not downright bizarre, phenomenon.

There is, of course, the issue of ethics. There seems to be a kind of unwritten, unspoken, and, for the most part, unquestioned rule about the ethics of sex in the field that all anthropology students somehow absorb during their graduate education. That rule can be summarized in one word: *Don't*. Tony Whitehead expresses this prohibition when he explains 'I considered myself to be highly ethical in sexual matters; among other things this meant not getting sexually involved with members of the study community' (1986: 217). Peter Wade writes 'I felt in an unarticulated way that in the anthropological community "sex with the natives" was considered improper and even unethical, as simply the gratifications of guilty lusts in an exploitative fashion' (1993: 211). Allen Abramson reports that sex in the field 'seemed to be in contravention of the unwritten ethnographic code' (1993: 75). Esther Newton tells us that, 'In graduate school in the early 1960s, I learned – because it was never mentioned – that erotic interest between fieldworker and informant either didn't exist, would be inapproriate, or couldn't be mentioned; I had no idea which' (1993: 4). And one of Wengle's anthropological informants seems to have gotten the message particularly clearly. She told him bluntly, 'You don't have an option, you must remain celibate. Sexual relationships in the field are going to be disastrous' (1988: 62).

Despite such firm *idées reçues* on the matter, it is not immediately apparent that having sex with anyone in the field is necessarily bad. In fact, as Dubisch points out in her contribution (Chapter 1, p. 31):

> We do almost everything else with our 'informants': share their lives, eat with them, attend their rituals, become part of their families, even become close friends, and sometimes establish life-long relationships. At the same time, we 'use' them to further our goals, writing and speaking in public contexts about personal and even intimate aspects of their lives, appropriating these lives for our own professional puposes. Could a sexual relationship be any more intimate, committing, or exploitive than our normal relations with the 'natives'? (In some societies, it might even be less so.)

In addition to being restrained by preconceived ethical restrictions, consideration of sex in the field seems also to be blocked by the fear that it may result in ejection from that field. One of the main things that graduate education in anthropology seems to do to students is instill in them severe anxiety they may be rejected by the people they have chosen to study. One of the women interviewed by Wengle expressed this succinctly when she told him that she 'went into the field frightened out of my mind and expecting to be rejected. Completely out of hand rejected' (1988: 44). This fear of rejection might be analyzed as the realization, on a personal level, of what Mary Louise Pratt has identified as the much larger issue of 'the sheer inexplicability and unjustifiability of the ethnographer's presence from the standpoint of the other' (1986: 42). But while this 'sheer inexplicability and unjustifiability' is routinely nodded at by members of the profession in seminars and scholarly papers, it seems rather unlikely that it would be very often invoked to account for actual cases of rejection. Instead, I conjecture that it would most probably be assumed that the rejected fieldworker, especially if that fieldworker is a graduate student on her first fieldtrip, was a failure. She failed to 'adapt', to 'establish rapport'. She failed to survive the mandatory initial 'gust-of-wind stage' that, once overcome, results in inclusion in the group and amusing post-fieldwork anecdotes.

Anxiety surrounding possible rejection is a paralyzing and extremely depressing situation for many young anthropologists, especially for heterosexual women, lesbians, and gay men, all of whom are likely to find themselves in the field afraid to 'be themselves' but quite unsure of who else they might be. The smooth advice they have read in field manuals – such as 'The fieldworker is obliged to adapt the most nearly comfortable version of the appropriate gender identity permissible in the host culture' (Angrosino 1986: 64) – turns out to be useless, because it ignores the extent to which a seemingly simple thing (for Angrosino, anyway) like 'gender identity' 'is not in itself a coherent subjective stance, but [is] rather a range of somewhat contradictory, conflictive and changeable positions' (Wade 1993: 207) enacted in situated contexts.

Significantly, it is in the vacuum created between leaving off being one's self and attempting to be someone else that many ethnographers begin to become very aware of, and very unhappy with, the pretense of anthropological 'rapport'. Where exactly is the rapport, one might ask, in a set of disciplinary practices that seems to demand (in order to avoid rejection and expulsion) evasion, concealment, and lying about one's opinions, identities, and activities outside the field (these are the practices usually lurking behind the glib phrase 'adaptation') – even as it conditions anthropologists to resist and resent it if local people do the same? For the problem is that in anthropology, other people's secrets are valuable commodities. Ethnographic success is often measured, and anthropological careers often made, by the extent to which the anthropologist gets others to 'open up', as this process is so benignly known, and reveal secrets – magical formulae, cult fetishes, esoteric myths, hidden rituals, private experiences, golden stools. But what about our own secrets? What would happen to the way we understand and practice our discipline if success was also seen to relate to the extent to which we revealed secrets of our own to the people with whom we work?

Of course sex, at least for Western subjects, is, as Michel Foucault has argued, '*the* secret' (1981: 35, emphasis in original). The various practices, feelings, and knowledges that have come to compose the domain of sex in Western societies are currently 'the medium through which people seek to define their personalities, their tastes' (Foucault and Sennett 1982: 3). Sex has become 'a constitutive principle of the self' (Halperin 1990: 24). It is experienced by many Western subjects as the core of their being, their essence, the privileged site in which the truth about themselves and their social relationships is to be found. 'Few people today would subscribe to Brillat-Savarin's dictum, "Tell me what you eat, and I will tell you who you are"', Richard Sennett comments, 'but a translation of this dictum to the field of sex does command assent: Know how you love, and you will know who you are' (Foucault and Sennett 1982: 3).

It is because sex has assumed a pivotal position in Western understandings of self that it would be analytically premature simply to accept at face value anthropological protestations that sex in the field is unethical, and leave it at that. To do so would forfeit the perception that by *a priori* defining sex as out of bounds for fieldworkers, anthropologists have engineered a silence; a kind of meaningful silence that could be analyzed in a Foucauldian spirit as constituting an integral part of the strategies that undergird anthropological claims to authority. The interface posited in Western societies between sex and self, and the purposeful and heavily guarded silence about the sexuality of the anthropologist, implies that looking at sex in the field could provide great insight into the anthropological self and the relations and processes implicated in the production of that self. For individual fieldworkers, as this volume documents, sexual desire in the field can call into question the boundaries of self, threaten to upset the researcher–researched relation, blur the line between professional role and personal life, and provoke questions about power, exploitation, and racism. All of this can be extremely difficult and anxiety-provoking. But instead of sealing it with the stamp of 'Unethical' and flinging it away to the extreme periphery of the discipline, as has been done until now, perhaps the time has come to acknowledge and explore it, not out of narcissism or a desire to gaze at navels, but, rather, as part of our ongoing critical enquiries into the basis for, and the production of, our knowledge.

Putting the self at stake

> To expose the Self and to open it to question is not merely to question the individual anthropologist or anthropology's specific theoretical hypotheses. Rather, it is to question the Self in its extended sense: that is, the anthropological effort itself, and social system that gives that effort its force.
>
> (Dwyer 1982: 256)

One nexus to look at, then, in order to be able to theorize sex in the field, is how sex and self intermesh. We can start that enquiry by focusing on the self. In her recent book *Sexing the Self: Gendered Positions in Cultural Studies* (1993), Elspeth Probyn argues a strong case for both theorizing the self, and theorizing from the self. Probyn critiques the way that the self has been deployed in reflexive cultural studies, and she is particulary dismissive of recent attempts within anthropology to discuss the self and insert it in ethnographic texts. In addition to repeating the familiar critique that a reflexive anthropology too narrowly focused on textual practices risks 'elevat[ing] the ethnographer and his subjects into the realm of pure discursivity' (1993: 72), Probyn faults self-reflexivity within anthropology for 'banal egotism' (1993: 80). She criticizes the way in which much of what passes for reflexive anthropology reifies the experiential for its own sake, and continues the tradition of reflecting on others only as a means of talking about the self.

Using the other only as a means to gaze back at the self is precisely the fault that I find with John Wengle's attempt to analyze the role and meaning of sexuality in the anthropological encounter. Wengle, I think correctly, interprets sex in the field as presenting 'the ultimate problem . . . of self-loss' (1988: 124) for the ethnographer. However, instead of seeing in that problem a potential for connection with others and for reflection on the anthropological self, Wengle's narrow focus on the individual researcher, and his understanding of self as something that 'strives to maintain a sense of continuity, coherence, and integrity' (1988: 7), lead him to see sex only as a threat. This causes him to shut down discusssion at precisely the point at which it should be opened up.

It also causes him to completely efface the potential sexual partners of fieldworkers from consideration. This is particularly evident in his discussion of Manda Cesara's account of her field experiences in Africa. Cesara (a pseudonym) is the first female anthropologist to have written openly about her sexual experiences in the field. While conducting fieldwork in Africa among the 'Lenda' people, Cesara had two affairs; one with a local magistrate and one with a government official. These relationships are described in warm terms, and Cesara clearly sees them as a central force in her transition from 'a female student of anthropology. . . into a woman and an ethnographer' (1982: vii).

In his analysis of Cesara's text, Wengle ignores this. Instead of taking Cesara at her word, Wengle throws her on his psychoanalytic couch and explains what she *really* means. Thus, where Cesara tells us that 'the emotion of love for a particular individual of a people among whom one conducts research aims at laying hold of the culture in its entirety through that particular individual' (1982: 60), Wengle explains that she has an 'identity need' (1988: 145). Where Cesara comments that 'Douglas [the magistrate] showed me the valley's beauty' (1982: 157), Wengle sees a 'narcissistic transference' (1988: 145). Cesara concludes that her affair with Douglas 'opened the gate to Lenda. I don't mean that he introduced me to his friends. I mean that he opened my heart and mind' (1982: 61). Wengle concludes that Cesara 'entered the field suffering from a particularly marked vulnerability in her self-representation' (1988: 150), and that her affair with Douglas was an attempt to 'use another person as a mirror to reflect a new sense of identity', something that 'had to fail' (1988: 148).

In this analytical makeover, the two men who become the objects of Cesara's attention and affection are nowhere to be found. Their roles are reduced (as are the roles of all the Lenda people) to nothing more than an angst-ridden backdrop for Cesara's 'new resolution of her life, a resolution found in her identification with her work and with anthropology' (1988: 150). A strong objection that could be raised against this kind of (psycho)analysis is that it reproduces and entrenches the idea that reflexive anthropology, which Cesara explictly sees herself to be enacting, is primarily about the self. The 'other', in Wengle's language, is divested of all materiality and subjectivity – he is transformed into a blank surface, 'a mirror', where all that is visible is the anthropologist herself.

Because he erases Douglas, Nyiji (the government official), and the other Lenda from consideration, Wengle is prevented from seeing the crucial point that, for Cesara, sexual relationships were illuminating. Her affairs with Douglas and Nyiji compelled reflections on the nature of fieldwork, relationships, and knowledge. They were an important part of the self-reflexive process that led Cesara to come to 'reject as dishonest the subject–object, self–other, introspective–empiricistic segregations' (1982: vii) on which anthropology rests. Cesara was not interested in upholding the boundaries between self and other that Wengle thinks are so necessary. Quite the opposite: instead of merely recording difference, Cesara wanted to 'confront their otherness, to hear their viewpoint and let it challenge mine' (1982: 217). To do so, she tells us that she 'risked involvement' (1982: 217).

Cesara's choice of the word 'risk' here is poignant, because it both foregrounds the insight that involvement with other people necessarily entails risk (not only for the anthropologist, as Cesara and others, such as Rabinow 1977 and Hastrup 1992 make clear), and it provides us with some sense of how the calls now emerging in the discipline for anthropology to 'make its own vulnerability central' (Dwyer 1982: 272) might be put into lived, instead of just textual, practice.

Partial selves

> Splitting, not being, is the privileged image for feminist epistemologies of scientific knowledge.
>
> (Haraway 1991: 193)

> Ethnographic truths are thus inherently partial – committed and incomplete.
>
> (Clifford 1986: 7)

In her discussion of reflexivity and what it can contribute to cultural studies, Elspeth Probyn emphasizes that her criticism that reflexive writings are often self-centered and sterile is not a criticism of reflexivity itself. 'It is not the process of being reflexive about one's research practices that is the problem', she stresses, 'it is the conception of the self at work within this reflexivity that is at fault' (Probyn 1993: 80). What Probyn is referring to is the tendency in anthropology to think that problems of power, privilege, and perspective can be defused simply by inserting the self into one's accounts and proclaiming that dialogue has occurred. To the extent that this move leaves unchallenged the epistemological basis of anthropological knowledge, all it does is subsume the other into the project of the self. It is like, in Graham Watson's words, 'play[ing] chess with oneself, making the moves for both black and white pieces' (1991: 85).

In order to push reflexivity beyond the bounds of self-absorption, Probyn explains that '[w]e need to ask what exactly a self reflecting self is reflecting upon' (1991: 62). Her suggestion is that the object of reflection should be a self understood as 'a *combinatoire*, a discursive arrangement that holds together in tension the different lines of race and sexuality that form and re-form our senses of self' (1991: 1–2). In this conceptualization, the self emerges 'as a speaking position that . . . is firmly based in an epistemological questioning of how it is that I am speaking' (1991: 80). It is a self that 'is both an object of enquiry and the means of analysing where and how the self is lodged within the social formation' (1991: 105). More than anything else, it is a self that 'must . . . be seen as a theoretical manoeuvering, not a unifying principle' (1991: 106). Need one add that it is a self very different from the object of concern to John Wengle?

I want to underscore the difference between Probyn's argument that the self is a politically situated discursive arrangement, and Wengle's definition of self as 'an autonomous and independent entity . . . [that] strives to maintain a sense of continuity, coherence, and integrity' (1988: 7), in order to highlight three points. The first is that while at first glance Probyn's ideas might seem, for some, slightly mystical and difficult to grasp, they are drawn from a well-elaborated current of feminist thought. In discussions about the self in a great deal of feminist writing, what gets consistently emphasized is openness and fluidity, not boundedness and 'integrity'.

A recent, rhetorically powerful, example of this is Jennifer Nedelsky's appraisal of Lakoff and Johnson's work on metaphor (Lakoff and Johnson 1980). Nedelsky is highly critical of the central thesis of this work that all people everywhere experience their bodies as bounded 'containers'. She refutes this proposition by juxtaposing it with alternative perspectives:

> [Lakoff and Johnson] treat the experience of the body as a 'container' to be . . . a self-evident, direct description of 'our' experience of the body. They assert that 'we are physical beings, bounded and set off from the rest of the world by the surface of our skins'. But

> Catherine Keller has a very different experience: 'Our skin does not separate – it connects us to the world through a wondrous network of sensory awareness . . . [T]hrough my senses I go into the world, and the world comes into me. It is precisely in embodiment that the many are becoming one and the outer becoming inner'. Lakoff and Johnson tell us that 'we experience the rest of the world as outside us'. But Susan Griffin reminds us, 'For the part of the mind that is dark to us in this culture, that is sleeping in us, that we name 'unconscious', is the knowledge that we are inseparable from all other beings in the universe. Intimations of this have reached us'. Lakoff and Johnson say, 'Each of us is a container, with a bounding surface and an in-out orientation'. But for Alfred North Whitehead, 'Each actual entity is a locus for the universe'.
>
> (1990: 178–9)

Nedelsky extensively cites the feminist writer Catherine Keller (Keller 1986) to argue the point that understandings of the self as separate and bounded are functions of a sexist apparatus intimately linked to practices of domination:

> The separative ego as we have characterized it – as self-objectifying and other-exclusive – cannot separate its strategies of self perpetuation from its drive to control. In its emphasis upon self-control, being 'on top of things', it is simultaneously keeping the influent others under control as well. Domination is the best defense, and retreat its familiar back-up plan. And these defensive strategies inadvertently confirm the truth of internal relations: that the world gets inside us, gets under our skin, does not keep a respectful difference.
>
> Control is the age-old alternative to connection. The denial of internal relations issues in external manipulation.
>
> (Keller 1986: 200, cited in Nedelsky 1990: 180)

My interest in these arguments is what leads to my second point, which is that viewing the self as unbounded and connected entails a view of the self as inherently incomplete and partial. This notion of partiality, and its significance for anthropological knowledge, has recently been developed in an especially focused manner in the work of Donna Haraway and Marilyn Strathern. Although their backgrounds and sources of inspiration are different (Haraway is an American historian of science who has critically studied research on monkeys and apes,

Strathern is a British social anthropologist with extensive experience working in the Highlands of Papua New Guinea), both writers invoke the notion of partiality, in order to rethink how anthropological work can be done. It is not necessary to go into the details of their respective arguments, which are far too rich to permit condensation here. It is enough to note that a central thought that structures their work is the idea that knowledge is, and must be, partial. This partiality is not a weakness or a flaw. It is, on the contrary, an epistemological strength. Strathern explains how an awareness of partiality entails an appreciation of social and political situatedness. She uses the example of feminist discourse to illustrate her point:

> Feminist discourse creates connections between the participants – but they remain partial insofar as they create no single entity between them. What each creates is an extension of a position, which could not have been done without the instrument of conversation but in the end is done from the position each occupies *for* herself or himself. 'Partial' captures the nature of the interlocution well, for there is no totality, each part also defines a partisan position. Ethnographic truths are similarly partial in being at once incomplete and committed.
>
> (1991: 39, emphasis in original, reference omitted)

Haraway speaks more directly about the self. 'The knowing self', she explains in prose similar to Probyn's, 'is partial in all its guises, never finished, whole, simply there and original; it is always constructed and stitched together imperfectly, and *therefore* able to join with another, to see together without claiming to be another' (Haraway 1991: 193, emphasis in original). Furthermore, this 'split and partial self is the one who can interrogate positionings and be accountable, the one who can construct and join rational conversations and fantastic imaginings that can change history' (1991: 193). Like Strathern, Haraway stresses that partiality means *positioned* – in every sense of that word (historically, socially, radically politically, economically, gendered, sexed, and so on). Both authors also argue that positioned selves are accountable selves and that partial knowledge 'promises a vision of the means of ongoing finite embodiment, of living within limits and contradictions, i.e. of views from somewhere' (Haraway 1991: 196).

At this juncture, I am ready to make my third point, which is, simply, that desire in the field seems to be one especially poignant means through which anthropologists become aware of themselves as positioned, partial, knowing selves. This is the case regardless of whether the desiring agent is the anthropologist or someone in the field. In this volume, for example, Morton, Gearing, and Moreno all reflect on how they as fieldworkers became quite firmly positioned with regard to gender, age, and sexual availability through the desire of others. Killick and Morton also discuss how their race and their nationalities, with everything that those signified, became salient as they found themselves fashioned into objects of desire by people in the field.

Other contributions discuss anthropological desire. Dubisch wonders whether one of the reasons she was initially reluctant to act on her own desire in the field was because she feared that a relationship with a Greek man might have threatened her 'privileged' position as an anthropologist. Morton frankly recognizes that her attraction to Tongan men may have in some senses been structured by racist desires to (sexually) possess the Other. Altork, Gearing, Bolton, and Killick all raise similar issues, and they all argue that the disciplinary silence about desire in the field is a way for anthropologists to avoid confronting issues of positionality, hierarchy, exploitation, and racism.

That issues such as these cannot help but arise once desire is acknowledged is perhaps clearest in Blackwood's essay, which explores the connection that mutual erotic attraction can forge between an anthropologist and a person in the field. Blackwood shows how this connection does not dissolve difference. On the contrary, it highlights it. She recounts how her relationship with her lover, Dayan, continually challenged her categories of experience, repositioned her into new spaces, and forced her to recognize her own privileged position. She writes that (Chapter 2, p. 68):

> The attractiveness and power of my status as a well-educated, middle-class, white American made me the dominant partner in our relationship. I had the money to pay for everything . . . the high-status job and time constraints that could not be neglected. Consequently, I was able to call the shots about when we saw each other and what things we did that cost money. She could refuse to meet my wishes, but she was invariably at home when I arrived on weekends. . . . When I told her I was doing research on lesbians in Indonesia, Dayan asked me if I was with her just so I could get data for my study. I told her no, that I did not have to be involved to get information, but I also gained much more information by being involved. Then I asked if she was with me because I was a 'rich' American who could offer more than the limited opportunities she now had. She was offended by my asking and reminded me that I was leaving in a few months and she would be left alone.

In the introduction to a volume that she recently co-edited on the topic of gender in the field, Pat Caplan mentions several contributions that recount experiences of sexuality in the field and discuss issues similar to those raised by Blackwood and other contributors in this present volume. However, Caplan's interpretation of those experiences is that sexuality between anthropologist and local woman or man 'enables a kind of transcendence of the self–other dichotomy to take place' (1993: 23). Caplan's point is taken, but it is important to the argument I am pursuing here to disagree with her characterization of the consequence of sexual union as a 'transcendence'. While individuals may very well use the language of transcendence to describe their experiences, I would suggest that, rather than transcendence (which Haraway 1991: 187 calls 'a story that loses track of its mediations just where someone might be held responsible for something'), what often happens when an anthropologist and a member of the local community engage in an erotic relationship can also be described in terms of a heightened awareness of the positioning and situatedness of relations. That is, desire, both in the accounts presented in this book and in the ones referred to by Caplan, seems not really to result in a Hollywood dream where differences in race, socioeconomic status, education, position in the global hierarchy, and culture suddenly fizz away into pink froth, leaving everybody living happily ever after. It seems, rather, to result, for both partners, in increased sensitivity to one another's position and role, and an increased awareness of – and stake in – how the other regards the self.

It is this increased sensitivity of position, this heightened awareness of partiality, and, perhaps most pertinent of all, this increased stake in the game that I would argue might well provide one possible springboard out of a reflexive anthropology caught up in 'banal egoism' and toward an anthropology capable of using the self in an epistemologically productive way. Dorinne Kondo makes this point when she explains that 'experience, and the *specificity* of my experience – a particular human being who encounters particular others at a particular historical moment and has particular stakes in that interaction – is not opposed to theory; it *enacts* and *embodies* theory' (1990: 24, emphasis in original). And both Haraway and Strathern argue at length that partial knowledge, positioned knowledge, can be epistemologically productive because of the connections and unexpected openings that such knowledges make possible. After all, Haraway sums up, 'The only way to find a larger vision is to be somewhere in particular' (1991: 196).

The same point is made by Probyn, who ends her book about the self with a chapter that directly links together positioned knowledge and sexuality. Probyn explains that the dilemma facing anthropologists and others interested in developing reflexivity is that they must somehow avoid the pompous Scylla of using the other only as a ventriloquist's dummy to talk about the self, and the patronizing Charybdis of thinking that we might speak in somebody else's voice. The way around this dilemma, she explains, is to develop a means of speaking 'within the space between my self and another's self' (1993: 145). The enunciations emerging from this space would neither privilege 'me' nor presume to speak for the other.

This space is created through a theoretically grounded reflexivity in which the self continually acknowledges and questions the historical and political conditions which must already be met for it to speak in the first place, as well as the conditions that structure and limit its interactions with an other. But in its interactions with others, the self must transgress onto a terrain of other selves, in the sense that it must imaginatively attempt to empathize with and participate in the feelings and ideas of others. In reaching out in this way, the goal is neither equality nor encompassment. It is, instead, to return to Strathern's imagery, the creation of an extension of a position, one that will yield different capacities (Strathern 1991: 38–9).

Sexuality can enter the discussion at this point as an especially powerful means through which transgression onto the terrain of other selves might be articulated. This is because, in Muriel Dimen's words:

> Erotic experience is extraordinary, lying somewhere between dream and daily life. Sped by desire, it knows no shame and no bounds. In it, pleasure and power, hurt and love, mingle effortlessly. It is a between-thing, bordering psyche and society, culture and nature, conscious and unconscious, self and other. Its intrinsic messy ambiguity confers on it an inherent novelty, creativity, discovery; these give it its excitements, its pleasure, its fearsomeness. Sexual experience entails loss of self–other boundaries, the endless opening of doors to more unknown inner spaces, confusions about what to do next or who the other person is or what part of the body is being touched or what part of the body is doing the touching or where one person begins and the other ends. This is sometimes pleasurable, sometimes painful, always unsettling.
>
> (1989: 46–7)

While one can disagree with Dimen that erotic experience in itself has any intrinsic capacities at all, and therefore modify her characterization by prefixing a 'can' to her verbs and changing all her 'is'es to 'can be's, it seems to me that this passage manages to capture the simultaneous sense of vulnerability and pleasure felt by many anthropologists who engage in erotic relationships in the field, regardless of whether or not those relationships are actually consummated sexually (as Altork's contribution to this volume makes especially clear). It is because erotic experience can be 'messy', 'unsettling', and a 'between-thing', capable of provoking a whole gamut of both pleasurable and painful feelings, that it has great capacity to prod us into moving, gingerly and with a lot at stake, onto the terrain of others, with the goal of extending positions, both our own and theirs. Elspeth Probyn sums up the idea like this, in prose that could serve as an epigraph for many of the chapters in this book: 'I want to acknowledge that her desire and mine are not enough but that at the same time they may constitute the only place from which to begin a drawing each other in' (1993: 162).

Conclusion

> In order to be utilized, our erotic feelings must be recognized.
>
> (Lorde 1978)

In reading the above passages, it would be unfortunate if readers were left with the impression that the purpose of this book is to encourage anthropologists to rush off into the field and try to have sex with their informants. Let me, therefore, plainly declare that that is not the point. Let me, furthermore, reassert that everyone contributing to this volume is cognizant of the fact that every fieldwork situation will include numerous circumstances in which sexual relations between anthropologists and individuals in the field would be unethical and exploitative. And lest this introductory chapter be accused of advocating a 'Pollyana' view of human relations, let me reiterate once again my understanding that the structural conditions that make sexual relationships between anthropologists and members of the communities they study possible in the first place are almost inevitably highly unequal and colonial.[1]

But having said that, I hurry to repeat that the point is precisely that sexuality seems to have the potential of bringing into theoretical and political focus exactly those asymmetrically ordered conditions. Perhaps more than any other type of interaction, sex can urge an exploration of the basis for, the nature of, and the consequences of relationships entered into in the field. It can be one way of putting the self at stake, and of 'working through the desire to imagine, to inhabit, to caress, to be and to be with the other' (Probyn 1993: 158), which, in turn, may allow for a qualified and cautious extension of position and permeation of the boundaries and roles on which anthropologists for the most part uncritically depend. The very idea of such extensions and permeations, let alone their consequences, may seem exceedingly threatening to many fieldworkers, and this may exacerbate the sense of what Wengle calls 'self-loss' that one may experience in the field. Unlike Wengle, however, one might perceive personal and epistemological possibilities in that loss. Disintegration, after all, as Nedelsky reminds us (1990: 184), entails promise.

I can end by repeating that despite my arguments about the potential for insight that I see in erotic subjectivity, I do not claim that it necessarily provides any insight at all. We are all only too aware that sex can be, and regularly is, used to thwart understanding, quash challenge, and fortify hierarchies of gender, class, and race. Furthermore, unless desire is made to work to examine critically the historical, cultural, and political conditions that make possible its production and expression, it remains analytically barren. For those reasons, it is not necessary to enter into debate about whether anthropologists should privilege accounts by fieldworkers who have had sexual relationships with the people among whom they have worked. Whether such accounts are more or less insightful than those produced by fieldworkers who did not have such relationships will depend on a lot more than the fact of sex.

The suggestion is that if we focus on it and put it to work, the erotic subjectivity of the ethnographer *can* be epistemologically productive. This does not mean that it has to be, or even that it necessarily should be, productive in this way – indeed, one potential pitfall in this entire project is that it may ultimately result in yet another exoticist discourse that invents a problem out of what for others is unproblematic, that draws the bodies of others still further into our own regimes of knowledge and power, ignoring their protests, or their disintrest, textually choreographing them, as usual, to satisfy our own desires. This risk makes it crucial that we critically discuss both the potential *and the limits* of the erotic subjectivity of the ethnographer. It is my hope that the questions posed and the issues raised in this book will help to structure that discussion among anthropologists, students, and people who work with anthropologists. Since the issue of the erotic subjectivity of the fieldworker has until recently been one of the few remaining tabooed topics within anthropology, we have a lot of talking to do about it. This book is a bid to get the conversation started.

Acknowledgements

I wish, first of all, to acknowledge my co-editor, Margaret Willson, and thank her for the extremely productive and stimulating working relationship that we have continued to develop since our initial drinking bout in Port Moresby, long ago, and for her critical comments on an earlier draft of this chapter. I also thank all the contributors to the volume – Kate Altork, Evelyn Blackwood, Ralph Bolton, Jill Dubisch, Andrew P. Killick, Jean Gearing, Eva Moreno and Helen Morton – for their incisive readings of an earlier draft of this chapter. In addition, I am very grateful to Karin Aronsson, David Behan, Jonathan Benthall, Ann-Christin Cederborg, Deborah Elliston, Kenneth Hyltenstam, Bengt Sandin, Bambi Schieffelin, Christopher Stroud, and Routledge's anonymous reader for their thought-provoking comments on that earlier draft. That the suggestions of my readers were too numerous to incorporate fully into this text testifies, I think, to the richness of this topic and its power to get people thinking about a wide variety of issues. My final thanks must go to everyone at the Department of Child Studies at Linköping University, where I worked until very recently, for having provided an extraordinarily supportive atmosphere throughout the production of this book, and to Heather Gibson of Routledge, for being a wonderful and supportive editor.

Note

1 Several readers have interpreted this sentence to mean that I believe that *the relationships themselves* between anthropologists and members of the communities they study must inevitably be unequal and colonial. This is not my point. Individual relationships are obviously the ongoing outcomes of dynamics that cannot be reduced to global political inequalities. My point concerns only the overarching historical, political, and socioeconomic conditions that make it possible for anthropologists to go where they go and come into intensive contact with the people whom they do. Those conditions, I think most would probably agree, are usually the result of exploitive and colonial histories, and they remain saturated with exploitive and colonial resonances. I would argue that those resonances cannot be ignored when considering individual relationships. However, they certainly do not determine, in any simplistic or straightforward way, the nature or tenor of people's erotic relationships.

References

Abramson, Allen (1993) 'Between Autobiography and Method: Being Male, Seeing Myth and the Analysis of Structures of Gender and Sexuality in the

Eastern Interior of Fiji', in Diane Bell, Pat Caplan, and Wazir Jahan Karim (eds) *Gendered Fields: Women, Men and Ethnography.* London and New York: Routledge.

Alloula, Malek (1986) *The Colonial Harem.* Minneapolis: University of Minnesota Press.

Angrosino, Michael V. (1986) 'Son and Lover: The Anthropologist as Non-threatening Male', in Tony Larry Whitehead and Mary Ellen Conaway (eds) *Self, Sex and Gender in Cross-Cultural Fieldwork.* Urbana and Chicago: University of Illinois Press.

Bell, Diane, Pat Caplan, and Wazir Jahan Karim (eds) (1993) *Gendered Fields: Women, Men and Ethnography.* London and New York: Routledge.

Callaway, Helen (1992) 'Ethnography and Experience: Gender Implications in Fieldwork and Texts', in Judith Okely and Hellen Callaway (eds) *Anthropology and Autobiography.* London and New York: Routledge.

Caplan, Pat (1993) 'Introduction 2: The Volume', in Diane Bell, Pat Caplan, and Wazir Jahan Karim (eds) *Gendered Fields: Women, Men and Ethnography.* London and New York: Routledge.

Cesara, Manda (1982) *Reflections of a Woman Anthropologist: No Hiding Place.* London and New York: Academic Press.

Clifford, James (1986) 'Introduction: Partial Truths', in James Clifford and George E. Marcus (eds) *Writing Culture: The Poetics and Politics of Ethnography.* Berkeley, Calif.: University of California Press.

——— (1988) *The Predicament of Culture: Twentieth Century Ethnography, Literature, and Art.* Cambridge, Mass.: Harvard University Press.

——— and George E. Marcus (eds) (1986) *Writing Culture: The Poetics and Politics of Ethnography.* Berkeley, Calif.: University of California Press.

Corbey, Raymond (1988) 'Alterity: The Colonial Nude'. *Critique of Anthropology.* Vol. 8, No. 3, pp. 75–92.

Davis, Angela (1981) *Women, Race, and Class.* New York: Random House.

Dimen, Muriel (1989) 'Power, Sexuality, and Intimacy', in Alison M. Jaggar and Susan R. Bordo (eds) *Gender/Body/Knowledge: Feminist Reconstructions of Being and Knowing.* New Brunswick and London: Rutgers University Press.

Donner, Florinda (1984) *Shabono.* London: Triad/Paladin Books.

Dwyer, Kevin (1982) *Moroccan Dialogues: Anthropology in Question.* Prospect Heights, Ill.: Waveland Press.

Elliston, Deborah (1993) 'The Dynamics of Difficult Conversations: Talking Sex in Tahiti'. Paper read at Panel on 'Methodological and Ethical Issues in the Study of Sexuality', 93rd Annual Meeting of the American Anthropological Association, 17–21 November, Washington, D.C.

Forge, Anthony (1967) 'The Lonely Anthropologist'. *New Society,* pp. 221–4.

Foucault, Michel (1981) *The History of Sexuality, Vol. 1.* Harmondsworth: Pelican Books.

——— (1986) *The Use of Pleasure. The History of Sexuality, Vol. 2.* New York: Vintage Books.

——— (1988) *The Care of the Self. The History of Sexuality, Vol. 3.* New York: Vintage Books.

——— and Richard Sennett (1982) 'Sexuality and Solitude', in R. Dworkin, K. Miller, and R. Sennett (eds) *Humanities in Review, Vol. 1.* Cambridge: Cambridge University Press.

Garber, Marjorie (1991) 'The Chic of Araby: Transvestism, Transsexualism and the Erotics of Cultural Appropriation', in Julia Epstein and Kristina Straub (eds) *Body Guards: The Cultural Politics of Gender Ambiguity*. London and New York: Routledge.

——— (1992) 'The Occidental Tourist: M. Butterfly and the Scandal of Transvestism', in Andrew Parker, Mary Russo, Doris Sommer, and Patricia Yaeger (eds) *Nationalisms and Sexualities*. London and New York: Routledge.

Geertz, Clifford (1983) '"From the Native's Point of View": On the Nature of Anthropological Understanding', in *Local Knowledge: Further Essays in Interpretive Anthropology*. New York: Basic Books.

——— (1984) 'Anti Anti-Relativism'. *American Anthropologist*. Vol. 86, No. 2, pp. 263–78.

——— (1988) *Works and Lives: The Anthropologist as Author*. Stanford: Stanford University Press.

Golde, Peggy (ed.) (1986) *Women in the Field: Anthropological Experiences*. Berkeley, Calif.: University of California Press.

Goldstein, Judith L. (1991) 'Sexual Phallacies'. *Reviews in Anthropology*. Vol. 16, pp. 203–10.

Goode, Kenneth, with David Chanoff (1991) *Into the Heart: One Man's Pursuit of Love and Knowledge among the Yanomama*. New York: Simon and Schuster.

Halperin, David (1990) *One Hundred Years of Homosexuality: And Other Essays on Greek Love*. London and New York: Routledge.

Haraway, Donna J. (1991) *Simians, Cyborgs, and Women: The Reinvention of Nature*. London and New York: Routledge.

Hastrup, Kirsten (1992) 'Writing Ethnography: The State of the Art', in Judith Okely and Helen Callaway (eds) *Anthropology and Autobiography*. London and New York: Routledge.

hooks, bell (1992) *Black Looks: Race and Representation*. London: Turnaround Press.

Hsu, Francis L.K. (1979) 'The Cultural Problem of the Cultural Anthropologist'. *American Anthropologist*. Vol. 81, No. 3, pp. 517–32.

Jarvie, Ian (1988) 'Comment on "Rhetoric and the Authority of Ethnography: 'Postmodernism' and the Social Reproduction of Texts", by P. Steven Sangren'. *Current Anthropology*. Vol. 29, No. 3, pp. 427–9.

Keller, Catherine (1986) *From a Broken Web: Separation, Sexism, and Self*. Boston, Mass.: Beacon Press.

Kondo, Dorinne K. (1990) *Crafting Selves: Power, Gender and Discourses of Identity in a Japanese Workplace*. Chicago: University of Chicago Press.

Lakoff, George and Mark Johnson (1980) *Metaphors We Live By*. Chicago: University of Chicago Press.

Lorde, Audre (1978) *Uses of the Erotic: The Erotic as Power*. Freedom, Calif.: The Crossing Press.

Malinowski, Bronislaw, (1967) *A Diary in the Strict Sense of the Term*. London: Routledge and Kegan Paul.

——— (1987) [1929] *The Sexual Life of Savages*. Boston, Mass.: Beacon Press.

Marcus, George E. and Michael M.J. Fischer (1986) *Anthropology as Cultural Critique: An Experimental Moment in the Human Sciences*. Chicago: University of Chicago Press.

Mead, Margaret (1949) [1928] *Coming of Age in Samoa: A Psychological Study of Primitive Youth for Western Civilization.* New York: Mentor Books.

Mercer, Kobena and Isaac Julien (1988) 'Race, Sexual Politics and Black Masculinity: A Dossier', in Rowena Chapman and Jonathan Rutherford (eds) *Male Order: Unwrapping Masculinity.* London: Lawrence and Wishart.

Nedelsky, Jennifer (1990) 'Law, Boundaries, and the Bounded Self'. *Representations.* No. 30, pp. 162–89.

Newton, Esther (1993) 'My Best Informant's Dress: The Erotic Equation in Fieldwork'. *Cultural Anthropology.* Vol. 8, No. 1, pp. 3–23.

Okely, Judith and Hellen Callaway (eds) (1992) *Anthropology and Autobiography.* London and New York: Routledge.

Padgug, Robert A. (1979) 'Sexual Matters: On Conceptualizing Sexuality in History'. *Radical History Review.* Vol. 20, pp. 3–23.

Patton, Cindy (1990) *Inventing Aids.* London and New York: Routledge.

Pieterse, Jan Nederveen (1992) *White on Black: Images of Africa and Blacks in Western Popular Culture.* New Haven and London: Yale University Press.

Pratt, Mary Louise (1986) 'Fieldwork in Common Places', in James Clifford and George E. Marcus (eds) *Writing Culture: The Poetics and Politics of Ethnography.* Berkeley, Calif.: University of California Press.

Probyn, Elspeth (1993) *Sexing the Self: Gendered Positions in Cultural Studies.* London and New York: Routledge.

Rabinow, Paul (1977) *Reflections on Fieldwork in Morocco.* Berkeley, Calif.: University of California Press.

Rubin, Gayle (1984) 'Thinking Sex: Notes for a Radical Theory of the Politics of Sexuality', in Carole S. Vance (ed.) *Pleasure and Danger: Exploring Female Sexuality.* London: Routledge and Kegan Paul.

Sangren, P. Steven (1988) 'Rhetoric and the Authority of Ethnography: "Postmodernism" and the Social Reproduction of Texts'. *Current Anthropology.* Vol. 29, No. 3, pp. 405–24.

Schneebaum, Tobias (1969) *Keep the River on Your Right.* New York: Grove Press.

Strathern, Marilyn (1991) *Partial Connections.* Savage, Md.: Rowman and Littlefield.

Torgovnick, Marianna (1990) *Gone Primitive: Savage Intellects, Modern Lives.* Chicago: University of Chicago Press.

Vance, Carole S. (1984) 'Pleasure and Danger: Toward a Politics of Sexuality', in Carole S. Vance (ed.) *Pleasure and Danger: Exploring Female Sexuality.* London: Routledge and Kegan Paul.

Wade, Peter (1993) 'Sexuality and Masculinity among Columbian Blacks', in Diane Bell, Pat Caplan, and Wazir Jahan Karim (eds) *Gendered Fields: Women, Men and Ethnography.* London and New York: Routledge.

Watson, Graham (1991) 'Rewriting Culture', in Richard G. Fox (ed.) *Recapturing Anthropology: Working in the Present.* Santa Fe: School of American Research Press.

Wengle, John L. (1988) *Ethnographers in the Field: The Psychology of Research.* Tuscaloosa, Ala.: University of Alabama Press.

Whitehead, Tony Larry (1986) 'Breakdown, Resolution, Coherence: The Fieldwork Experiences of a Big, Brown, Pretty-talking Man in a West

Indian Community', in Tony Larry Whitehead and Mary Ellen Conaway (eds) *Self, Sex and Gender in Cross-Cultural Fieldwork*. Urbana and Chicago: University of Illinois Press.

——— and Mary Ellen Conaway (eds) (1986) *Self, Sex and Gender in Cross-Cultural Fieldwork*. Urbana and Chicago: University of Illinois Press.

Chapter 1

Lovers in the field

Sex, dominance, and the female anthropologist

Jill Dubisch

'Your friend is very nice.' The woman to whom I had just been introduced smiled at my companion and myself from the doorway of the village cafe. 'Is she married?'

'She's engaged', my friend, an anthropologist whose village I was visiting, replied quickly.[1]

'That's too bad', the woman said, laughing. 'If she weren't, we would find someone from the village for her.'

Marry a village man? When I was first doing fieldwork in Greece, over twenty years ago,[2] the idea would have seemed quite strange, even unthinkable. Villagers belonged to a world very far from mine, and we were further separated by education and by class. And although Greek men in tourist areas might have affairs with foreign women, most of the village men I knew were excluded from such activities by their lack of knowledge of foreign languages and their lack of contact with tourists. As for myself, not only was I married and accompanied by my husband when I first went to Greece, I was also determined that, married or not, I would cause no scandal or gossip within the village, and so was very careful in all my behavior, but especially my behavior with men.[3]

Greece has changed since that time. The village in which I did my original fieldwork, like many villages throughout Greece, has become greatly depopulated through out-migration. Tourism has increased in many areas and invaded the once relatively untouched island where my fieldwork village was located, and there is more awareness of, and contact with, the outside world even among Greeks still living in such small communities.

During this period, I have changed as well. When I visited the village where my friend was working in 1986, both she and I had anticipated and prepared for the village woman's inevitable question about my marital status, and had decided in advance that 'engaged' would be the term which best described this.[4] What I had not entirely anticipated, however, was my own response to the woman's joking remark. Although quite aware that I would be a failure as a Greek housewife, I could not help wondering a little about the village man the woman might have selected for me, a thought I doubt that I would have had at an earlier time.

This chapter is about such thoughts and about some of the ways in which my reactions to being a woman in Greece, and more specifically to being a foreign woman (*kseni*), have led me to reflect on the female anthropologist as both sexual actor and sexual object in the context of doing anthropology in Europe. My discussion covers three main topics: (1) sex in the field, (2) cultural domination and the nature of the exotic/erotic Other, and (3) the implications of both of these in the particular context of fieldwork in Europe. I conclude by relating all of these to my own experience working in Greece.

Sex and the single anthropologist

A basic tenet of my graduate education was: 'You can't teach fieldwork.' All I received in the way of advice prior to beginning my own field research were a few informally transmitted guidelines for personal conduct and a little practical advice for settling into the field situation. And certainly there was no advice about sex, not even for those who were going alone into the field and would presumably be facing a long period of sexual abstinence in addition to the other hardships which we all assumed fieldwork would entail (cf. Newton 1993: 4).[5] The only mention of the topic that I recall came from a professor in another department, who, when I informed him that I would be working in Greece, remarked with a faint suggestion of a leer that Greek men would, of course, try to 'lead me up the garden path' (his phrase).

Yet despite this lack of explicit instruction or advice on the matter, I think it is safe to say that I and most of my fellow graduate students absorbed the idea that sexual relations with members of the community in which we were working would be neither appropriate nor wise. (Although underground stories of the sexual escapades of certain famous anthropologists circulated among us, there was a flavor of scandal about them.) It is difficult to know the extent to which all of us followed this implicit directive in our own fieldwork.[6] However, it appears that celibacy is probably the norm during fieldwork, at least in the fieldwork location itself. Accounts of exceptions to this have occasionally appeared in print, and informal conversations with friends may reveal other instances as well, but celibacy, it would seem, is more common than not.[7]

Why would this be so? Is it a matter of ethics? We do almost everything else with our 'informants': share their lives, eat with them, attend their rituals, become part of their families, even become close friends, and sometimes establish life-long relationships. At the same time, we 'use' them to further our goals, writing and speaking in public contexts about personal and even intimate aspects of their lives, appropriating these lives for our own professional purposes. Could a sexual relationship be any more intimate, committing, or exploitive than our normal relations with the 'natives'? (In some societies, it might even be less so.) Or is it really ourselves we are trying to protect?

There are, or course, practical problems which sexual relationships can create. In societies in which female sexuality is restricted, a male anthropologist's sexual advances to a local woman might have unpleasant results, and even necessitate the termination of fieldwork. In the same circumstances, the lone female anthropologist might feel that it was necessary to remain not only celibate but circumspect in her dealings with men in order to retain her standing and respect in the community (a standing which may already be compromised by her very presence there as a single woman). Certainly this is how I felt in my early fieldwork in Greece. Even though I was married and accompanied by my husband during my first stay in the village, I knew how villagers and townspeople regarded 'loose' foreign women (indeed 'loose' and 'foreign' were very nearly synonymous).

Yet there are many societies studied by anthropologists in which such restrictions are not present. In some cases, the anthropologist's celibacy may even pose a problem, since puzzled local people cannot understand why such a state would be assumed voluntarily, and they may seek to 'fix up' the anthropologist with a partner (e.g. Whitehead 1986). Or they may, as Cesara found in her work in Africa, regard a sexually deprived person as unhealthy and likely to exhibit erratic behavior or even go mad (Cesara 1982: 146). Why, under such circumstances, would the anthropologist say no to a sexual relationship? (In fact Cesara did not.) Yet when such incidents are described in the anthropological literature, the reasons why the anthropologist says no are not analyzed; they are assumed to be obvious.

Anthropological abstinence by no means implies a lack of temptation, however. Consider the following excerpt from Malinowski's diary:

> A pretty, finely built girl walked ahead of me. I watched the muscles of her back, her figure, her legs, and the beauty of the body so hidden to us, whites, fascinated me . . . I was sorry I was not a savage and could not possess this pretty girl.
>
> (Malinowski 1967: 255)

Malinowski's diaries are filled with accounts of erotic dreams and fantasies, indications of the sexual frustrations and longings which afflicted him in the course of fieldwork. (I suspect that the same is true of many other anthropologists' diaries as well.) Hsu (1979) interprets Malinowski's refusal to follow through on his attraction to Trobriand women[8] as an indication of his feelings of racial and cultural superiority, feelings which made it psychologically impossible for him to contract such a liaison (though such feelings of superiority have hardly deterred other European men from affairs with 'native' women). Wengle offers another interpretation of Malinowski's celibacy, suggesting that it was an attempt to preserve self-identity in the context of an alien culture by avoiding the surrender of self that sex would represent, and to maintain a link with home by directing his sexual fantasies and longing there (Wengle 1988: 123–5).

There may be elements of truth in both interpretations. The anthropologist may feel that a sexual relationship is too great a surrender of self in a context in which that self is already threatened or blurred, or that, at the least, intimate contact with someone so different would be too great a source of confusion in an already confusing situation. However, in addition, there may be implicit hierarchies of relationships which lead the anthropologist to see the people with whom she or he works as unsuitable sexual partners. Significantly, the people with whom we work may see us as less different, and more equal, than we see them. Hence, local mores permitting, they may regard sexual liaisons as more acceptable and less problematic than we do.

The problem presents itself differently to male and female anthropologists. This difference is the consequence not only of differences which may exist in permissible sexual behavior for men and women in the society in which the anthropologist is working, but also of the cultural baggage which the anthropologist carries into the field from her or his own society. In this baggage notions of gender, hierarchy, dominance, and sexuality are inextricably and sometimes very subtly mixed. Manda Cesara, the only female anthropologist to publish a frank account of her sexual experiences in the field[9] (and even then, only under a pseudonym; cf. Rabinow 1977), suggests another source of confusion which the female anthropologist may experience. This is a confusion which may originate in the anthropologist's own society, specifically, in her socialization into the male-dominated world of academe. Cesara described herself thus: 'More and more I came to see myself as anatomically woman but emotionally and intellectually man' (1982: 6). She admits to fearing sex as a conflict between mind and body and fears that an attraction to men compromises and even threatens her mental powers. Such mind–body conflict is not unique to women (indeed Cesara quotes Sartre extensively on this topic), but it assumes a particularly pertinent form for the female anthropologist in the field for whom the people she is studying must remain, to some extent at least, intellectual objects.

This issue of dominance and 'objectivity' is in turn related to the issue of the erotic 'other'.

Sex and Orientalism

The exotic and the erotic are often intertwined in Western conceptualizations of the Other. In Edward Said's analysis of Orientalism, we see repeated examples of the ways in which the mysterious and sensuous oriental woman embodies the essence of the Orient itself as the West 'invents' the 'mysterious east'. In Flaubert's writings, for example, 'the Oriental woman is an occasion and an opportunity for Flaubert's musings' and the Egyptian dancer and courtesan with whom Flaubert has an affair is '[l]ess a woman than a display of impressive but verbally inexpressive sensuality' (Said 1978: 187). Said does not attempt to analyze why the Orient is so often associated in the Western mind with a deep, alluring, and occasionally threatening sexuality (nor will I attempt to do so here). What is important to my own argument, however, and to the analysis of my own experience, are two features of Otherness: first, the sexual temptation posed by the exotic Other in Western discourse, and secondly, the fact that this erotic Other is usually portrayed as female, at least in the dominant male discourse. Moreover, this female Other often represents, ironically, the very impenetrability of the exotic, oriental culture. Less frequently portrayed or examined, however, is the sexual male Other. When he is portrayed, such portrayal often reveals the threatening dimension of erotic sexuality which Said mentions – for example, the insatiable and in-exhaustible oriental potentate with his harem of wives and concubines.

The threat, however, is usually for the Western *male*. The muted, generally unacknowledged side of erotic Orientalism is the exotic male

Other's potential attraction for the Western female. It is the consequences of this 'muted model' of attraction (to borrow E. Ardener's term; Ardener 1975) that I wish to explore here. As I will argue, the mutedness of this model both affects and reflects the nature of fieldwork as well as revealing the implicit hierarchies of dominance which govern its conduct. Moreover, I suspect, it greatly affects the way in which women view their own experiences in the field. It certainly did for me.

The Other is more forbidden to the Western woman than to the Western man. Indeed she is often assumed not to be attracted to the male Other in the way in which the Western man may find himself drawn to the female Other. Richard Lee, for example, comments upon the attractiveness of a Dobe !Kung woman who was placed in the 'wife' category to him through the complex !Kung naming system into which he was incorporated, noting the mild sense of titillation he felt thinking about the possibility of her in this role (Lee 1984). It is difficult to imagine a similar response from a female anthropologist placed in the same situation; or at least, it is difficult to imagine her writing about it. The reasons for this, I would suggest, lie in the confusion of hierarchies which underlies a sexual liaison for a female fieldworker, a confusion which makes liaisons with the male Other problematic generally (and the more 'other' the Other is, the more problematic). Moreover, as Newton points out, 'a veil of professional silence covers the face of indulgence toward men's casual sex with women in the field' (Newton 1993: 5). Female anthropologists, as females, have not been granted such professional indulgence, whether their sexual encounters occur in their own society or in the field.

Beneath erotic attraction lies a double set of dominance relations, those of gender and those of cultures. The availability, in both ideology and fact, of women of colonial or politically subordinate cultures to men of dominant cultures presents a consistent set of dominance relations. The sexual availability of such women is both a consequence and a representation of these dominance relations, and reproduces them. Sexual relations of women of the dominant cultures with men of the subordinate cultures, however, confuse dominance relations, for the gender hierarchy in such a relationship (from the point of view of the dominant Western society) contradicts the hierarchy of the cultural relationship by making the dominant women 'available' to subordinate men.[10]

And yet, as Cesara points out, such relationships are becoming more and more likely as the degree of 'difference' diminishes: 'The "native" of the non-Western world has become far more sophisticated and educated' and hence 'it should not be surprising that more anthropologists will have affairs with, or will marry, members of the society in which they conduct research' (Cesara 1982: 144). And since, as Cesara also points out, Western ideas of gender dominance and sexual relations may not be shared by those who are one's research subjects, the confusion for the female anthropologist in such situations may become even more acute.

All of this takes on a particular significance in the European context.

Gender and dominance in the European context

Europe presents the anthropologist with an anomaly, for it offers the unfamiliar in the deceptive guise of the familiar. As Ernestine Friedl put it in *Vasilika*, her now-classic study of a Greek village: 'We had two opposite reactions to the way of life in the village; one was a strong sense of familiarity, and the other was a surprised awareness of its strangeness' (Friedl 1962: 5).

From the point of view of the subject of this chapter, what may be confusing for the female anthropologist working in Europe is that, at first glance at least, the men may not seem very different from the men of her own society. In addition, the familiarity of the European background may not pose the challenge to identity maintenance which Wengle suggests often lies behind the practice of celibacy in the field. And especially when one is dealing with people who are knowledgeable, sophisticated, and highly educated, it may be particularly difficult to draw the line between self and other. The confusion of sexual attraction in such a situation is further compounded when the men in question cannot see a difference which, for the anthropologist, has defined one person as researcher ('superior') and the other as the object of her research (by definition somehow 'inferior').

The confusing sense of difference – which conflicts with the simultaneous sense of cultural familiarity – embodies an implicit hierarchy which is twofold. It resides first in the hierarchy of an anthropology which sees others as the object (a view which may, particularly in the European context, inspire resentment from those whom we research – see, for example, Danforth 1989). And second, it resides in an *intra*-European hierarchy of difference. The latter emerges with a particular clarity when we begin to contemplate the issue of sexuality. Popular sexual images attached to both male and female alter as one moves from north to south (and to some extent from east to west) within Europe. There is a movement from relative 'sameness' (at least for the

Western European or American anthropologist) and toward 'otherness', from superior (but somewhat passionless and boring) civilization to the inferior (but enticing and passionate) primitive. (This set of images may also be employed by those on the 'margins' of Europe as they themselves debate their own Europeanness – see Herzfeld 1987; also Gilmore 1987). Interestingly, for Northern Europeans and Americans, the exotic European Other here is often embodied in the male, and particularly in the Mediterranean male.[11] He is more sensual, more passionate, more emotional, more 'primitive' than his Northern European counterpart, a stereotype which he himself may play into and use as a means of self-contrast (Gilmore 1987). (The negative side of this stereotype is the sleazy sexual predator, the gigolo, which may represent a Western – and especially male – defensiveness against the image of the 'virile' Latin male.)

Turning to Greece, the site of my own fieldwork and of my own encounter with these issues, we see a clear illustration of some of the points I have made above.

The restrictions placed by the sexual code upon Greek women have made them generally inaccessible to the foreign male, and also to the Greek male except in the context of marriage. Although the situation is changing among young people today, liaisons between foreign men and Greek women still appear to be a rare occurrence. Greek men, on the other hand, like men in other countries of Mediterranean Europe, may initiate sexual relationships with visiting foreign women (especially Americans and Northern Europeans). So institutionalized is this practice in Greece that it even has a name, *kamaki*, which literally means 'fishing spear'. Anthropologist Sofka Zinovieff suggests that, among other things, *kamaki* reverses the relationships of nations, for in *kamaki* the men of the society which is subordinate (politically, economically, culturally) dominate the women of the dominant societies (Zinovieff 1991). Implicit in such an interpretation, of course, are certain notions regarding sexuality and hierarchy, notions which Greek men may share, to some extent at least, with other European and European-derived cultures. From the point of view of the foreign women, however, such a sexual adventure with an exotic Mediterranean male may be exactly what they are looking for as an added spice to their holiday (a possibility which Greek men may overlook or deny, since it diminishes their own role as the sexual predator). Thus there is a mutual feeding on stereotypes (as, for example, in the movie *Shirley Valentine* in which a love-starved Englishwoman has a brief but revitalizing affair with a simple but passionate Greek fisherman).

Since I was married and lived in a village during my first fieldwork in Greece, I seldom had to confront the situations created for the foreign woman by the practice of *kamaki*. However, in 1986 when I returned to Greece after a long absence to do further research, I had been divorced for a number of years, and although I was involved in a steady, long-term relationship, my partner did not accompany me on this trip (though he did visit me for several weeks during the summer). In this return trip I found myself not only in a different kind of fieldwork situation from that in which I had done my earlier research, but also in a Greece which had changed considerably in the intervening years. Not only was I conducting my fieldwork alone (for the most part), I was now living in a busy island town rather than in a small village. During the early 1970s, the town had been visited mostly by pilgrims and occasional adventurous foreign tourists. When I returned in 1986, however, it had become bustling and cosmopolitan. There were signs in English at shops and restaurants, there were discos and bars, there was topless bathing at the beaches, and there were many more foreign tourists. A number of townspeople now spoke at least a smattering of foreign languages, and tourist items in shops were selected to appeal to foreigners as well as Greeks. There were even *kamaki*, previously all but unknown on the island. (Indeed the term itself was one I had not encountered during my earlier fieldwork.) My return thus found me working in a more complex environment than the one which I had experienced earlier, acting within multiple contexts and in contact with a wide range of people, from pilgrims at the island's famous church (which was the focus of my research) to shopkeepers and other townspeople, to villagers who had jobs or relatives in the town, to foreign tourists.

In these multiple contexts I found myself being multiple people, and I was often confused about which person was the appropriate one, and – perhaps more importantly – which one was really 'me'. Was it the person who followed the daily crowds of pilgrims streaming up to the church, a person who dressed in such a way as to blend in and not offend? (And in so doing often dressed more modestly than many of the pilgrims themselves.) Or was I the person who, rather differently attired, trudged off to the beach for sun and relaxation in the late afternoon after my day's work was done? And where was the person who had lived and made friends in a small island village, a village which now seemed quaint after my life in the bustling, more cosmopolitan town? And what did I, living alone in my rented apartment, say to my landlady when a single male friend came to visit me (as happened on several occasions)? And – to get to my subject here – how was I to respond to the island *kamaki*, to whom I was just another *kseni* (foreign woman), albeit, as they discovered, one who could speak Greek? These men were, after all, an element of the community I was studying, but I did not want to be relegated to the identity of available foreign woman, either by them or by other townspeople, since I had seen how that category of person was treated – dismissed or ignored by local people other than the *kamaki* themselves.

In addition to all of this, I faced the twin problems of loneliness and sexual frustration. The crowded, anonymous summer atmosphere of the town was quite different from the small, rather intimate village setting in which I had first done fieldwork. In the village it had been virtually impossible to be anonymous, and opportunities to socialize could be found in any stroll down the village street or in any village shop or café. In the town it was different. I was just another visitor, and my ability to speak Greek, and my somewhat more prolonged stay, set me apart only marginally from other tourists. Moreover, the townspeople were extremely busy during the summer, and any inclination they may have had for a closer acquaintanceship was generally thwarted by the sheer volume of strangers with whom they had to deal. And since most of the subjects of my research were the shifting population of pilgrims, they provided me with no social life or companionship either. I felt such deprivation all the more acutely because I was working in a place where many people had come for fun, accompanied by friends, families, and lovers. Alone, and working, I felt particularly isolated.

Under such circumstances, why not respond to the advances of local men? This is not to suggest that such advances were a constant part of my experience on the island. They were merely occasional – a waiter in a café with whom I struck up a conversation, a man at the beach, another man who began talking to me while I was photographing pilgrims disembarking at the waterfront. During the height of the summer, large numbers of foreign tourists visited the island, and many of the women were more noticeable and attractive than I was (particularly since most of the time I was dressing to 'blend' in a manner appropriate to my subject matter, which was religious activities). In fact, not attracting undue interest from *kamaki* was something of a relief, since I had worried about such attention when I was contemplating doing fieldwork alone in Greece.

But why was it a relief? And why not respond to such advances as were made? As I look back I see several reasons for my own reluctance.

The first has to do with my own attitudes toward sexual relations. The kind of encounter offered by *kamaki* was not attractive to me – at least not initially – because it did not represent the sort of relationship to men that I was accustomed to. I have never been interested in 'pick-up' sexual encounters or one-night stands. In order even to feel sexual attraction to someone, I have to have some sense of knowing the person and being comfortable. Being approached by someone of another culture was being approached by a double stranger, our only immediate bond our being in the same place at the same time and our being of the opposite sex, enough perhaps for the other person but not enough to make me feel comfortable, or even interested.[12]

The second factor in my discomfort with *kamaki* was that their approaches generated anxiety in me, anxiety related to fieldwork. In part this may have been a residue from earlier fieldwork, when all of my reading about 'honor and shame' and the Greek sexual code of behavior for women made me perhaps excessively anxious not to cause any local scandal or offense. Hence I was worried about consequences should I undertake an affair with a local man and the effects that this might have on my ability to carry out fieldwork. I also felt anxiety about coping with an intimate relationship in a foreign language and with someone of another culture, and about whether the demands of such a relationship would distract me from, or interfere with, my fieldwork. Added to this was the confusion posed by these men, who were both part of and not part of my research universe. Were they 'informants' or potential companions? Could they be both without violating one or the other status? Was I afraid of the implications of the sexual dominance hierarchies which both I and the island men shared (albeit in different degrees) as members of a common Western tradition, and hence afraid of the threat to my 'privileged' position as an anthropologist?[13]

At some deeper level, was I perhaps afraid of being myself, or at least of being the self I was used to 'back home'? One of the problems of fieldwork, one of the things which makes fieldwork difficult for many of us, is not simply having to deal with strange people and unfamiliar behavior and having to express ourselves in a language which is not our native tongue. More basic than all of these, as Wengle and others have pointed out, is the difficulty of being ourselves under such circumstances – or at least of being any self which is recognizable. Hence we experience loss of, or at least uncertainly about, our own identities. But perhaps it is not so much difficulty of being ourselves but the *fear* of being ourselves in a strange setting which is paralyzing, for we do not know how that self – which we experience as 'authentic' – will be received. And in a sexual encounter, of course, the self stands particularly revealed, both literally and metaphorically. Here the issue of sameness and difference is starkly revealed as well, as the presumed universality of sexual attraction and of maleness and femaleness (presumed by those of other cultures as well) is confronted with the reality of cultural otherness. Will what may have seemed familiar prove to be strange? Will what is unfamiliar reveal itself to be known after all? To put it very simply, does one do what one normally does in bed, or will one's 'normal' behavior prove culturally inappropriate, and in a particularly embarrassing way?

The issue of sameness and difference is related to the issue of inside and outside, of engagement and detachment – in other words to the whole dilemma of participant observation itself. Before I discuss my responses to this particular dilemma in my recent fieldwork, I would like to describe an earlier encounter in which my separation was clearly marked and never called into doubt, in which I was clearly an observer rather than a participant. This encounter serves as an important point of contrast to my later experience.

This earlier incident took place in 1975, when for the first time I returned to the village by myself. I was recently separated from my husband but had decided not to tell the villagers yet, uncertain of how they would react. (I simply said that he was unable to accompany me because of his limited vacation time, a situation with which they were already familiar.) After a very enjoyable stay with my friends in the village, I took a boat to the nearby island of Syros, where I planned to make connections to another island to visit other friends. As I sat in a café by the waterfront with several people from the village waiting for the boat, we were joined by the village schoolteacher (male) who, as it turned out, was also going to Syros. 'How nice, you will have company on the trip', one of the women sitting with me commented. I was a little surprised by her remark, as I might have thought that our traveling together would have been problematic – a man and a woman, each married to someone else, going to another island where we would both be staying overnight. But no one at the table seemed to put such a construction the situation, so I decided to treat it as entirely innocent as well.

Costas[14] and I sat together on the deck for the short trip to Syros, and we conversed on entirely innocent topics. However, he had pulled his deck chair close to mine, and periodically reached over to touch me as we talked. This was much more intimate body language than he would have employed in conversation with me in the village. (Such closeness and touching might have been part of my conversation with a village woman but not a man.) It was obvious that he was taking advantage of the opportunity provided by our being alone together and away from the village to flirt with me. Although I was in no way physically attracted to him, I did not draw away. I was not put off or threatened by his behavior, but instead was simply amused. I did worry a little bit, however, about what would happen when we landed in Syros, especially since he had proposed that we go together in search of hotel rooms. Would I end up in an awkward situation, I wondered, if we had rooms next to each other in the same hotel?

As it turned out, I need not have worried. While I waited at the waterfront, Costas set out in search of rooms. I had not realized that the cheese merchants were in Syros that week (the island has a large dairy industry) and that rooms would be hard to find. When Costas finally returned, he had located rooms in two different hotels, graciously allocating to me the better of the two. He saw me to the hotel but made no mention of further plans, and any anxieties I might have had were thus alleviated.

Later that evening, while I was sitting at a restaurant by the waterfront having dinner, I saw Costas passing by with a friend. I called out a greeting to him and he acknowledged it in a somewhat restrained fashion. As he moved away, I saw him responding with what appeared to be a certain embarrassment to a question which his friend, eyeing me curiously, had asked him. I have no doubt that the question was about me, and that Costas was explaining how he came to know this foreign woman. The next morning I saw him again (alone) as I was eating breakfast and we conversed normally for a while, Costas complaining of the mosquitoes which had infested his hotel room.

My responses to all of this were detached. Although an actor in the little 'drama', and indeed the reason for its occurrence, I was not emotionally involved (apart from my anxiety about the hotel rooms). Costas' distancing himself from me later that evening when he was out with his friend, and his obvious reluctance even to acknowledge me, let alone introduce me or converse, did not offend or bother me. I viewed the whole incident anthropologically, noting the behavior of the native male who was willing to flirt with me when we were alone but inclined to ignore me as a *kseni* with whom a relationship would be questionable when in the company of his friend. (I should add here that my interactions with Costas also grew out of our previous relationship, a respectful one between the educated village schoolteacher and another educated person whom he saw as someone to whom he could talk. While our travelling together was an opportunity for him to flirt, my sense is that the situation created for him a certain confusion or ambiguity in our roles.)

Eleven years later, when I returned to the island for a longer period of fieldwork, I found myself in a different situation – one which was not so emotionally detached, as I eventually became involved with two different men, one on the island, one in Athens. The first was an island *kamaki*, Nikos, a man of about my own age, divorced, involved in a variety of businesses which put him in regular contact with tourists. Although he spoke several languages (including some English), my own conversations with him were in Greek. Indeed, from the beginning we spoke nothing else, as he made his first advances to me in that language. (Later he told me he couldn't determine what nationality I might be and so decided to try Greek – which worked.)

I have said I became 'involved' but that is perhaps too strong a term to use here. Nikos first simply called greetings to me at a distance as I passed his shop. At that point it was near the end of my stay on the island and near the end of the tourist season as well. Although we had minimal conversation in this fashion, it gave him the grounds for approaching one day as I was busy photographing pilgrims. I had just fended off another persistent (younger) *kamaki* earlier (the tourist season was drawing to a close and foreign women were becoming few and far between). But when Nikos came up to me and very politely asked if he could treat me to coffee later, I thought 'What does it matter?' I was leaving the island for Athens the next day, it was my last night on the island, and after a long, lonely period of fieldwork, I did not want to spend my last evening by myself. When we met for coffee, we chatted a while and I agreed to join him later in the evening. I had no illusions about what I was agreeing to, but I also felt that it was, in some sense, 'safe'. I was leaving, there could be no repercussions for my fieldwork.

Later, however, at Nikos' house, I didn't feel comfortable staying the night, and I persuaded him to take me back to my apartment, hoping that my landlady would not see me getting out of his car at such a late hour. (Sensitive to this consideration, Nikos dropped me off a block away.) The next morning, I awoke with a sense of anxiety, even panic, afraid that I had done something that would 'spoil' my fieldwork site. In retrospect, I am not entirely certain what I feared – the town was certainly no small village, and while I was not anonymous, my life was not of that much concern to most of the townspeople. In any case, by the time I left that afternoon, much of my anxiety had subsided. As I stood on the deck of the boat watching the island fade into the distance, I felt a mixture of sadness over the end of my stay there and pleasure at the thought that I had spent my last evening on the island with Nikos.

I saw Nikos once more, in Athens, and we spent the evening at a small hotel in the Plaka (the old area of the city). Although we tried to continue our sexual relationship on subsequent visits to the island, it became obvious that we had different approaches to, and different expectations of, such a relationship, and eventually we gave up. We remain friends, however, and I drop by his office to say hello and to have a cup of coffee on my return visits to the island.

My second encounter was more worthy of the term 'involvement'. It took place in Athens, during the month I spent there following my fieldwork on the island. Yanis was also my age and also in a tourist business, but he differed from Nikos in that he had been married to a non-Greek woman and had considerable experience not only with tourists but also with students and professors, particularly Americans. His English was excellent and we generally conversed in a mixture of English and Greek. Our relationship was deeper and more long-lasting than the one I had with Nikos (continuing in subsequent visits until 1990, when he had apparently become involved in a full-time relationship with someone else). Yanis, although not highly educated, was intelligent and interested in intellectual topics. He also had a delightful sense of humor (which Nikos lacked) and we had good times together. Apart from these personal characteristics, however, I think we got along well because we met each other half-way. His experience with Americans and British and my knowledge and experience of Greece and Greeks allowed us to cross each other's cultural boundaries. Although there were differences – of culture, of class, and of personality – these only made things interesting for us. Our expectations were compatible and our pleasure in each other's company was mutual, and although our relationship was not romantic, there was intense affection and a strong liking for each other. When I finally left Athens, it was hard to part. Perhaps this is the negative side of an intimate involvement during fieldwork – it is difficult for both parties when the anthropologist leaves. And yet in this respect it may be no different from other relationships we develop in the course of our research. I cried in 1970 when I left the village after thirteen months of fieldwork, and so did some of the women with whom I had become friends.

What did I learn from these two involvements? Certainly they did not solve the dilemmas I have discussed in this chapter. On the contrary, it was through these relationships that I became aware of many of the issues I have articulated, and they provided part of the impetus for writing this account. Nor did Nikos and Yanis solve the fieldwork confusion of 'Who am I?' In fact, they added to the confusion by giving me yet another set of fieldwork identities, identities which had to take account of my own sexuality (hitherto suppressed in most of the fieldwork situations in which I found myself). In addition, these two relationships made even more complex the issues of sameness and difference and the question of the point at which I stopped being a researcher and simply became my private self (or of whether there even is such a point). They also made me aware of my own hitherto unexamined and unconfessed notions of hierarchy in the field.

To analyze all of this: the relationships I have described here might be said to fall along a continuum with respect to the participant/observer split. The brief flirtation of Costas the schoolteacher would fall at one end of this continuum, an encounter in which I, though involved as the object of the flirtation, was removed from it by my own lack of sexual attraction to Costas and therefore able to view it simply with anthropological interest. With Nikos my interest was obviously not that of an observer – I hardly said yes to his invitation my last night on the island out of a desire for an ethnographic experience. Nonetheless the differences between us were great enough for me to have to bring my own anthropological understanding to bear upon the relationship. For him, our being a man and a woman was sufficient basis for our encounter. My own requirements were more complex, in part due to my own personality and personal preferences, in part to my society's views that there *ought* to be more to such a relationship, especially for a woman.[15] By 'more' here I do not mean that I expected a long-term commitment, or even anything very serious – only an interest in each other that went beyond sex. Though I thought my expectations minimal in this respect, they apparently did not appear so to Nikos, for I earned from him the comment (almost an accusation) that I was 'romantic'. In part the differences between us also stemmed from the fact that while for me our encounter was something different and daring, for Nikos it was almost routine, given his regular contact with female tourists of all ages and nationalities.

I do not wish here to make totalizing generalizations about 'Greek men'. Indeed my point leads in the opposite direction. Nikos and Yanis, though both Greek men my age, used to encounters with foreigners, and similar in class and education, were nonetheless quite different, even in their Greekness. Moreover, even though I have labelled Nikos a *kamaki* and even though he exhibited behavior that fits well with what Zinovieff has written about the phenomenon (Zinovieff 1991), I suspect that in other ways he might be unusual for that category.[16]

I have mostly analyzed my relationship with Nikos so far, putting an element of the observer into it. Because of the differences between us, it was easier (and sometimes necessary) to detach in this fashion. With Yanis, however, it was not only less necessary, it was also more difficult. I cannot claim that he was not part of my 'fieldwork' insofar as a sexual relationship, like any relationship, illuminates both similarities and differences across cultures, and within them. Reflecting on those differences and similarities has led to insights about my research in Greece, insights by no means limited to the relationship itself. In addition, Yanis, familiar with both anthropology and my own research, frequently offered information and comments which were of direct help to me in my work. In that respect, he was less 'informant' than friend and collaborator.

Sex, fieldwork, and the 'authentic' self

Earlier, in discussing the uncertainties about 'Who am I?' engendered by the fieldwork situation, I utilized such phrases as 'being myself' and 'what was really me'. The concepts which these phrases reflect derive from a particularly Western – and perhaps more specifically American – concept of the self, a dualistic concept in which a stable, authentic, interiorized self confronts an objectified, exterior world. If, however, we begin to question this concept and to speak of multiple, culturally constituted *selves* rather than of *the* self, some of the difficulties posed by fieldwork become clearer (see Kondo 1990). Different selves are constructed in the fieldwork process, different from those we have come to know in the context of our own society. These selves have some elements which are familiar to us, and some which are not. Since sexuality often seems to us especially characteristic of the 'interior', basic self, sexual activity which crosses cultural lines, and hence creates new sexual selves, may be particularly confusing to the sense of self and hence particularly threatening.

Although in some way we are always basically 'ourselves' (how can we not be?), the cultural idea of an authentic, 'real' self is nonetheless important in the fieldwork experience and in our reactions to what happens to us in the context of another culture, particularly as we feel this real self being lost or blurred (cf. Kondo 1990). It is in this way that the *idea* of a self has reality and impacts on the nature of our fieldwork and the relationships we develop there. At the same time, the concept of an interiorized, stable, consistent self may not be characteristic of the society in which we work, adding further to the confusion and difficulty.

With these ideas in mind, I would like to end with the following story, a story that kept coming back to me as I was writing this chapter. It both reveals and sums up several important points about self, hierarchy, and sexuality in the context of my own fieldwork experience.

The story concerns a village man I have known since the time of my first fieldwork, almost twenty-five years ago. My former husband and I had been good friends with Marcos and his wife, a couple a little older than ourselves, and we frequently had dinner and made excursions together. When I returned one summer to the island, I found Marcos working at the island's famous church, where I was doing research.[17] We greeted each other with mutual pleasure and he invited me up to the village for dinner at their house. After learning his schedule at the church, I sometimes timed my visits there so that I could talk to him, happy to see a familiar face in the constantly changing crowds of pilgrims. He proved a valuable informant, and from him I learned many interesting things 'behind the scenes' at the church. It was an odd situation for us, however, because although we had known each other for some time, we had always been in the company of our spouses whenever we conversed and had never had any lengthy conversation alone together. We also received some curious glances from Marcos' fellow employees at the church. I'm sure they were wondering who the foreign woman was. We were both conscious of the oddness of our situation, and a little uneasy, perhaps, because for the first time we were forced to be aware of each other as a man and a woman in ways we had not been before.

I had rented an apartment in town where I lived alone. One afternoon shortly before I was due to leave the island, Marcos unexpectedly dropped by. He had been confused about which day I had said I was leaving, he told me, and concerned that I might have left without saying goodbye. I was caught off guard by his visit, dressed more casually than I might have been either at the church or in the village (though by no means indecently). But I was also – and I think more importantly – caught off guard by this visit in a private setting which none of the islanders I knew (except my landlady) had entered to that point. He was a little uneasy as well, perhaps aware that he had surprised me in a different persona, one with which he was unfamiliar.

My first thought, however, when I saw Marcos at the door revealed my own socialization into a different aspect of Greek gender roles. The apartment was a mess, I thought in dismay, and Marcos would think me a poor housekeeper. I then sought to cope with the situation through further 'Greekness', taking refuge in rituals of hospitality. I insisted that Marcos sit down and have an ouzo, preparing a small plate of food to go with it, despite his protests. These roles exhausted, I had to confront his presence in my hitherto private space. At that point, I decided that all I could do was relax and be what I thought of as myself, a woman in her apartment talking to a male friend. I even accepted Marcos' offer of a cigarette, though I had always made a point of not smoking in the village.[18] This acceptance was a subtle signal of a different relationship between us, and I think we both sensed this as I let him light my cigarette. We talked for a while (or mostly he talked), and after several ouzos, he finally got up to leave. We shook hands firmly in farewell, and I had a momentary impulse to give him the brief hug and ritual kiss on both cheeks I might have given an Athenian male friend in such a situation. But I knew that it was not appropriate behavior with a village man.[19] We said goodbye and he was gone.

To an outside observer, nothing happened in this brief visit. But for Marcos and myself, something had changed, for I had let myself be myself in a way which acknowledged our sameness and at least a small degree of attraction between a male and female friend. What was important was that by letting myself reveal what I experienced as my 'authentic' self to a degree I had not before, and by acknowledging, however subtly, that we were a man and a woman in a sexual way, I was treating Marcos more as an equal, more as I would treat a man in my own society than I ever had before. Yet, significantly, I had never recognized that I had not been doing so until then.

Conclusion

James Clifford has observed that 'every version of an "other", wherever found, is also the construction of a "self"' (1986: 23). What I might add, based on my own contemplation of the issues of gender, sexuality, and otherness, particularly in the European context, is that our own 'self' in the field helps to create the 'other'. Sexuality is one dimension of self, and a dimension which may be particularly challenged in the field, whether by the felt necessity for abstinence, the sexual temptations offered to us, the fears of professional consequences of sexual indulgence, and/or the reactions of those we encounter to our perceived nature as sexual beings. At the same time, nothing in our training as anthropologists truly prepares us for dealing with these issues, a fact that reflects our own society's deep ambivalence about sexuality (and particularly female sexuality).[20] Thus sexuality can confuse – sometimes subtly, sometimes obviously – the sense of self and other, of sameness and difference, which we experience in the course of our fieldwork. To the degree that the female anthropologist takes account of her own sexuality in the field, she may create or enable contexts in which a more 'authentic' self can be revealed, and thus perhaps a more authentic 'other' as well.

Acknowledgements

I would like to thank Mari Clark, Ray Michalowski, and Don Kulick, as well as various friends and lovers in Greece, for their help with my research and/or the preparation of this chapter.

Notes

1 I was researching pilgrimage on the island of Tinos at the time (1986–7), and had visited this village to talk to villagers who had made such a pilgrimage. Funding for research during this period was provided by the Fulbright Foundation and by a faculty research grant from the University of North Carolina and the UNCC Foundation.

2 This was fieldwork for my doctoral dissertation at the University of Chicago, carried out in 1969–70, under a fellowship and grant from the National Institute of Mental Health.

3 Compare Conaway 1986: 59–60; Giovannini 1986: 110.

4 Though unmarried, I was living with someone in a long-term relationship. In Greece engaged couples often travel and even live together.

5 Esther Newton and I attended the same graduate school (University of Chicago) at about the same time, and our experiences regarding this issue appear to have been similar.

6 The only one of my contemporaries in graduate school who has publicly revealed sexual encounters during fieldwork is Rabinow (1977).

7 I have now come to wonder if sexual relationships in the field are quite as uncommon as we assume. After I presented an earlier version of this paper at the American Anthropological Association meeting in Chicago in 1991, several people, both male and female, both friends and people I did not know, come up to me to talk about their own affairs in the field.

8 It is not clear whether Malinowski was entirely abstinent in the course of his fieldwork. It appears Malinowski's widow censored the diary before publication (see Newton 1993 for a further discussion).

9 For an account of a lesbian anthropologist's erotic (though not sexual) relationship with her female 'best informant' see Newton 1993.

10 Often such sexual contact may be part of dominant discourse only in the form of rape, or the expressed fear of rape.
11 Though there is a female counterpart in the Carmen image.
12 This is not unique to Greece or Greek men, as evidenced by singles bars and one-night stands in my own society.
13 I might mention that this was never a problem for me in relationships with Greek men who were academics.
14 All names used here are pseudonyms.
15 At least those were the expectations for people of my generation. Although I had always considered myself less bound by such expectations than other women my age, perhaps I was more bound by them than I thought.
16 For example, he was interested in talking about sex (including my sex life), almost obsessively so (at least to my mind). He sometimes seemed bored with 'ordinary' sex and liked to tell me about his relationship with a French doctor (female) who visited him on a regular basis. She was bisexual and liked to introduce another woman into their encounters. (They have since had a child together, as I learned during a visit in 1993.)
17 For accounts of my research see Dubisch 1990, 1991.
18 When I first worked in the village, smoking had not really been acceptable among village women, and although things have changed since then, even now none of the village women my age smokes.
19 At least it would not have been an appropriate behavior with a man my own age. I have hugged the elderly husband of my landlady in the village, a man with whom I had an almost grandfather–granddaughter relationship.
20 See Newton 1993: 4–5.

References

Ardener, Edwin (1975) 'Belief and the Problem of Women,' in S. Ardener (ed.) *Perceiving Women*. London: Malaby Press.

Cesara, Manda (1982) *Reflections of a Woman Anthropologist: No Hiding Place*. New York: Academic Press.

Clifford, James (1986) 'Introduction: Partial Truths', in J. Clifford and G.E. Marcus (eds) *Writing Culture*. Berkeley, Calif.: University of California Press.

Conaway, Mary Ellen (1986) 'The Pretense of the Neutral Researcher', in T.L. Whitehead and M.E. Conaway (eds) *Self, Sex, and Gender in Cross-Cultural Fieldwork*. Urbana and Chicago: University of Illinois Press.

Danforth, Loring (1989) *Firewalking and Religious Healing: The Anastenaria of Greece and the American Firewalking Movement*. Princeton, N.J.: Princeton University Press.

Dubisch, Jill (1990) 'Pilgrimage and Popular Religion at a Greek Holy Shrine', in E. Badone (ed.) *Religious Orthodoxy and Popular Faith in European Society*. Princeton, N.J.: Princeton University Press.

——— (1991) 'Gender, Kinship, and Religion: Reconstructing the Anthropology of Greece', in P. Loizos and E. Papataxiarchis (eds) *Contested Identities: Gender and Kinship in Greece*. Princeton, N.J.: Princeton University Press.

Friedl, Ernestine (1962) *Vasilika: A Village in Modern Greece*. New York: Holt, Rinehart and Winston.

Gilmore, David (1987) *Aggression and Community: Paradoxes of Andalusian Culture*. New Haven: Yale University Press.

Giovannini, Maureen (1986) 'Female Anthropologist and Male Informant: Gender Conflict in a Sicilian Town', in T.L. Whitehead and M.E. Conaway (eds) *Self, Sex and Gender in Cross-cultural Fieldwork*. Urbana and Chicago: University of Illinois Press.

Herzfeld, Michael (1987) *Anthropology Through the Looking Glass: Critical Anthropology on the Margins of Europe*. Cambridge: Cambridge University Press.

Hsu, Frances (1979) 'The Cultural Problem of the Cultural Anthropologist'. *American Anthropologist*. Vol. 79, pp. 805–8.

Kondo, Dorinne (1990) *Crafting Selves: Power, Gender, and Discourses of Identity in a Japanese Workplace*. Chicago: University of Chicago Press.

Lee, Richard (1984) *The Dobe !Kung*. New York: Harcourt Brace Jovanovich.

Malinowski, Bronislaw (1967) *A Diary in the Strict Sense of the Term*. New York: Harcourt, Brace and World.

Newton, Esther (1993) 'My Best Informant's Dress: The Erotic Equation in Fieldwork'. *Cultural Anthropology*. Vol. 8, No. 1, pp. 3–23.

Rabinow, Paul (1977) *Reflections on Fieldwork in Morocco*. Berkeley, Calif.: University of California Press.

Said, Edward (1978) *Orientalism*. New York: Vintage Books.

Wengle, John (1988) *Ethnographers in the Field: The Psychology of Research*. Tuscaloosa, Ala.: University of Alabama Press.

Whitehead, Tony Larry (1986) 'Breakdown, Resolution, and Coherence: The Fieldwork Experiences of a Big, Brown, Pretty-talking Man in a West Indian Community', in T.L. Whitehead and M.E. Conaway (eds) *Self, Sex and Gender in Cross-cultural Fieldwork*. Urbana and Chicago: University of Illinois Press.

Zinovieff, Sofka (1991) 'Hunters and Hunted: *Kamaki* and the Ambiguities of Sexual Predation in a Greek Town', in P. Loizos and E. Papataxiarchis (eds) *Contested Identities: Gender and Kinship in Modern Greece*. Princeton, N.J.: Princeton University Press.

Chapter 2

Falling in love with an-Other lesbian

Reflections on identity in fieldwork

Evelyn Blackwood

> Being the supreme crossers of cultures, homosexuals have strong bonds with the queer white, Black, Asian, Native American, Latino . . . We are a blending that proves that all blood is intricately woven together, and that we are spawned out of similar souls.
>
> (Anzaldúa 1987: 84–5)

I conducted fieldwork in a rural Muslim Minangkabau village in West Sumatra, Indonesia.[1] I went there in 1989 to study social change, gender and power, but I was also interested in exploring the gender identity of lesbians in West Sumatra.[2] I was fortunate to meet several lesbians, and in the process fall in love with one of them. An already challenging field experience then became more complicated as I shifted between the professional, straight identity I maintained in my research village, and the closeted, lesbian identity I possessed with my lover in her village. The instability of my identity and the necessity to reconstruct it in relation to the people with whom I interacted forced a recognition of the differences and similarities between us.

The question I want to explore here is how one's subjectivity in the field, in this case my own subjectivity as a lesbian and an anthropologist, exposes and challenges issues of exoticizing and identity in ethnographic fieldwork. I attempt to understand the ways we reify distance between ourselves and our 'subjects' to avoid asking uncomfortable questions about our presence in other cultures and the ways we exoticize Others. If the denial of our subjectivity enables exoticizing in anthropology, how does recognition of our subjectivity, our agency in relationships in the field, counter that practice? In particular, how does the subjective experience of sexuality in the field challenge the distance between 'us' and 'them'?

I will explore these issues through the disjunctures of the familiar and the alien that I encountered in my field experience. I was alternately a young, unmarried daughter who professed to be sexually naive and engaged to be married, and also a lover, who fell in love with an-Other lesbian. This essay is a reflection on life in the borders of gender and sexuality and how conflicts of identity lead to new meanings and deeper understandings of cultural differences and similarities.

In this essay I do not want to speak for my lover, although in my recounting of our relationship I ultimately represent her. These recollections, however, are my interpretation of our experience, not hers. Her experience of me differed from my experience of her; her conflicts and disjunctures may be other than the ones I highlight here. (It might have been troublesome to her that I was non-Muslim, but I do not raise that issue here.) Further, I do not pretend to understand precisely how she felt being with a lover whose affluence and power as a member of a First World country set the terms of the relationship. This essay, then, is an excursion into the subjectivity of the anthropologist. It is an attempt to recognize the multiplicity of genders, sexualities, and classes within which we operate as anthropologists and the ways in which we can use our subjective experience of these domains as a bridge to challenge the distance inscribed in ethnographic fieldwork.

Anthropological privilege

Anthropology has long been accused of being a discourse in which the anthropologist holds a privileged position as bearer of the right to ask questions and make claims to knowledge about others. As Trinh so potently writes, anthropology is:

> a conversation of 'us' with 'us' about 'them', of the white man with the white man about the primitive-native man . . . a conversation in which 'them' is silenced. 'Them' always stands on the other side of the hill, naked and speechless, barely present in its absence.
>
> (1989: 65, 67)

This statement questions our right to speak for others and to assume in speaking that we convey some truth. As Trinh suggests, in the relation between anthropology and its subject there are two separate and distinct entities, a self and other, one unmarked, the other marked. This construction reinforces the distance between anthropologists and the people they 'study'. In his *Diary*, Malinowski (1989) expressed in contemptuous terms the gap he felt between himself and the Trobrianders. Dubisch (in this volume) notes that, twenty years ago, she felt as if she occupied a different world from that of the people in Greece she went to study. As Kondo points out, 'ethnographies commonly convey a subtle sense of superiority over the "people studied". . . All too often, standards of scientific objectivity in ethnography have masked points of view that are merely distant and unsympathetic' (1986: 84). Haraway eloquently defines this scientific objectivity as:

> the gaze from nowhere. This is the gaze that mythically inscribes all the marked bodies, that makes the unmarked category claim the power to see and not be seen, to represent while escaping representation. This gaze signifies the unmarked positions of Man and White.
>
> (1988: 581)

As anthropologists, our presence in other cultures and our subjectivities as members of the First World elicit certain responses that are understandable only if we know how we are perceived. In reference to informants, the metaphor of 'friend' appears frequently in writings about fieldwork by American anthropologists (see, for example, Geertz 1968). It is one way we define our relationship with the Other (and a way to find some solace for the loneliness we feel and replace relationships we had at 'home'). We constitute ourselves as 'friend', a neutral entity that embodies our belief that the relationship between ourselves and at least some of our informants is one of equality. But the category of 'friend' that we so readily apply to cross-cultural situations actually masks a much greater complexity in our field relations.

The problems that arise from lack of recognition of one's position in fieldwork are apparent in Rabinow's *Reflections on Fieldwork in Morocco* (1977). In this book Rabinow uses his experience of fieldwork as a way to describe his initiation into, and growing understanding of, the ways of another people. Such confessional writing has become a standard genre for critical anthropologists; sometimes it provides other revelations than those intended. Rabinow argues that fieldwork is an experiential activity conducted by a 'culturally mediated and historically situated self' (1977: 5). So far, so good. But he fails to acknowledge the superior position from which he is operating. Further, he assumes that Moroccans are relatively unreflective about things that anthropologists want to know. Rabinow writes that the process of fieldwork requires a building up of common experiences in order for the informant to speak so that the anthropologist can understand (1977: 152). In other words, the informant must come to see things in the way the anthropologist sees them to make their conversations intelligible. For Rabinow, it is his (male) informant who is required to bridge the gap, who should be brought to the (higher) level of understanding where the anthropologist dwells. Though Rabinow insists he only arrived at 'a partial understanding' of his informants (1977: 162), as with most ethnographies, it is nevertheless this partial understanding that is enshrined as true knowledge brought home from the field.

It is in part Rabinow's inability or refusal to position himself that creates the distance between himself and his subject. Rabinow established what he considered to be a friendship early on with the man who was his Arabic teacher. 'Basically I had been conceiving of him as a friend because of the seeming personal relation we had', he stated (1977: 29). His first disjuncture, which he identified as 'one of my first direct experiences of Otherness' (1977: 28), happened when his friend/teacher treated him as an exploitable source of income (someone who could provide a certain amount of status and financial reward), rather than the 'friend' that Rabinow had convinced himself that he was. This disjuncture made him realize that they were operating under different assumptions, which he assumed meant something about his teacher's culture. On the contrary, Rabinow's disjuncture came from being reminded that he was not a neutral Self but a situated Other (the wealthy white man from America), something he attempted to downplay but which his informant understood quite well. Rabinow described this disjuncture as a meeting with 'culture', thus failing to recognize it as the result of his own positioning within another culture. By setting their interaction aside as distinctly belonging only to his informant's culture, he denies that they are both players at some level in the same world; his statement relegates his teacher to a cultural backwater that operates without connection to the larger world.

In contrast, Favret-Saada (1980) insists that there can be no ethnographic statement that is not upheld by its relation to the two (author and subject). Her work on witchcraft among French peasants caused her to rethink the relationship of the author and the subject. To understand, one has to 'become one's own informant, to penetrate one's own amnesia, and to try to make explicit what one finds unstatable in oneself' (1980: 22). She was forced to understand her own motives, to question why she wanted to understand her subject; for her, simply seeking knowledge was not enough.

Reflexive anthropology, of which Favret-Saada's is one example, seeks to counter criticism 'of the truth claims of Western representations of the "other"' (Mascia-Lees *et al.* 1989: 9) by bringing the anthropologist into the text and highlighting the interaction between anthropologist and subject. In another such attempt, Dwyer (1979) argues that understanding the dialectical relationship between Subject and Object provides an alternative to traditional anthropological practices. Dwyer implies a connectedness between Self and Other by suggesting that as ethnographers we are 'at home' everywhere (1977: 150). His vehicle for connection, a dialogic approach, goes a long way toward bridging difference. It is insufficient, however, because it only takes into account the will and subjectivity of the Other in the anthropological project, without fully accounting for the position of the anthropologist in this 'confrontation with the Other' (1979: 211).

It is not enough for the anthropologist to be visible asking the questions; we must acknowledge the position from which we ask our questions and make our interpretations. Our subjectivities form the core of anthropological theory and method. Haraway's challenge to feminists to search for situated knowledges is equally applicable to anthropological knowledge: 'feminist objectivity is about limited location and situated knowledge, not about transcendence and splitting of subject and object' (1988: 583). The position and identity of the ethnographer, as a member of a certain Western intellectual tradition and citizen of the 'First World' (with all the implications of hierarchy that term carries), are critical to the shape of our work and the meaning it expresses. We have to locate ourselves because, as Kondo writes in her confessional on fieldwork, 'knowledge is always knowledge from a particular perspective. Understandings are situated within culture, history, and biography' (1986: 84). But the ethnographic experience is more than an identification of positionality or subjectivity; we occupy multiple positions and identities that transform over time, forcing us constantly to reconstruct who we are in relation to the people we study. Disjunctures, the moments at which we find ourselves uncomfortable, point the way to understanding these transformations and the differences between ourselves and others.

Marked identities

My identity as a lesbian, feminist, and woman prevented me from assuming in the field situation that I was simply a neutral figure observing culture. As a lesbian, I am aware that I move in a world partially alien, one where the norms of heterosexuality and femininity are at odds with self-image. I have the sense that any role I take on is 'drag', a costume one puts on to suit the occasion, not some inborn, natural part of me. As a lesbian and member of a marginalized community, I move within the dominant, straight (white) culture without comfortable inclusivity in it.

Consequently, I come to anthropology as an insider/outsider, an insider who was indoctrinated in American culture and its intellectual tradition, yet whose marginality as a lesbian makes me an outsider in many contexts. I am not allowed the luxury of perceiving myself as the center of the world, or as the 'man' against which all others are measured, the person able to speak Truth (Trinh 1989). From a marginalized position on the borders of the dominant system, it is easier to recognize the categories that shape all of us and not just those categories that come under our scrutiny as anthropologists; it is harder to claim that one sees all, as Haraway's imagery of the Eye suggests (1988: 581), and deny that one has any position relative to those being studied. Whitehead (1986), writing from a similarly marginalized position as a black American anthropologist, could not maintain the fiction that he occupied an unmarked, non-problematic identity in his fieldwork. Instead, he used his identity and people's responses to him to gain a better understanding of Jamaican culture.

My lesbian identity was not openly part of my field identity, as Whitehead's identity as a black person was. I used it not as a personal criterion to judge other people's reactions but, rather, as an internal monitor that keyed me to the margins and disjunctures of culture. It made me extremely aware of the dominance of heterosexuality in Minangkabau culture and the careful gender distinctions that mark men and women as different. Later, when I met my lover, it also keyed me to the differences between her life and other women's lives and the forces that shaped her identity as a lesbian.

In preparing for fieldwork, I decided it would be better to hide my lesbian identity. I assumed Muslims would not accept an openly gay person and I did not want to hurt my chances of completing my research successfully. To those who asked, I identified myself as unmarried (I was, in fact, single at the time). I also allowed the cultural assumption of heterosexuality to slot me as heterosexual. Because my marriageability and high status as a foreigner made me a supposedly desirable target, it was suggested to me by other Indonesianists that I maintain a story about a fiancé whom I would marry as soon as I finished my dissertation. This story would hopefully discourage unwanted male advances and proposals of marriage. Since it is acceptable now in West Sumatra for women to finish their education before marriage, my excuse made sense to people in the village, although they still considered me to be rather old for an unmarried woman. I maintained this story throughout my fieldwork, although I was uncomfortable with it. It was a flimsy disguise at best (since I had no pictures of my fiancé and never received any letters from him) and at worst established my superiority over the people in the village because it implied they should not, or did not need to, know such things about 'their' anthropologist. This notion that I was the knower and they the known reflects one of the ways we as anthropologists distance ourselves from those we study.[3]

As an unmarried, supposedly heterosexual woman living with an Indonesian family, I was expected to fulfill the ideals of the gender category to which I was ascribed. This situation is common for women anthropologists and always problematic. In many cases women anthropologists are forced to accept restrictions of movement as well as an inferior status vis-à-vis men that confronts a deeply held sense of self.[4] I tried to meet the expectations of people in the village concerning my gender because I wanted to maintain good relations, acquire access to any information I wanted, and, most of all, gain their love and acceptance. In a Minangkabau village, these expectations are not overly burdensome; within the rank hierarchy relations between women and men are egalitarian (see Blackwood 1993). As heads of lineages and controllers of ancestral houses and lands, women have power over the labor and activities of their kin; no decisions are made within the lineage without their consent. Consequently, women are prime movers in village social life, which is, however, sex-segregated in most social contexts. Unmarried women in particular must protect their reputation and not associate freely with men, nor should they engage in activities typically identified with men, such as smoking, drinking, or gambling. I maintained these conventions quite easily in addition to my story that I had a 'boyfriend' back home. At least my unavailability was amply supported by my lack of sexual interest in men in the village. I treated men my age as peers and older men as seniors and did not have to struggle with my sexual identity in relation to them.

At the same time I resisted constructing a field identity that conformed to their expectations for an unmarried woman. Although I cleaned my room and sometimes swept the floors in the house, I never cooked or did my own laundry; instead, I paid other women to take care of these domestic duties for me. This failing did not surprise my host, however, who assumed that 'rich', privileged Americans would not be well trained in such matters. Where the gendered dress code was at odds with my lesbian self, however, I developed the most resistance to reconstructing my identity. I could not force myself to wear skirts, as any proper Indonesian woman does, except very occasionally. My host sometimes remarked on this lapse because it raised deeper questions for her about my womanhood. She expressed great satisfaction when I wore local dress on ritual occasions but eventually decided that my proclivity for pants was a harmless American custom. Her tolerance of my behavior showed a willingness to understand and overlook the differences between us that I had not expected.

My marginality in two cultures and my inability to conform to gender categories helped me to feel at ease moving between men's and women's spaces. At ceremonies I bridged the distance between men and women with equanimity. Women and men physically occupy different parts of a room during ceremonies. In some instances, I sat with the women and listened to their conversations, but when I had permission I would sit between the two groups. On one occasion I attended the male-only part of a ritual. My presence with the men unnerved my Indonesian mother, who was helping with food preparations at the ceremony, yet she understood my need to collect data and sought to support me by crossing the boundary herself and sitting with me and the men.

While I recognized my own marginal gender identity, I resisted coming to terms with my privilege. Beside being a daughter to my Indonesian family, I was also the white American woman scholar, who, as a representative of the First World, had certain privileges and power over other people's lives. I was honored in a welcoming ceremony and sat in high-status positions at rituals. I was embarrassed by this treatment but took full advantage of it by boldly walking into anyone's house and asking them questions that were important only to me.

As have other women anthropologists during their fieldwork, I continually tacked back and forth between various assigned and constructed identities: researcher, friend, daughter, professional, American. I seemed to have no single identity but many, and none of them fit neatly into any of the ascribed categories for me. It was ultimately the instability of my identity that forced my awareness of the complexity of my position:

> Sept. 7, 1989: I have to be here a year – make this my home and I'm such a stranger. Just dropped in on their world – I can share it but

> not really be a part of it. At another level I am just a researcher. I will go home again and leave all this behind – their worries, problems, needs. What an ambiguous role . . . I have to live with people who don't really understand who or what I am and have their own agendas in dealing with me. As I have mine. This is not my universe.[5]

In my journal I expressed the unease I felt in terms that emphasized the distance between myself and them: 'their world', 'not my universe'. To me there was my home and this place that had no connection to it, that occupied a different 'universe'. The problem of feeling alien was intensified, however, because I was a lesbian in a heterosexual world. I did not share a common sexual identity with the people in the village, which most ethnographers take for granted (although this assumed commonality has to be problematized, as other chapters in this volume point out). I felt as if I no longer recognized myself. My lesbian identity had totally disappeared:

> Jan. 31, 1990: And who am I, this amorphous creature with few reality markers to cling to, yet somehow conspiring to present a self acceptable to people here. Much of who I am, or considered myself to be, goes unrecognized . . . My gay identity is lost and crying out for recognition.

As Newton (1993) aptly points out in her discussion of the 'erotic equation in fieldwork', there are few gay zones to retreat to in foreign field locales and thus no opportunity for lesbian or gay male anthropologists to relax in a safe and accepting environment. Every day I played the nice, polite, naive, heterosexual American woman and was thereby unable to share with anyone the part of my life that was about my lesbian identity and family. Indonesians always ask about family, parents, siblings, husband, and children; the silence I imposed on my own life story was a constant and painful reminder of my separateness; the denial of a significant part of my life was a tremendous blow to my self-esteem.

I lived with one family during my stay in Indonesia and the greater the emotional attachment between my Indonesian mother (whom I called Ibu, which means mother) and me, the more painful it was not to talk about my life. I cared deeply for Ibu; she was a guardian and good friend who willingly confided in me her hopes and fears, happinesses and sorrows. I tried to repay her for her kindness to me and did so through the best means available to me, by lending her money to keep her business solvent. Although this action played on the inherent inequality in our positions, it nevertheless seemed to restore some balance in my debt to her as my host and did not cause any rupture in our relationship, as it did with Rabinow.

Despite Ibu's friendship and the companionship of other women in the village, I felt cut off from myself and deeply lonely:

> Nov. 2, 1989: Right now I want to go home. I want to be me again, with my friends, my house, my dyke world. I'm not tired of being here but I miss my life back home. I miss being in a familiar world where I know who I am . . . I can't talk about my lovers, about half my family experiences and that's what people relate to here. How can I share my life with Ibu who tells me all her life?

I missed everything that was part of the self I left behind. I was tired of being someone for somebody else, for professing to being sexually naive to suit Islamic notions of womanhood, for claiming to be engaged to avoid possible suitors, and for not being able to share who I was with people who shared so much of themselves.

In desperation one day, when Ibu and I were having a long conversation about American sexual practices, I told her I was a lesbian. I was tired of the deceit and the pretense of having a boyfriend. Instantly, I was afraid that I had lost the one person I could count on in the village. To my great relief, however, Ibu told me she was not upset. 'That's what you do in America', she said, again refuting my understanding of the knower/known categories implicit in anthropology. She went on to warn me, however, that I should not engage in such practices here (meaning both her house and her country), effectively asserting the dominance of her cultural ideology and cutting off any further attempts to engage my vision of the world. Her response affirmed at once her own tolerance as well as the Islamic admonition to guide others in the right way, since according to Islam, homosexuality is a greater sin than adultery. She was also protecting herself and me, as a member of her household, from possible shameful repercussions. I adhered to her edict while I remained in her house, but her position on this issue later caused a strain in our relationship. Although I remained fearful for several days that the village head would come to my house and ask me to leave the village, nothing happened, and Ibu did not bring up the subject again.

The need to have my lesbian identity recognized, and the need for physical and emotional intimacy beyond the friendships I had, ultimately led me into a relationship with a Minangkabau woman in a village about an hour from my fieldsite. The significance of this relationship was far from clear to me during the nine months we were together. While I struggled to create a safe place and a new 'home' where I felt sure of my identity, my relationship with an-Other lesbian decentered and displaced me, forcing me to recognize and resist the differences between us. At the same time, it helped me to regain my sense of self and establish a bond that bridged the distance between us.

Love in the field

I had been in Indonesia for nine months before I was introduced to Dayan (a pseudonym). Early in my field stay I met several young gay men in town through a woman friend of mine. I asked this friend if she knew any lesbians, and when she said she did, I asked her to help me meet some of them. Months passed but nothing came of my request. Finally, I went into town one day and begged my friend to take me to see a friend of hers who she said was a lesbian. She collected another friend and after half an hour's bumpy ride on the local bus to a neighboring village, we got off the bus and walked a short distance down a dirt road to a dilapidated wood and cement house. We were greeted by a woman in her early thirties, Dayan's older married sister. Dayan was outside working on her chicken coop; she came in after a few minutes and shyly shook my hand. She had on shorts and a T-shirt, wore her black hair short; I thought she had a beautiful smile. We left her sister and several curious onlookers and children behind, and went up to her room.

Her room contained a small bed, a bureau, a chair, and a guitar (and, I later noticed, the largest spider I'd ever seen, hanging in its web about 12 feet above the bed in the rafters). Dayan's family owned some riceland but were not well off. She had posters of rock stars plastered on her walls: Billy Idol, Madonna, Sting. My friends went out for a short while to get cigarettes while we talked; Dayan asked me if I had some erotic photos of women that I could give her. She couldn't get any in Indonesia. Then my friends were back and it was time to leave – the buses don't run at night and they needed to get back to town. We said goodbye and I promised to come see her again.

My friends were pleased with their role in helping me meet Dayan. Young people in West Sumatra are generally more open about sexuality than the older generation, although most people in West Sumatra are aware that homosexuality exists. The words *lesbi* and *gay* have entered their lexicon through the national media, which frequently report on the lesbian and gay movement in Europe and America as well as provide portrayals of Indonesian lesbians. Lesbianism has been a topic in the media since the early 1980s. While some of the articles attempt to be sympathetic, most tend to criticize or condemn it as abnormal, deviant, or a reflection of Westernized lifestyles (Gayatri 1993). The Indonesian Criminal Penal Code does not forbid homosexual or same-sex relationships, however (Gayatri 1993). West Sumatran (and Indonesian) categories of gender and sexuality differ from the Western categories labelled 'lesbian' and 'gay', which refer to sexual identity. In West Sumatra, alternatively gendered males are called *bujang-gadis* (a term meaning boy-girl) or *bencong*. Both terms refer to a male transvestite or drag queen (in our terms), usually a male who dresses and acts like a woman; the term *banci* is also used, but more commonly in Java. Alternatively gendered females are called *supik-jantan* (a Minangkabau word meaning girl-boy) or *tomboi* (a more recent term from the English for a male-like woman). These terms are now used alternately with *lesbi* and *gay*, due to the close connection of alternative gender with homosexuality in West Sumatra and Indonesia (see also Gayatri 1993).[6] Alternatively gendered individuals find partners among same-sex individuals who appear straight-looking and are usually bisexual. The masculine (*jantan* or *tomboi*) partner in a lesbian couple is also called *cowok*, an Indonesian slang term for a young man meaning 'guy', or *laki-laki* (man), while her feminine partner is called *cewek*, Indonesian slang for a young woman meaning 'girl'. This usage reflects the direct application of terms for man and woman to an alternatively gendered individual and her partner. Due to the tremendous pressure on children to marry, most bisexual individuals and some alternatively gendered individuals in Indonesia marry at some point in their lives and later may become involved with a lover of the same sex.

Homosexuality and alternative gender are more or less tolerated in rural West Sumatra as long as the person fulfills his or her duty to family by marrying and having children. Although Islamic law explicitly forbids homosexuality and Minangkabau are devoutly Muslim, Minangkabau tend to look the other way on this issue unless the individual strongly resists his or her marriage obligations. Pressure to marry and the strength of Islamic proscriptions, however, mean that most gay people conduct their relationships secretly to avoid shaming themselves and their families. According to Gayatri's study of lesbians in Java, whose lives have close parallels to those in West Sumatra,

> the biggest risk is that they will be labeled as lesbian, scorned by friends and acquaintances, considered as sick, and thus become

> isolated within their own society. [They could also] lose their good name, especially if they happen to be public figures. The family name is also important, [as is] their respect for their parents.
>
> (1993: 13)

Those who cannot conform to the heterosexual model move away from their families to urban areas to live with their lovers, if they can afford to. Others may be forced to marry and raise children, and only later be able to live with a lover, though they keep such a relationship hidden. Although gay people I met usually knew others in the area, there is no gay community as such, even in the large towns in West Sumatra. *Bencong* may have quite a following of bisexual men, and the parties they throw draw many other *bencong*, bisexual men, and some women. I met few lesbians in West Sumatra, a fact that probably attests to the greater pressure on women to marry and the fewer options for single women in rural communities.

Dayan, who grew up in a small rural town, was not open about her sexuality; in her village only her best friend knew she had women lovers, although several gays and bisexuals in the area knew she was a lesbian. All of Dayan's lovers were feminine. Dayan considered herself masculine. Some of her neighbors called her *cowok* ('guy') because of her masculine appearance. At 28, Dayan was well past marrying age and not living up to the model of womanhood expected of her as a Minangkabau woman. Because her family constantly pressured her to get married, she would leave home for months at a time in search of acceptance in urban areas. But she was never successful in finding decent employment, since she would not accept traditionally female jobs, and would be forced to return home.

When I met Dayan, she had recently returned from a several-month long stay in Jakarta, where she had been involved with a very feminine-looking woman (who, shortly after Dayan's departure, started seeing a man). She was in the middle of a new project to support herself: she was building a small chicken coop to house hens to collect their eggs for sale. Later I wrote in my journal about that meeting:

> Jan. 29, 1990: I finally met my first gay woman – and I don't know how to write about it – because it was more personal than I expected. I don't want to make her a research object. I expected a mannish woman because [a friend] said they look like men, but [Dayan] wasn't at all . . . I didn't understand some of what she said – I don't know the language of emotions and lovers here.

> What would I do – I can easily imagine being lovers . . . I'm tired of only half of me being alive here.

Our meeting made me anxious and happy at the same time. Here was someone I could share myself with, yet I wondered how to negotiate a cross-cultural relationship in which our common language was Indonesian, not English, and in which our ethnic and sexual identities were so different. I thought at first that it would be best to remain friends. I did not know whether I would have much time to spend with her, given the demands of my fieldwork and the necessity of maintaining secrecy. Further, I would be leaving in less than a year and was unsure what expectations might arise if we established a sexual relationship. But the bleakness of my daily life and my need and desire to be intimate overcame my caution and we became involved.

At first we saw each other infrequently, but as our relationship developed, I began to spend nearly every weekend at Dayan's house:

> May 7, 1990: Sunday morning she asked when I was coming back and I said I didn't know. I felt torn by the expectations of people in [my fieldsite] and didn't think I should spend every weekend with Dayan. But the thought of not seeing her upset me so . . . that I decided[,] one week. I surprised myself at how achingly bad I wanted to be with her.

I worked furiously all week so I could catch the bus on Saturday afternoons to go to her village. Monday mornings came too soon and I would reluctantly head back to pick up my research tasks again.

Dayan rarely visited me at my house. From the first time she met her, Ibu disliked Dayan. Feeling Ibu's antipathy, Dayan would only stay a short time and refused to eat with us, which Ibu took as a sign of disrespect. Ibu's rejection of Dayan highlighted for me how carefully distinctions are drawn between men and women. Ibu pointed out to me that Dayan never wore skirts, she drove a motorcycle, she smoked cigarettes and played cards, and she went out at night alone. All of these acts crossed the boundaries of gender and raised Ibu's suspicions that Dayan was not a proper woman. But her rejection of Dayan also came from a number of other sources. People tend to view outsiders, even other Minangkabau, with a certain level of mistrust; family ties, friends in common, or knowledge of a person's family background provide the foundation for acceptance, none of which Ibu had with Dayan. Further, Ibu's suspicions about Dayan were fueled by my own earlier confession and my frequent trips away from her home. Ibu asked me why I went to Dayan's village so often. Although I never talked to Ibu about my relationship with Dayan, in distancing Dayan from her house, Ibu indirectly communicated her discomfort with Dayan's presence in my life and her loss of my complete attention.

On our weekends together we stayed at her sister's, where Dayan had her own room slightly apart from the rest of the house. Her sister welcomed me but Dayan and I were very careful not to let her know that we were lovers. We maintained this secrecy because Dayan did not want her family to know she was a lesbian and was fearful of her family's reaction, particularly her brothers', if her identity became known. Dayan's male friends, who treated her as a *cowok*, visited her frequently to play cards or sing bluesy Minangkabau folk or pop songs. Sometimes we drank beer with her friends and listened to tapes of American rock music. Occasionally, she and I took off on her motorcycle, driving up into the nearby hills for a view of the checkerboard valley of rice fields and palm trees below.

When I met Dayan, I felt an instant bond with her. Here, I thought, was a woman who loves women: 'January 29, 1990: Looking at her, I felt like I was with a sister, we both spoke the same language. Yes, she likes women.' But beyond that simple identification lay a whole range of cultural differences and sexual expectations of which I knew little. From the start our relationship was not easy. When we talked, I struggled to understand her. The vocabulary of love and feelings was unfamiliar to me. Several times I had to wait until I returned home to my dictionary to find out what I had missed of her conversation. I did not know how to make small talk very well, much less express romantic feelings in Indonesian. The sense I had of not being clearly understood nor of clearly understanding her created a distance between us that I found frustrating. But missing the nuances of language helped me initially to overlook the differences in our lesbian identities.

In addition to the constant vigilance to keep our relationship secret, there were cultural practices that I found at times burdensome and other times useful. Women's practice of walking hand in hand was useful to me because it allowed us some freedom in public. On the other hand, cultural practices enjoining politeness and circumspection were burdensome when my actions or comments were misunderstood and I was accused of being rude. Our arguments sometimes left me bewildered and unable to bridge the gap in our differing expectations. When I once got tired of trying to resolve a misunderstanding, I made a show of leaving but then realized I did not want to return to my fieldsite, my only other option. Instead I walked in the woods near

Dayan's house, to the dismay and embarrassment of her sister, who sent Dayan out to collect me on her motorcycle.

Little about our identities as 'lesbians' coincided. I clung to a sense of our sameness, represented by our shared love of women, as the anchor to my lesbian identity and the means to assure me that I was operating in a familiar world. I resisted the knowledge of her difference and her attempts to make me fit her image of women lovers. But the differences in our lesbian identities continually decentered me even as I tried to construct our relationship to my own image. Dayan placed women into two categories, masculine and feminine, or *cowok* ('guy') and *cewek* ('girl'). We were forced to negotiate the differences between our lesbian identities because, although she was masculine, or 'butch', as I persisted in calling her, I was not clearly 'femme'. I introduced the terms 'butch' and 'femme' to Dayan and used them partly to fit my own frame of reference and partly because she did not use any label for herself except *cowok*, which I resisted using. 'Butch' and 'femme' do not directly correspond with the cultural categories of *cowok* and *cewek* (or *tomboi* and woman).

On one occasion Dayan asked me if I was attracted to a rather pretty and feminine woman we both knew. I blithely said yes, not knowing I was slotting myself into a category. To Dayan, my response meant that I was *cowok*, since I clearly liked *cewek*, a perception that confused her because she was attracted to me. According to her understanding, *cowok* are not attracted to other *cowok*. When I later discovered my mistake, I told her I only meant that the woman was pretty, not that I was sexually attracted to her. I said I was attracted to Dayan, and that she was not so butch, using my categories, and I was not particularly femme. She politely ignored my slight to her identity and seemed to accept the notion that I might not be the model of womanhood she was used to.

Our differing gender and sexual identities turned out to be less easily managed than I imagined, however. We decided to have a party for Dayan's birthday. As the day approached, and her sister made the arrangements for the food, Dayan became increasingly offended that I was not taking charge of the preparations as a good wife should. I, however, was unaware of her expectations; once I began to understand, I tried to explain that I was abysmally ineffective in cooking or shopping, and preferred simply to pay for the food and drink. She interpreted my lack of participation as a lack of desire for her; her disappointment cast a pall over the entire day.

On another occasion we went to visit another lesbian and friend of

Dayan's, a *cowok* who was living in a nearby town with a woman whose husband had died a few years earlier. Dayan had not wanted me to meet her friend because she was afraid I might find her more attractive. I remember feeling embarrassed and offended by the questions asked about me. Her friend asked if I was a good cook, if I was good in bed – questions that constructed me as *cewek* and reinforced their sense of being *cowok*. When I spoke to Dayan using her name, her friend raised her eyebrows and said, 'She calls you Dayan?' Again I had stumbled on a practice of which I had no knowledge and embarrassed Dayan before her friend and rival by situating Dayan as a younger 'friend' rather than an older male lover. Lovers calls each other Ma and Pa (or other endearments), according to their gender identity in the relationship. When I later started to call Dayan Pa in an effort to please her and conform more to her expectations of me, she smiled with delight. The term, however, grated against my lesbian feminist sensibilities and my belief that we were both equal and both women.

Other disjunctures brought similar responses of disbelief and discomfort on my part. I was surprised on another occasion by Dayan's strong reaction to my presence in a male friend's hotel room. I had gone to the port town in West Sumatra on business and while there stopped to visit a friend of mine from the U.S., who was staying temporarily in town. Dayan was to meet me at my hotel room, but, arriving too late, she was given the message that I had gone to visit Bob. When she arrived at Bob's hotel room, she had little to say and I could sense that she was angry. We left shortly after and then she began to pester me with questions. Why hadn't I waited for her at my hotel? What had I been doing there in Bob's room? Were we lovers? Had we made love? I was shocked that she should even question that I might be attracted to Bob. I'm a lesbian, I said, as if that explained it all. But to her I was *cewek* and *cewek* all too often leave their female lovers for a man. She believed that I was bisexual and could not be convinced that I had no ulterior motive in visiting Bob.

It surprised me even more to find out that Dayan actually wanted to be a man. As a lesbian, I was repelled by her *cowok* identity and persisted in calling her butch to suit my own perceptions. The butches I knew back home did not really want to be men and I was not interested in a male lover. To me Dayan seemed soft and sweet, not at all like her *cowok* friend, whom I found too masculine. Dayan told me she had bound her breasts in high school so they would not get large. She wanted to be tough and enjoyed working with her hands and doing the things that men do. She regretted being female, she said, and wanted an operation to change her sex. I had to resist the temptation to talk her out of what I thought an odd desire.

Our sexual practices were informed by these differences in gender identity and gave me further insights into the gender distinctions that Dayan drew for herself. She preferred to take the 'male' role in sex, as she understood it from men she had talked to, and was little interested in being touched. Acts that emphasized her female body made her uncomfortable; she perceived them as corporal negations of her maleness. My own practices reflected an American lesbian feminist's rejection of male-defined and hierarchical sexuality; however, my attempts to negotiate greater latitude in lovemaking, in effect, to insert 'equality' into sex, were generally unsuccessful.

I tried to efface the differences between us even as I resisted her attempts to define me as *cewek*. Ultimately, it was the ethnic and class differences between us that defused her attempts to define our relationship as *cowok* and *cewek* and enabled me to set the boundaries of the relationship. The attractiveness and power of my status as a well-educated, middle-class, white American made me the dominant partner in our relationship. I had the money to pay for everything (I paid for her motorcycle and bought her cigarettes, among other things), the high-status job and time constraints that could not be neglected. Consequently, I was able to call the shots about when we saw each other and what things we did that cost money.[7] She could refuse to meet my wishes, but she was invariably at home when I arrived on weekends. When we were together, Dayan had greater control of our movements and activities. She determined the pace of our days and where we went or who we visited in her village. Though in some ways I reversed the *cowok/cewek* relationship, in other social and sexual contexts mentioned above her desires as *cowok* took precedence. Above all, I was dependent on her for creating the space for our relationship.

The struggle over our identities created a certain level of doubt about the meaning of our relationship. Was I exploiting her? Were we taking advantage of each other? When I told her I was doing research on lesbians in Indonesia, Dayan asked me if I was with her just so I could get data for my study. I told her no, that I did not have to be involved to get information, but I also gained much more information by being involved. Then I asked if she was with me because I was a 'rich' American who could offer more than the limited opportunities she now had. She was offended by my asking and reminded me that I was leaving in a few months and she would be left alone.

Despite the differences in our identities and the struggles to understand each other, I felt closely bonded with Dayan at some basic level. With Dayan, I felt at ease in a way I never did with my Indonesian mother in her heterosexual world, even when I rubbed Ibu's arms and legs for her when she was ill, or plucked (timidly) at the grey hairs on her head that she insisted on having removed. For me Dayan represented a place to get away, to be lesbian, and to stop feeling so alien. I felt safe with her; when I buried myself in her arms, I could forget the loss of identity and loneliness I felt every day. We spent much of our time alone in her bedroom because it was only there that I truly felt at peace with myself and the knowledge of my lesbian identity. I resented the visits of her friends and the intrusions of her relatives, who came in even when the door was barricaded. I did not want to talk to anyone else, leave her house, or even go downstairs to eat with her family, because I felt exposed, vulnerable, and out of place. Any excursion threatened the fragile hold I had managed to gain on my lesbian identity. I needed to be with Dayan to remove the physical and emotional isolation I felt. She validated that part of me that went unrecognized everywhere else.

To me Dayan was a hero because she dared to believe in herself and maintain an identity for which there was no validation. I shared her pain when she talked about past lovers who had left her for boyfriends or marriage, or of the isolation that she increasingly faced in the village because she was not like other women, who at her age were all married and raising children. Yes, she was different from me and saw life as a lesbian differently from the way I did. But her love of women was unmistakable. Recognizing that similarity between us, I was able to move into a space that was at once familiar and alien, to find security and compassion in something that was and was not 'lesbian'.

By establishing a relationship with an-Other lesbian, I became both an insider and an outsider: an insider because I shared her marginalization as a lesbian and her love of women, and an outsider because of our different sexual identities and cultural frameworks. In a similar manner Rosaldo (1984) consciously uses his own experience of grief at his wife's untimely death to understand the Ilongot headhunter's rage and thus find a sense of shared humanness that recognizes the Other in ourselves. In a fascinating exposé of her own field experience, Kondo argues that some elimination of difference, openness to Otherness, and a willingness to traverse the distance can be productive in fieldwork (1986: 84). Her physical resemblance to the Japanese she studied and their assumption that she shared an identity with them helped her to bridge some of the differences between them. Yet she still carried with her her specifically American cultural framework. So I carried with me my Otherness to Dayan, my American tactlessness and refusal to be *cewek*, and she her Otherness to me, her desire to be a man and to make me her wife. But in our struggles together we found common ground and new meanings.

Conclusion

It has been five years since I returned to the U.S. alone, unable to bring my lover with me because she had no legally recognized relationship to me. Although some of my heterosexual colleagues have returned from the field with their partners, I was forced to leave Dayan behind, effectively severing our relationship, because the U.S. Embassy would not grant her a tourist visa. Since that time I have sought to understand the meaning of our relationship and the questions of identity and distance that it raised. I find it difficult to expose the wonderful and painful memories of our relationship, and yet am compelled to write about them to resolve my own confusion. My relationship with Dayan coalesced the identity conflicts that plagued me during my fieldwork. It helped to ease my sense of being ungrounded, restored to me my lost lesbian identity. I found a deeply rewarding and loving relationship that helped me survive the anomie and isolation of fieldwork, an isolation made more difficult by the need to keep my lesbian identity invisible.

My field experience revealed that identities are never stable, never simply undefined. Even the marked categories of gender, sex, race, and class are constantly shifting as our understanding of and distance from another culture shift. Manalansan's (1993) excellent piece on transmigration and the postcolonial bodies of Filipino gay immigrants shows that contact with another culture produces a new vision, a shift in perspective, and a need to make sense of one's place in the world that creates new distances and categories in the collision of race, class, ethnic, and gay identities. As anthropologists we may attempt to preserve unblemished our vision of culture from the top by remaining alien, but as with other travelers across cultural borders, we do not remain alien or undefined; we are forced constantly to reconstruct who we are in the field in relation to the people with whom we interact.

As an American in Indonesia, I felt strongly the loss of my lesbian identity. Thinking I had found it again with Dayan, I attempted to reconstruct that identity in a way that resonated with my own familiar categories. I wanted my relationship to be safe, to be home, and thus resisted many of Dayan's efforts to make me more familiar to her and construct me as her wife. By refusing the knowledge of her identity, and seeking, instead, comfortable familiarity, I reinscribed the distance and asymmetry between us. Because our negotiations were subtle, often sub-verbal, there was space for me to imagine a shared identity and overlook the differences between us. But while I persisted in defining our relationship and providing the categories, it refused to be simply 'lesbian'. Our relationship challenged my categories of experience as it continually decentered and repositioned me into new spaces. I was forced to examine our differences and recognize my privilege in relation to her. It was perhaps our sexual space that evoked the deepest expression of Dayan's identity and the clearest recognition of our different yet similar desires. Ultimately, in our mutual resistance we refashioned each other.

As members of a culture that downplays class differences, American anthropologists in particular tend to emphasize the egalitarian nature of relationships, assuming that in fieldwork most people will be friends or equals. Within the global context, however, anthropologists occupy a position of dominance that transcends attempts to be defined otherwise. If anthropologists are unable to erase differences of power, will recognition of these differences and positionalities bring greater understanding? I can use my position as an American woman and member of a minority in my own culture to sensitize me to the ways identities are shaped. I still speak for others, as ultimately I choose to do for Dayan, but in recognizing my position and the inequalities of power between us I can make choices about how I represent people and how I talk about their lives.

I have tried to situate myself in this encounter, to reflect on the power imbalances that existed within the relationship and what they meant for my relation to others in my fieldsite. My relationships with both Dayan and Ibu brought into view the boundaries of gender in West Sumatra, the assumption of heterosexuality, the dominance of marriage, and the masculine/feminine model of alternative gender relations. They also kept me from seeing the Minangkabau simply as Alien or Other. I could not and did not want to remain alien or undefined. I was not just an observer; I constructed a family for myself, Dayan's family. Ultimately, it was this relationship that brought to the fore issues of identity and subjectivity that permanently altered my vision of myself in connection with an-Other lesbian.

I would suggest that many male anthropologists tend not to make the connection between their privilege and identity and the women with whom they have been sexually involved in the field. Rabinow (1977), who has been one of the few male heterosexual anthropologists willing to write about his sexual activities in the field, describes his sexual experience with a Moroccan woman as a one-night encounter noteworthy because it better secured his identity with other men. Whitehead (1986), who avoided involvements in the field, was surprised when he returned home to hear from a male colleague that 'everybody gets laid in the field', a casual statement that carries all the overtones of the anthropological conquest of the Other, the Alien, Woman. Many male anthropologists, through their silence on the subject of sexuality in the field, have failed to make connections between their own privilege and power as situated (rather than unmarked) men and the very personal experience of sexual involvement. The paucity of articles by heterosexual men in this volume speaks to an unwillingness to acknowledge or question sexual and gender definitions. Having assumed the naturalness of gender categories, many heterosexual male anthropologists tend to be less able than those of us who are marked in our own culture to bridge the gap between Self and Other, particularly when Other is female. Reflexive anthropology is thus necessarily limited to the extent that its advocates are unwilling to situate themselves as gendered or ethnic beings (this criticism applies to, for example, Crapanzano 1977; Dwyer 1979; Clifford 1983).

Sexual connections do not always provide the insights I am suggesting, as any viewing of David Hwang's play *M. Butterfly* makes clear. In this play, a French diplomat falls madly in love with an image of exotic, submissive, oriental, feminine sexuality without ever piercing M. Butterfly's disguise until the truth of her gender is dramatically forced on him (Hwang 1986). (Did he ever understand 'the Oriental'? See Kondo 1990 for further discussion of this point.) To find these insights, or at least make a beginning, we must be willing in our writing to expose our own privilege and power, and our own assumptions about the categories we occupy, whether they be categories of race, class, gender, or sexual orientation.

The ethnographic experience is about experiencing oneself with others, of knowing we are all different, yet recognizing the bonds among us rather than reifying the difference to make Others exotic or inferior. Finding the common ground through our subjective experience is the basis from which to build understanding and knowledge, as Haraway suggests (1988), and thus to avoid the stance that exoticizes other cultures. Anzaldúa (1987) argues that all people are border people, all sharing multiple selves, multiple identities. In recognizing our positions, our identities and shared humanness, we can displace the centrality of 'the male, heterosexual cultural ego' of anthropology (Newton 1993) and replace it with many different marked perspectives.

Acknowledgements

I conducted fieldwork in West Sumatra for a year and a half during 1989 and 1990. I am extremely grateful to the people who gave comments on this chapter. They have pushed me (at times unwillingly) to explore and articulate more fully the meaning of my relationship with Dayan, a process that has been painful and rewarding. My heartfelt thanks go to Deborah Amory, Deborah Elliston, Patricia Horvatich, Joel Striecker, Mildred Dickemann, and Ellen Lewin. A special thanks to Don Kulick and Margaret Willson for excellent comments that carried this chapter to its final form.

Notes

1 The Minangkabau, comprising predominantly rural agriculturists, are one of the larger ethnic groups in Indonesia, numbering 3.8 million. They are also the largest matrilineal group in the world and devoutly Islamic. Descent and inheritance are reckoned from mother to daughter (see Blackwood 1993).

2 I use the term 'lesbian' here with reservation because I do not wish to subsume other cultural categories under Western labels. The term 'lesbian' does not adequately represent the women I met in West Sumatra, whose gender, and sexuality encompass a range of categories, including alternative gender, bisexuality, and homosexuality. Indonesians do use the term *lesbi* for female homosexuality, which is why I chose to use the term 'lesbian' in addition to local terminology (cf. discussion on p. 61–2). Some Indonesian women, however, are uncomfortable with the label because of its association in the Indonesian media with Western sexuality and promiscuity (Gayatri 1993).

3 It also reflects a reality of being lesbian or gay: it is sometimes safer to hide one's identity than to risk the rejection and even physical harm that could result if such were known. I could not say even now whether I would go to a fieldsite as an openly gay person.

4 See, for example, Abu-Lughod's (1987) experience conducting fieldwork in Bedouin culture and articles in Goldet (1986), Whitehead and Conaway (1986), and this volume.

5 All dated entries are from my field journal.

6 In addition to local terms, I also use the terms 'lesbian' and 'gay' in this chapter to refer to alternatively gendered individuals and their partners.

7 This situation is actually more complex. Although a Minangkabau husband is expected to provide money for his wife, most Minangkabau women make their own income as well. A wife may provide as much as or more than her husband to the household.

References

Abu-Lughod, Lila (1987) *Veiled Sentiments: Honor and Poetry in a Bedouin Society.* Berkeley, Calif.: University of California Press.

Anzaldúa, Gloria (1987) *Borderlands/La Frontera: The New Mestiza.* San Francisco: Spinsters/Aunt Lute.

Blackwood, Evelyn (1993) 'The Politics of Daily Life: Gender, Kinship and Identity in a Minangkabau Village, West Sumatra, Indonesia.' Ph.D. dissertation, Department of Anthropology, Stanford University.

Clifford, James (1983) 'On Ethnographic Authority'. *Representations.* Vol. 1, No. 2, pp. 118–46.

Crapanzano, Vincent (1977) 'On the Writing of Ethnography'. *Dialectical Anthropology.* Vol. 2, No. 1, pp. 9–73.

Dwyer, Kevin (1977) 'On the Dialogic of Fieldwork'. *Dialectical Anthropology.* Vol. 2, No. 2, pp. 143–51.

——— (1979) 'The Dialogic of Ethnology'. *Dialectical Anthropology.* Vol. 4, No. 3, pp. 205–24.

Favret-Saada, Jeanne (1980) *Deadly Words: Witchcraft in the Bocage.* Trans. Catherine Cullen. Cambridge: Cambridge University Press.

Gayatri, B.J.D. (1993) 'Coming Out but Remaining Hidden: A Portrait of Lesbians in Java.' Paper presented at the International Congress of Anthropological and Ethnological Sciences, Mexico City, Mexico.

Geertz, Clifford (1968) 'Thinking as a Moral Act: Ethical Dimensions of Anthropological Fieldwork in the New States'. *Antioch Review.* Vol. 28, No. 2, pp. 139–58.

Golde, Peggy (ed.) (1986) *Women in the Field: Anthropological Experiences.* 2nd edn. Berkeley, Calif.: University of California Press.

Haraway, Donna (1988) 'Situated Knowledges: The Science Question in Feminism and the Privilege of Partial Perspective'. *Feminist Studies.* Vol. 14, No. 3, pp. 575–99.

Hwang, David (1986) *M. Butterfly.* New York: Plume.

Kondo, Dorinne K. (1986) 'Dissolution and Reconstitution of Self: Implications for Anthropological Epistemology'. *Cultural Anthropology.* Vol. 1, No. 1, pp. 74–88.

—— (1990) 'M. Butterfly: Orientalism, Gender, and a Critique of Essentialist Identity'. *Cultural Critique.* Vol. 16, pp. 5–29.

Malinowski, Bronislaw (1989) *A Diary in the Strict Sense of the Term.* Trans. Norbert Guterman. Reissue. Stanford: Stanford University Press.

Manalansan, Martin F., IV (1993) '(Re)locating the Gay Filipino: Resistance, Postcolonialism, and Identity'. *Journal of Homosexuality.* Vol. 26, Nos 2/3, pp. 53–72.

Mascia-Lees, Frances E., Patricia Sharpe, and Colleen B. Cohen (1989) 'The Postmodernist Turn in Anthropology: Cautions from a Feminist Perspective'. *Signs: Journal of Women in Culture and Society.* Vol. 15, No. 1, pp. 7–33.

Newton, Esther (1993) 'My Best Informant's Dress: The Erotic Equation in Fieldwork'. *Cultural Anthropology.* Vol. 8, No. 1, pp. 3–23.

Rabinow, Paul (1977) *Reflections on Fieldwork in Morocco.* Berkeley, Calif.: University of California Press.

Rosaldo, Renato (1984) 'Grief and a Headhunter's Rage: On the Cultural

Force of Emotions', in Edward M. Bruner (ed.) *Text, Play and Story: The Construction and Reconstruction of Self and Society.* Washington, D.C.: American Ethnological Society.

Trinh, T. Minh-ha (1989) *Woman, Native, Other: Writing Postcoloniality and Feminism.* Bloomington: Indiana University Press.

Whitehead, Tony Larry (1986) 'Breakdown, Resolution, and Coherence: The Fieldwork Experiences of a Big, Brown, Pretty-talking Man in a West Indian Community', in Tony Larry Whitehead and Mary Ellen Conaway (eds) *Self, Sex and Gender in Cross-cultural Fieldwork.* Urbana and Chicago: University of Illinois Press.

——— and Mary Ellen Conaway (eds) (1986) *Self, Sex and Gender in Cross-cultural Fieldwork.* Urbana and Chicago: University of Illinois Press.

Chapter 3

The penetrating intellect

On being white, straight, and male in Korea

Andrew P. Killick

Anthropology was once defined as 'the science of man embracing woman' (McLuhan 1965: 226). The homology between ethnographic knowledge and carnal knowledge has not escaped the notice of reflexive anthropologists and literary analysts of anthropological texts, while ethnographic film has been critiqued as 'a kind of legitimated pornography, a pornography of knowledge' (Hansen *et al.* 1991: 210). We can no longer hide from ourselves the sexual symbolism by which the ethnographic Other, the erotic–exotic, is imagined as inhabiting an enclosed space, the field: stronghold of cultural secrets, breeding ground of experience, virgin territory to be penetrated by the ethnographer's interpretive thrust. Vincent Crapanzano has suggested seeing this act of penetration as not merely intellectual, but phallic: 'We say a text, a culture even, is pregnant with meaning. Do the ethnographer's presentations become pregnant with meaning because of his interpretive, his phallic fertilizations?' (1986: 52).

Such imagery may help sensitize us to 'the issue of power as symbolized in the subject–object relationship between he who represents and she who is represented' (Tyler 1986: 127); but the metaphor may also serve to forestall a literal reading: to make unthinkable the idea of an anthropologist's actual sexual involvement with informants. For even as the ethnographic literature becomes ever more explicit about the manner of its production, the anthropologist's sexuality remains a subtext that is systematically erased. Self-searching reflexive analyses give the impression that they tell all and, conversely, that what they do not tell does not exist; thus, the ethnographer is constructed as an objective observer, free from distracting desires, not merely celibate but asexual. Texts are ideologically structured in part by what they omit and, by implication, deny (Cormack 1992: 31–2); and in much of the reflexive literature, sex is a structuring absence.

I will be concerned with both the metaphorical and the literal levels of sex in the field as reflected in my own research on Korean music as an unmarried, Caucasian, heterosexual male. These aspects of my identity are relevant not only because of their implications for my fieldwork experience, which would have been markedly different if any one of these parameters had been reversed, but also because the initiative to examine the issues of sex in the field has come from writers who were female, gay, black, or some combination of these. One of my aims in this paper, therefore, is to consider whether there might be a specifically white-straight-male (henceforth WSM) perspective on the subject. The 'straight' and 'male' aspects will obviously be the most prominent in an article on sexual issues, though ethnicity also enters the picture in the context of colonial relations of sexual dominance – a context not without relevance to my own fieldwork situation. Other aspects of identity, such as social class, nationality, and regional background, will enter into the discussion when this seems necessary, hopefully without clouding the issue.

In seeking a WSM perspective I make no claim, of course, to represent *the* WSM perspective, nor do I wish to essentialize identity on the basis of ethnicity, or gender, or sexual orientation. On the contrary, it is my view that as cultural anthropologists we should be especially alert to the constructedness of these categories, and problematize them as part of our subject matter rather than assuming them as stances that predetermine lines of inquiry. I will treat the WSM identity, therefore, not as given and self-evident, but as achieved and ascribed through narratively structured experience, including that of the anthropologist's legitimizing myth: fieldwork.

I will argue that a WSM subject position is required by the narrative structure of fieldwork accounts, and is therefore not exclusively an issue for the WSM ethnographer: that the unequal relationships implicit in the concept of 'the field', though rooted in anthropology's colonial and patriarchal traditions, will apply regardless of the identity of the ethnographer, as long as fieldwork experiences are predetermined by a male-oriented narrative structure that is still largely unchallenged. My analysis of that structure approaches the topic of 'sex in the field' first by considering how 'the field' is constituted as a significant unit of experience – a unit which, as my own narrative will suggest, need not be taken for granted.

My autobiographical account will be framed by theorizing, and deployed as a hinge between theoretical angles. Reflecting on my position as author of this chapter, I suggest reasons why WSM authors in general have been slow to address erotic subjectivity as a factor in fieldwork. I then argue that the narrative structure of fieldwork accounts is based on a sexual metaphor that typically assigns to the ethnographer a plot-function that is heterosexual and masculine, regardless of his (*sic*!) actual gender and sexual orientation. My own narrative is introduced first as an instance of the problem, rarely made explicit, that the fieldworker faces in accommodating to the pre-existing norms for relations (including the sexual) between locals and outsiders. I describe my research context in Seoul, where there is a stable if heterogeneous community of expatriates with their various discourses about Korea and about their relations with Koreans; and I reflect on the connections between my academic life and my history of relationships, not with Korean women in Korea, but with Korean American women in both Korea and America. Noting the pattern that emerges only when I look beyond the boundaries of what anthropology has traditionally designated 'the field' and 'fieldwork', I return to theory by claiming that these notions of a 'field' impose unnecessary preconceptions and are in danger of becoming, for postmodern ethnographers, an arbitrarily framed and homogenized background to their own self-absorbed 'experience'.

In the ensuing discussion, therefore, I use the terms 'fieldwork' and 'the field' in the specific sense of a construct that has been evolved by anthropologists to designate the locus of their constitutive experience *as* anthropologists; it is only to avoid being tiresome that I have refrained from putting these terms in quotation marks at every occurrence. One of the dangers of discussing 'sex in the field' is that the scrutiny of highly charged sexual issues pushes the equally contestable concept of 'the field' into the background, taking it for granted as a mutually understood delimitation of the terms of the debate. When this happens, an undue degree of unity is conferred on 'the field', resulting in the disregard of crucial differences in local conditions and individual personalities, and there is much bland talk of the ways in which the generic fieldworker is presumed to interact with the generic field. That which is taken for granted can be more insidiously persuasive than the surface argument; and the reader of fieldwork accounts would do well to remember the words of Lawrence Sterne: 'Every man will speak of the fair as his own market has gone in it' (*Tristram Shandy*, I.5).

What follows, then, is a discussion not so much of sex in the field as of the field in sex: of the position filled by the field in an overarching metaphor of sexual penetration that is only sometimes translated into actual sexual experience, but is always present in the narrative structure of fieldwork.

The silence of straight men

When I was invited to contribute to this volume, I was excited by the opportunity to be involved in such a timely and important project, and readily saw the need for at least one contribution from a WSM author to maintain balance and avoid any unintended suggestion that gender is only an issue for women, ethnicity for people of color, or sexual orientation for gay people. But I had to ask: why me? There had to be others who were more eager to publish the details of their personal lives than this bashful Englishman. In addition, I was bemused by the prospect of being seen as a 'token' straight white guy: was *I* supposed to represent the mainstream against which the marginality of women, blacks, and gays was defined? I had long felt, on the contrary, that I was a marginal figure myself: an alienated intellectual, disadvantaged by my regional and class background, and working in a discipline – ethnomusicology – that hovers on the margins of anthropology.

True, I had done fieldwork as a heterosexual male, though not an exceptionally active one, and I had written about sexual relations between locals and outsiders in my field area, albeit in the form of unpublished fiction. But sex had formed no part of either my academic subject matter or my relations with people directly involved in my fieldwork. Indeed, I had done my research in precisely the situation that is supposed to eliminate any interference from the erotic: as a heterosexual researcher among informants of my own sex. My thesis topic had been contemporary music for traditional Korean instruments, and my chief informants had been male composers.

Moreover, it is rare for a Western man to spend any length of time in Korea without marrying a Korean woman. I had done so. What was wrong with me? More to the point, what was there to say, that would interest anyone but a few close friends, about my romantic encounters in the field? I was puzzled by the task of writing about my love life in a way that would be honest and explicit, but would not read as either confessional, pornography, or an extended singles ad. Only when I stretched the terms of my brief, when I looked beyond the boundaries of the field, did I realize what should have been obvious: that my academic life had not been independent of my emotional life, that I might, after all, have a story to tell, but that the time I spent in Korea was merely a vital chapter in a longer story which neither began with my arrival nor ended with my departure. Clearly, I would have to write about the field, and why it was the wrong frame for my story, before I could reach any conclusions about *sex* in the field.

My initial reactions to the prospect of writing this chapter are, I suspect, among the considerations that have often deterred WSM anthropologists from reflecting in public on their sexual behavior during fieldwork. The subject may simply have struck them as one on which they had nothing much to say, or in which their readers were not particularly interested; or it may have seemed to attract too much attention to the researcher and away from the subjects.

A more powerful disincentive today, however, may be the fear of being identified with an image of the WSM as sexual exploiter of the exotic – an image that has a firm basis in both colonial history and current reality. In the nineteenth century, Orientalist writers like Richard Burton could gloat over exotic sexual experiences with a frankness that affronts our notions of Victorian prudery, because they were sure of their superiority and of their right to possess the Other (Burton 1967). This attitude, though still common, has given rise to a critical school of analysis with its paradigm formulation in Edward Said's *Orientalism* (1978). As Rana Kabbani, an important contributor to that school, has eloquently shown, 'These responses to other peoples were an intrinsic part of the imperial world-view. To perceive the East as a sexual domain, and to perceive the East as a domain to be colonised, were complementary aspirations' (1986: 59).

If this imperialist erotic–exotic construct still represents the mainstream (in however sublimated a form), there may be many ethnographers like myself who, bearing a sense of their own marginality, resent being identified with it solely because they are white, straight, and male. There is no reason to simply assume that a WSM ethnographer cannot, *ipso facto*, experience or understand marginality. Indeed, it may be hard to find an ethnographer who does *not* feel marginal, at least in some contexts. We study things to the extent that they seem problematic, and a frequent motive for studying culture is the sense of our own problematic relation to the culture in which we live; in this case the study of other (typically underprivileged) cultures may be a compensation for the anthropologist's own sense of otherness, a search for an external other against which the marginal anthropologist can attain selfhood. If there is a group of anthropologists that is not (in its own estimation) marginal, it is so small as to be marginal by that very fact.

It would be paradoxical, no doubt, to say that there can be a mainstream of anthropology while there are no mainstream anthropologists. I would merely suggest that it is more helpful to speak of mainstream anthropology than of mainstream anthropologists if the latter are to be defined by their gender, ethnicity, or sexual orientation rather than their opinions. I am far from denying, of course, that there is *some* correlation between identity and opinions: there does exist a powerful current in anthropology that was set up primarily, though not exclusively, by and for WSM anthropologists, and that has attracted some well-warranted criticism for its complicity with the imperialist project of mapping sexual and cultural domination onto each other. It is this fact, as much as any, that necessitates a WSM contribution to the present volume, for it has caused many WSM students of other cultures, myself included, to become sensitive to the issues of appropriation, embarrassed by our forebears, and inhibited by the widespread perception that we are always in a position of power and eager to exploit it. What keeps sex out of the picture may sometimes be a refusal to acknowledge this power, but it may also be a defense against the anticipated assumption that we are guilty until proven innocent. This defensiveness has made self-justification a recurrent theme in fieldwork accounts, and causes me some trepidation in approaching the current topic.

The remedy for the WSM guilt complex has often been to assume a monastic exclusion of sexuality, at least from our public personae, and often in private too. While in the field, the fear of upsetting the delicate balance of relationships with informants is likely to be a significant curb on the libido. But even those who remain sexually active have every reason to keep quiet about it if their behavior is likely to be seen as either uninteresting (a possibility we should not discount) or reprehensible. There has not yet been a crop of publications with titles like 'How I Used the Ethnographic Power Differential to Gain Sexual Favors'; after all, who wants to publish *and* perish?

This is not, of course, the exclusive concern of the WSM; but it is a concern of a special kind for him because of the patriarchal tradition of anthropology and the position of exploiter which he can hardly avoid stepping into. Confronted with the question, 'Have you stopped exploiting your informants?', he remains silent since any answer would condemn him. A WSM author must now be especially wary of the condemnation that can arise, not from the evidence of his own text, but from certain widely held and not totally unfounded assumptions: for instance, that any white man who sleeps with an Asian woman is by definition exploiting her. Again, it is not only the WSM whose sexual revelations are vulnerable to his readers' prejudice; but the particular form of that vulnerability may have discouraged WSM ethnographers from publicly addressing the issue of their sexuality.

Whitehead and Price may be right to observe that 'male writers . . . feel freer to address sexual desire and behavior in fieldwork than do female writers' (1986: 302), a point that has recently been echoed by Esther Newton: 'In print, and probably much more so in life, the men feel freer' (1993: 14). (In both cases the examples cited are straight, white men.) But this generalization is based on a tiny sample, and if it is true that *some* men 'feel freer' to discuss their sexuality in fieldwork accounts, it cannot be the *same* men who have made sex in the field a taboo topic. We need to distinguish between 'all' and 'some' more than Newton does when she states that 'a veil of professional silence covers the face of indulgence toward men's casual sex with women in the field' (p. 5). This line of argument treats heterosexual men as a more homogeneous group than they really are, and tends to exclude the possibility that the 'veil of professional silence' might often cover nothing but celibacy.

Later, Newton rightly remarks:

> the sexuality of heterosexual men – however much a puzzle or pain on a personal level – is the cultural 'ego', the assumed subjectivity; and it was predictable that women and gays, for whom matters of sexuality and gender can never be unproblematic, have begun to address these issues for the discipline as a whole.
>
> (1993: 8)

But the 'puzzle or pain' should not be underestimated: all cultures impose gender roles on men as well as women, and the penalties for not living up to them can be severe, whether one is straight or gay. Heterosexual men in the West (to say nothing of other cultures, Korea among them) are often too busy establishing and reconfirming their masculinity to be honest about their insecurities, and this is a precedent I am here trying to break with. To imagine that these insecurities do not exist is to be taken in by the macho rhetoric that dominates public male discourse while weakness and uncertainty emerge only in private documents like Malinowski's notorious *Diary* (1989).

Sexuality was anything but unproblematic for Malinowski, and his field diary was to a great extent a tool for grappling with his conscience over sexual matters in which he was a harsh judge of himself: 'I realize that purity in deeds depends on purity of thought, and I resolve to watch myself right down to the deepest instincts' (1989: 181).

Admittedly, as Newton points out, 'Malinowski struggled for restraint to keep *himself* pure' (1993: 14–15; italics in original): his sense of responsibility was toward his absent fiancée, not toward the native and missionary women who became the objects of his lust. Nonetheless, his efforts to reconcile his sexuality with the demands of his work stand as a rare testament to the specificity of a male heterosexual subject position in fieldwork.

James Clifford has pointed out the general failure to identify such a position in the cultures we study:

> If women's experience has been significantly excluded from ethnographic accounts, the recognition of this absence, and its correction in many recent studies, now highlights the fact that men's experience (as gendered subjects, not cultural types – 'Dinka' or 'Trobrianders') is itself largely unstudied.
>
> (1986: 18–19)

Similarly, the pioneering work of female and gay writers on the relevance of their sexuality to their field experience makes it necessary to examine the position of a straight male ethnographer as something more than the 'cultural ego' or unmarked case.

The specificity of that position is, however, inextricably bound up with its having been the one that determined the normative structure of the fieldwork experience, a structure that ascribes essentially the same subject position to all fieldworkers. It does so by homogenizing 'the field' as a place to which the fieldworker must relate in specific and predetermined ways, suppressing both local and personal distinctions. Fieldwork narratives show little variation at the level of plot-structure, regardless of the author's identity; and it is to this plot-structure that I now turn.

Narratives of penetration

Jurij M. Lotman, building on the work of Vladimir Propp and others in the formal analysis of mythic plot, has published a stimulating article entitled 'The Origin of Plot in the Light of Typology' (1979), in which he proposed a 'primordial mythological type of structural organization' (p. 168) that reduced Propp's thirty-one plot-functions to a generative opposition between just two fundamental types of character:

> It is not difficult to notice that characters can be divided into those who are mobile, who enjoy freedom with regard to plot-space, who

> can change their place in the structure of the artistic world and cross the frontier, the basic topological feature of this space, and those who are immobile, who represent, in fact, a function of this space.
>
> Looked at typologically, the initial situation is that a certain plot-space is divided by a *single* boundary into an internal and an external sphere, and a *single* character has the opportunity to cross that boundary.
>
> (Lotman 1979: 167; italics in original)

The applicability of this binary model to fieldwork narratives, in which the ethnographer is the solitary traveller, and the ethnographic subjects the immobile plot-space, becomes even more obvious when Lotman describes the basic action of his primordial plot:

> The elementary sequence of events in myth can be reduced to a chain: entry into closed space – emergence from it (this chain is open at both ends and can be endlessly multiplied). Inasmuch as closed space can be interpreted as 'a cave,' 'the grave,' 'a house,' 'woman,' (and, correspondingly, be allotted the features of darkness, warmth, dampness), entry into it is interpreted on various levels as 'death,' 'conception,' 'return home' and so on; moreover all these acts are thought of as mutually identical. The birth-resurrection consequent upon death-conception is linked with the fact that birth is thought of not as the act of emergence of a new, previously non-existent personality, but as the renewal of one which has already existed.
>
> (p. 168)

This entry into closed space is given meaning by interpretation, which is itself an act of penetration in Crapanzano's view; and the differing interpretations of penetration in Lotman's mythic scheme match the contrary forces that Crapanzano ascribes to interpretation itself: 'Interpretation has been understood as a phallic, a phallic-aggressive, a cruel and violent, a destructive act, and as a fertile, a fertilizing, a fruitful, and a creative one' (1986: 52).

The specifically sexual implications of Lotman's plot-structure have been spelled out by Teresa de Lauretis:

> In this mythical-textual mechanics, then, the hero must be male, regardless of the gender of the text-image, because the obstacle, whatever its personification, is morphologically female and indeed, simply, the womb. The implication here is [that] the primary distinction on which all others depend is not, say, life and death, but

> rather sexual difference . . . Opposite pairs such as inside/outside, the raw/the cooked, or life/death appear to be merely derivatives of the fundamental opposition between boundary and passage; and if passage may be in either direction, from inside to outside or vice versa, nonetheless all these terms are predicated on the *single* figure of the hero who crosses the boundary and penetrates the other space. In so doing the hero, the mythical subject, is constructed as human being and as male; he is the active principle of culture, the establisher of distinction, the creator of differences.
>
> (1984: 118–19; italics in original)

In the same way, when ethnographic texts and fieldwork accounts describe how the researcher 'penetrates the other space', either physically or intellectually, to become the 'creator of differences' between self and other, they automatically place that researcher in a heterosexual-masculine subject position, 'regardless of the gender of the text-image'. This is why Crapanzano, in his comments on interpretation, explains, 'I have insisted here on using the masculine pronoun to refer to the ethnographer, despite his or her sexual identity, for I am writing of a stance and not of the person' (1986: 52). It is no accident that George E. Marcus, in the same volume, writes of the 'seminal' role of the ethnography produced from fieldwork in 'inaugurating careers and creating a certain ideological community of shared experience among anthropologists' (1986: 265). There is probably no way to avoid this sexual modelling of anthropology's interpretive practices as long as they remain tied to a myth of the field as a place to be penetrated by the heroic figure of the lone anthropologist in search of self-renewal.

This is so even if we question (as I would) de Lauretis' view that, in Lotman's model, sexual difference should be considered 'the *primary* distinction on which all others depend' (de Lauretis 1984: 118, my emphasis). In speaking of metaphor, it is common to make rash assumptions as to which is the literal and which the figurative meaning; but the idea that boundary and passage stand for sexual intercourse does not preclude the possibility that sex is itself a metaphor for something else – perhaps for a dominant, 'heroic' relation of self to other. If this self–other distinction is primary, the sexual imagery is nevertheless a powerful means of conceptualizing it, through identifying the self with the penetrating male hero. The act of 'interpreting' the other then constitutes not only a symbolic sexual penetration, but a construction of the self as masculine and dominant.

Rabinow has succinctly stated: 'Culture is interpretation' (1977: 150).

That is, the data that the ethnographer gathers (typically, as in Rabinow's case, from male informants) are themselves interpretations; and it is tempting to situate all interpretations in the familiar and putatively universal model of masculine culture penetrating feminine nature. However, it remains to be asked how culture-specific is the plot-type proposed by Lotman, on which such elaborations would depend. A culture based on Confucianism, such as that of Korea, is likely to emphasize narratives of filial self-sacrifice and marital fidelity which are not easily conformable to Lotman's scheme of penetration. Indeed, the most frequently told story in Korea is that of Ch'unhyang, in which it is precisely the resistance to penetration (or domination) that is celebrated: Ch'unhyang remains faithful to her absent lover in the face of demands, threats, and actual violence from a lustful magistrate. The lover finally returns to rescue Ch'unhyang and punish the magistrate; but in the telling, his exploits always receive less attention than her constancy. This is a far cry from the tales of difficult seduction, of male triumph over female resistance, that have been staple fare in Western fiction from *The Taming of the Shrew* to *Guys and Dolls* – notwithstanding the stories of martyrdom that show the 'Ch'unhyang' type of plot-structure but form a relatively inconspicuous part of the Western store of tales. Narratives of penetration could well turn out to be normative only for certain cultures, notably European and Euro-American; and this would not be without relevance to the fieldwork practices and ethnographic discourses through which members of those cultures define themselves in opposition to others.

There is as yet little sign of a change in the way the field has been *conceived* – a word whose polysemy between sexual and psychological realms reminds us of Crapanzano's point about the phallic nature of interpretation (1986: 52). That ethnographic interpretation remains structurally phallic is evidenced by the position that fieldwork continues to hold in the value system and career path of academic anthropology. That position has been identified by Susan Sontag, who referred to what was already an old idea when she wrote in 1963: 'Anthropologists are fond of likening field research to the puberty ordeal which confers status upon members of certain primitive societies' (1990: 71). Puberty is the life-crisis through which one becomes fully gendered and mature; and the anthropologist does so through a rite of separation from, and reincorporation into, an academic community. Fieldwork is the liminal phase of this rite of passage, thought of (in Lotman's phrase) as 'the renewal of [a personality] which already existed' (1979: 168). Thus, Rabinow recalls, 'In the graduate anthropology department at the University of Chicago, the world was divided into two categories of people: those who had done fieldwork, and those who had not' (1977: 3). The latter type could only hope to become true anthropologists through 'the alchemy of fieldwork' (ibid.) – an interesting metaphor with its implication that the fieldwork experience can magically transform human base metal into gold. The anticipation of that experience, as one in which fledgling anthropologists renew their personalities and 'find themselves' professionally, continues to be a self-fulfilling prophecy.

It is not only straight male ethnographers who have thought of fieldwork in this way. An examination of the ways in which female and gay ethnographers have been incorporated into the same plot-structure is more than I can attempt here, but a single example should at least indicate that the straight men have no monopoly. 'Manda Cesara', writing under a pseudonym, introduces her narrative as being 'about a female student of anthropology, who, on her first field trip, becomes an accidental witness of her own transition into a woman and an ethnographer' (1982: vii). Although she defines her achieved femininity as a rejection of 'the subject–object, self–other, introspective–empiricistic segregations' (ibid.), her narrative retains the male-oriented structure of personal renewal through penetration of other space. Her affair with an African man turns out to be the means of that penetration: before it, she had been alienated and depressed, driving through a barren landscape while murmuring to herself, 'Oh my god, oh my god, oh my god' (1982: 45); after it, she 'had to admit that Douglas opened for me the gate to Lenda' (1982: 61). The predetermined narrative structure of the fieldwork experience ascribed to Cesara a plot-function that was morphologically masculine, and resulted in her reproducing that structure, for all her intended opposition to it. The WSM position vis-à-vis his subjects may have originally been the creation of WSM anthropologists; but it is no longer unique to the WSM: it is inscribed in the myth of the field, and affects the experience of all ethnographers whether or not the metaphor of sex as ethnography becomes a literal reality.

This type of narrative structure, inherent in anthropology's 'fieldwork' construct, is one of the two overarching structures that govern the researcher's relationships with subjects, including the possibility of erotic encounters. The second is the pattern of interaction with foreigners that already exists in the community we are studying. Since this can only be discussed with reference to specific places, I will now describe the situation in Seoul which forms the context of my own field experience.

Expatriates in Seoul

When we go to the field, we are entering a situation where norms governing relationships between locals and outsiders are already in place. These norms include sexual mores. The failure to address this fact in fieldwork narratives, even in those few that describe the researcher's sexual experiences, has hindered the adequate understanding of fieldwork dynamics.

Local people make sense of the ethnographer's presence in terms of their culture's accumulated store of encounters with outsiders; and ethnographers cannot make sense of their own presence without considering its position in the larger pattern of those encounters. There has been a great deal of discussion (e.g. in Whitehead and Conaway 1986; Bell *et al.* 1993) of the degree to which the researcher can or should adopt local gender roles in various fieldwork situations; but one finds only passing reference to the issue of local expectations toward the researcher as a *foreign* man or woman.

For me, this was a far more relevant concern, since no one expected me to act like a Korean man; indeed, Koreans seemed to find it funny or even threatening when I came too close to doing so. In their eyes, the appropriate way for me to behave was in accordance with their clear if overgeneralized notions of Western culture. This meant primarily the American culture to which they had been exposed through films and television and, less frequently, through personal interaction with civilian or military expatriates. As a Caucasian I was always assumed to be American, and when I revealed my actual nationality, stereotypes of the 'crass American' tended to be swept away, only to be replaced by equally restricting ones of the 'English gentleman'. Such local perceptions are bound to affect fieldwork in places where there is a large and visible expatriate community, where the culture of the expatriates has been a powerful influence on the locals, and where sexual relationships across community boundaries are a common occurrence – all of which is true of Seoul.

A thoroughgoing ethnography of Seoul's expatriate community has yet to be attempted. It would be a fascinating project, since this is a case where a surprisingly coherent culture has been created by people of diverse backgrounds whose only common bond is not being Korean. The relative ethnic and cultural unity of Koreans throughout their long recorded history, and their desire to protect it from more powerful neighbors, has meant that assimilation has rarely been an option for foreigners living there. As a result, the latter have turned to other expatriates, often to those with whom they have little in common besides *being* expatriates, to create a stable community of their own – stable in the sense that its cultural patterns are reproduced even as individual foreigners come and go, rarely staying more than a few years.

There have been people of European extraction in Korea since the seventeenth century, stranded by shipwrecks, prospecting for gold, or missionizing for converts to Christianity; and Japan's colonial rule from 1910 to 1945 introduced another kind of foreign presence. But for my purposes, the Second World War takes the role of the Big Bang beyond which it is needless to enquire, since it forced the British, French, and American missionaries to leave as enemies of Japan, and in its aftermath the Korean War of 1950–3 established a new expatriate community centered on the American military. The armed forces, though largely isolated within the compounds and surrounding areas, had their own ways of relating to local people, including sexual contacts that ranged from rape and prostitution to life-long marriage; and these relationships have shaped perceptions of inter-ethnic sex from both sides.

Prostitution in military contexts has been dealt with in depth by Sturdevant and Stoltzfus (1992) and by a contributor to their volume on the subject, Cynthia Enloe, who perceptively asks, 'Without myths of Asian women's compliant sexuality would many American men be able to sustain their own identities of themselves as manly enough to act as soldiers?' (1992: 23). The military also accounts for as many as 95 per cent of marriages between Koreans and Americans, and these have been the subject of various studies (e.g. Lee 1991). Of more immediate relevance to my own experience, however, is the civilian community that arose during the 1960s through American businesses eager to reap the benefits of Korea's cheap skilled labor, and through the growing numbers of Peace Corps volunteers working in Korea after 1966 (Clark 1993: 192). Male Peace Corps volunteers have often married Korean women and, unlike most military personnel, have remained in Korea and been able to communicate with their wives and in-laws in Korean.

This community was considerably augmented during the 1970s and 1980s when Westerners travelling in Asia discovered that there was money to be made teaching English in Korea, even for those who had no qualification to do so other than being fluent speakers of the language. I myself found employment (on the strength of a bachelor's degree in music) as an English teacher at one of the more respected institutes during my three years in Korea, and most of the expatriates I knew there were English teachers, though many had Peace Corps experience.

The vast majority of these expatriates are male, heterosexual, and transient. Not surprisingly, their sexual attentions are focused on local women, and they are usually more interested in good times than commitment. Although happy marriages and long-term relationships do occur, a more typical pattern is formed by one-night stands with hostesses and prostitutes in that hub of the expatriate community, an area of money changers, masseuses, and ribald night life known as It'aewon. Foreigners of the It'aewon set often seem to carry over the attitudes of commercialized sex into their non-commercial affairs with Korean women, treating them as an amusement rather than a responsibility, and giving them little thought when it is time to leave. An archetype of sexual cross-purposes in Western culture – she wants security, he wants freedom – is thus exaggerated by the relation of geographical penetration that further feminizes the other: by the mobility of the male traversing the immobility of the female, who is to him, as Lotman would say, merely part of the plot-space.

The notion of a 'sexual career', a series of partners tried and rejected until one finds a compatible permanent mate, may seem natural to most Europeans and Americans, but it has not been generally adopted by Koreans, who continue to think of marriage as the normal outcome of any relationship between sincere and well-meaning lovers, and among whom matchmaking and arranged marriages are still fairly common. A relationship that does not lead to marriage is felt to be a failure, and in the case of an inter-ethnic relationship, the breakup is nearly always more painful for the Korean woman than for the Western man, since she does not share his view of the normal relationship as one of a series. (Relationships between Western women and Korean men are too rare for me to make any confident general statement about them, though I suspect that here too, and for the same reasons, the Korean would suffer more, other things being equal.)

Many Western men in Korea regard the idea of marriage to a Korean woman as a potential trap, claiming that Korean women are out to use American husbands as a means of entry to the States, and that as soon as they have a green card, they will sue for divorce and start bringing their relatives over. Korean women are thus represented as a menace to American masculinity because they threaten to reverse the relations of penetration by making America their plot-space and populating it with their own kind: a new incarnation of the 'yellow peril' paranoia. American masculinity therefore has to be protected by a macho discourse that keeps Korean women literally *in their place*. This discourse is shared by Western males of other nationalities, and is as contemptuous of Korean men as it is demeaning to Korean women. It posits sex, and primarily emotionless, anonymous sex, as the only mode in which expatriates would want to interact with locals; it reduces women to their bodies, and men to an unwanted intrusion. No wonder Korean men tend to regard inter-ethnic sexual relations in a wholly negative light: in a recent study of 'Korean Perceptions of America' by Kim Kyong-dong, for instance, sexual relations between Koreans and Americans are mentioned three times, and in each case linked to violence and crime (1993: 164, 170, 173–4). The expatriates' patterns of sexual contact with local women, and of discourse about that contact, could hardly fail to promote hostility toward themselves in a culture that has made homogeneity a means of self-defense, and that was already disposed to look askance on sexual relations with outsiders.

Bruce Cumings has argued persuasively that the expatriates in Seoul maintain a 'colonial culture and racist discourse' (1992: 174) in which sexual subordination and cultural disparagement continually reinforce each other. Published accounts of expatriate life in Korea had previously stopped short of revealing the sexual component in its true colors. In the journalistic literature, Simon Winchester (1988: 74) and Michael Stephens (1990: 31–2) both relate encounters with prostitutes that were interrupted by a Korean male who came in to stop the fun – a role that many expatriates see as typical of Korean men in general. Cumings himself tells of the attempts of Korean men to provide him with prostitutes, deterred only by his announcement that his wife would soon arrive (1992: 169, 172–3). The oral histories of the It'aewon set paint a fuller picture – not excluding what Richard Burton described a hundred years ago as 'the pleasures which the mouth or the hand of a pretty woman can give' (quoted in Kabbani 1986: 65), and indeed, reproducing his Orientalist discourse. These narratives reveal that commercialized sex is the principal recreation for a substantial portion of Seoul's expatriate community, and is, as Cumings has said, 'the most common form of Korean–American interaction' (1992: 169).

While I would stress that these comments do not apply to *all* the foreigners I met in Korea, it is certainly possible to identify a mainstream. The expatriate community in Seoul is predominantly white, straight, and male. Its relations with the host population are, on the whole, those of the archetypal WSM in the East: sexual domination and cultural disparagement, penetration of the feminized other in the interest of the self. These relations, I felt, were unacceptable as a basis for the study of culture; but as a WSM arriving in Seoul, I had to situate my own project against the pre-existing norms for interaction between locals and outsiders. This had implications not only for my professional, but for my personal life.

Learning to love/loving to learn

In the nine years since I began studying Korean culture and Korean music, I have been involved in several relationships with Korean women, each of whom had, however, lived for a number of years in the United States and become an American citizen. While these were not my only relationships, they were the most sustained and intense, and they clearly form a pattern that cannot be dismissed as coincidence. These women were in many ways very different from each other, but the portraits that emerge here must necessarily be lacking in individuation, not only to protect their privacy but because what I am looking for is an explanation of the aspects common to each relationship. Since only one of these relationships was initiated in Korea, it would be pointless to restrict my account to the time I spent there: the pattern emerges only when I expand the frame to include the whole history of my 'love affair with Korea'.

Seen in that light, the connections between my academic life and emotional life become so obvious that I now feel as if their previous invisibility was a result of my having been carefully trained not to see them. Even my initial attraction to the field of ethnomusicology now appears as a response to emotional needs traceable back to childhood. Growing up as a shy boy and as the youngest of my peer group (my brother and two playmates next door were all one or two years older), I had learned to play the piano and used it increasingly as both a means of self-expression and a source of approval. Our next-door neighbors on both sides were international couples: a Greek husband on one side, and a Dutch wife on the other, each married to an English spouse; and my father, being a church minister, was often visited by missionaries and other church workers from exotic places like America. We never travelled abroad ourselves, due to financial constraints and my mother's precarious health, but as a result, the wide world as a place of adventure and potential romance was implanted in my youthful imagination, unsullied by actual experience. Meanwhile, the early realization that I could not accept the belief system in which I was being raised gave me that compulsion to figure things out for myself (which is probably a prerequisite for any successful academic work); and the development of omnivorous reading habits was encouraged by living in a house that was always full of books. It was some years, however, before I discovered how to combine all these tendencies in a single program of activity.

As a student of classical music at the University of Edinburgh, in a department where most students and faculty were from upper-middle-class backgrounds, self-consciousness about my northern working-class accent and gauche manners reinforced my introvert tendencies and encouraged me to concentrate with greater intensity on the piano. But I had also developed an interest that combined music with the exotic, and that therefore proved more satisfying to me in the long run: the concerts of Indian classical music that catered to Britain's large South Asian immigrant community. It may be that frustration with the elitism of the Western classical music world, where I often found that I was not taken seriously because of my accent, encouraged me to pursue an interest in a non-Western music tradition which, though equally elitist in its original context, was as accessible to me as to any other Western person. At these concerts I was as much excited by the sense of participating in another cultural world as by the adventure of learning a new way to listen to music – and certainly by the beauty of the women, whose modes of self-adornment struck me as highly artistic. In the winter after my graduation I travelled to India to study vocal music, and the experience made me decide to pursue ethnomusicology as a career and exile as a lifestyle.

When I told my friends I was going to graduate school in Hawaii, most of them refused to believe there was a university there, so strong was their association of those tropical islands with sunshine and romance. I cannot deny that in the back of my own mind Hawaii was attractive partly because it seemed to offer the prospect of finding the satisfying romance that had so far eluded me in my own country (and in this I was not disappointed). Americans would not notice my regional accent (which need not have been as great a social handicap as I made it, even in Britain): as far as they were concerned, I spoke the Queen's English, and to be British was to be special. Among the diverse cultural contexts in this quintessential melting pot, there would surely be one in which I could feel at home.

I arrived in Hawaii with the desire to study world music in general; I wanted to repeat my experience with Indian music, but had not yet chosen an area for field research. (From my point of view, Hawaii was already the field.) A number of factors pushed me in the direction of Korean music. The distinguished Korean scholar Lee Byong-won was on the ethnomusicology faculty, and was to become my advisor; I knew that Korea was a place where I could support myself by teaching if necessary, and I was tired of being poor; but not least, I was romantically interested in a Korean-American woman. Although she had come to the States as a child and was more or less bilingual, I wanted to speak Korean with her and to be with her in Korean social contexts – a side of her identity that had so far been a mystery to me. Shy people often find it easier to express themselves in foreign languages; but there was no way I could justify taking the time to learn Korean unless Korea was going to be my area of specialization. And that may have been the deciding factor.

Manda Cesara, citing Sartre, argues that 'the emotion of love for a particular individual of a people among whom one conducts research aims at laying hold of the culture in its entirety through that particular individual' (Cesara 1982: 60), and adds that this 'laying hold' is probably an illusion. I do not think I was under this particular illusion, but I am convinced that my feelings toward the individual with whom I was most intimately involved had a strong effect on my feelings toward her culture as a whole, and that this effect was transmitted to my research, even though she was not directly involved in it. In different contexts, this was true for both the Korean and the American aspects of her cultural identity. At low points in the relationship, I often wondered whether I had made the right choice either in coming to the States or in focusing on Korean music. At high points, I found myself emulating either American or Korean cultural traits myself. But perhaps the psychology of the matter is simpler than either Cesara or I have realized: love makes you feel good about yourself, and therefore about whatever projects and ambitions you are pursuing.

The relationship turned out to be a tempestuous one, for reasons that are best forgotten. I do not think I could present both sides of the story even-handedly, and it would be unedifying to give only my own. By the time it was over, I had taken several courses related to Korean music and art, and was able to hold a simple conversation in the language. This probably helped make me attractive to a second Korean woman, who was herself a musician and dancer, and was also interested in learning Western music. We began by exchanging piano lessons for instruction on a traditional Korean instrument, and often called each other in the evenings to chat in both Korean and English. Although she was widely acknowledged to be beautiful and gifted, and received the constant attention of numerous men, I think what made me stand out from the crowd was primarily my interest in Korean culture and music.

This was to be my deepest relationship to date; I do not know whether she would say the same. But it began just a few months before I was due to leave Hawaii, and the prospect of parting was a constant anxiety. The following summer, she came to England to meet my parents, who fell in love with her immediately and were strongly in favor of her becoming their daughter-in-law. I did not feel ready for marriage, or keen to settle in Hawaii, where she seemed to be very much at home. It was hard to see a way that we could be together in the long term, since our career goals were pulling us in different directions. We would have had to make our relationship the top priority in our lives, and it became apparent that neither one of us was ready to make the sacrifices that would have been involved. And so, shortly after I went to Korea to begin my research, I wrote to suggest that we no longer regard ourselves as committed, and she agreed. We have remained friends. The relationship was one in which love for an individual and the desire to understand her culture have constantly reinforced each other.

My successive involvement with two Korean-American women undoubtedly played a role in my selection of a specific thesis topic once I had decided on the general area of Korean music. Rather than study one of the many indigenous genres that have been somewhat artificially preserved through government sponsorship, I chose to focus on contemporary composers writing new music for Korean instruments. One of my central points was that 'composition', in this sense, had not existed in Korean music before contact with the West, since the repertoire of traditional music had been created by successive generations of musicians reworking material of ultimately unknown origin. A Korean musician who set up as a 'composer', therefore, was committed to some degree of compromise with the influence of Western music, and it was the different forms of that compromise that became the subject of my enquiry (Killick 1991). Though I had not consciously chosen this topic on the basis of my love life, it seems likely that my interest in cultural compromise was in part motivated by my desire to understand the biculturalism of the women with whom I was involved. In the light of this experience, it comes as no surprise to me that Malinowski, having striven to repress his own sexual impulses during fieldwork, chose to write about 'sex and repression in savage society' (1955).

In Korea, I first experienced a period of torpor in which I hesitated to embark on the research I had planned. I was under no obligation to do so, since I was supporting myself by teaching English rather than being funded by a grant, and was at liberty to adjust to my new surroundings in a general way until I felt ready to pursue more specific goals. It seems to me in retrospect that I was undergoing a crisis of selfhood that many anthropologists and others have endured when suddenly transposed from one cultural context to another – a crisis that was particularly acute because of the culture-shock I received from the expatriate community as well as the host population. Helen Morton (in this volume) discusses the loss of self that many fieldworkers feel as a danger, particularly when they are sexually involved with people from the culture they are studying; and it was probably as a response to this anxiety that I spent much of my free time during my first few months in Korea learning about Buddhist philosophy and meditation rather than gathering material for my thesis. Buddhism, with its doctrine of the self as illusion, and of attachment to the self and its desires as the cause of pervasive suffering in life, had a particularly therapeutic value for me as I struggled to make sense of the contradictory roles in which I found myself – or rather, didn't. I still often think of the self as nothing more than a convenient fiction for maintaining continuity between one interaction and another.

Meanwhile, I had gone from a physical environment of celebrated beauty into one of stress, overcrowding, and ugliness. A great deal of my difficulty in adjusting to life in Seoul, and probably in embarking on my research there, arose from the need to build up a tolerance for the noise, air pollution, jostling, traffic jams, and unrelieved concrete surfaces that characterized the city's impact on my senses. This was not the teeming, bustling vibrancy I had experienced in India, which had been exciting if at times overwhelming; it was an assault without any compensatory benefits, from which I felt a need to close off my sensory and psychological receptors. For this reason, I would not have been able to follow Kate Altork's recommendation (in this volume) that fieldworkers open their senses and allow themselves to be penetrated by the field, much as I am intrigued by her reversal of the relation that constitutes conventional fieldwork narratives. A state of heightened physiological stimulation was undoubtedly appropriate to her work among firefighters in a natural wilderness; but for myself, I felt that the only way to survive the grating physicality of Seoul was a deliberately dulled sensitivity. The shell I built around my senses, however, tended to limit receptivity on a personal and cultural level too, and this was a dilemma with which I grappled throughout my time in Korea, since I knew that present-day Seoul was just as much a part of Korean culture as the music I was studying.

A consideration that put me further on my guard in personal interactions was the realization that, in certain circumstances, Western men are regarded as desirable husbands for Korean women. The women in question are often those who have been unable to make a desirable match in the Korean 'marriage market' (a term that is widely used by Koreans themselves) because of qualities that would not necessarily be considered disadvantages in a Western context. Women who are highly educated, career-oriented, or even unusually tall may be regarded as unpromising home-makers by traditionally-minded Korean men; and when they reach their late twenties, their marriage prospects decline rapidly. I had the painful experience of seeing several of my female Korean friends and former students become increasingly desperate, seeking long-shot introductions and attending etiquette schools to enhance their wedding appeal, well aware that unless they were exceptionally talented there were no other avenues of success open to them than to impress an eligible male with their worth in such ways. Sometimes I suspected that I was one of the eligible males.

My first inkling of this possibility occurred soon after I arrived in Korea, when I was invited to dinner by one of the professors to whom I had a letter of introduction. We went to a Japanese seafood restaurant, which means an expensive restaurant; and he brought his younger sister. I was slow to perceive the logic in this, since I had thought we were going to talk about music. Instead, it seemed he had to steer the conversation toward general and personal topics to enable her to participate. She made polite suggestions, such as that next time I go to a concert I should invite her. It was only toward the end of the evening that I realized what was happening: she must have been around thirty, despairing of finding a suitable Korean husband, and her older brother had been given the brief of introducing her to any bachelor who sounded promising. As a prospective academic, I fitted that category. She seemed nice enough, but I did not quite feel unattached yet, and I had no wish to raise false hopes. I ended up not using that particular contact.

Entanglements that could have had a direct effect on my research, like this one, remained potential rather than actual. But their possibility brought home the fact that the agenda I had in mind for my informants might be different from theirs with regard to me, and that I could not adequately take account of the difference without considering myself as a sexual being. That my sexuality was part of my identity in Korean eyes was evident from one of the questions I was infallibly asked by new students, whether male or female: 'What do you think of Korean women?' Celibacy may be the usual condition for fieldworkers, but in most cultural contexts, to be asexual is abnormal, and therefore suspect: one is assumed (quite reasonably) to have sexual interests that might be engaged by others for their own purposes. These purposes range from profit by prostitution to sincere and permanent loving relationships. They may be at odds with our research goals, but we deflect them only at a price: that of losing potentially helpful collaborators, of missing romantic opportunities, and of being regarded as unmanly (or unwomanly) and hence, in many cultures, unworthy of trust or respect. (Male anthropologists who have written of their informants' need to see them as sexually active include Michael Angrosino 1986 and Peter Wade 1993.)

Nevertheless, despite some near misses, I did not date Korean women in Korea, excepting one who had been raised in the States and was an American citizen. My abstinence seemed strange to other expatriates, and also to some of my Korean friends, who thought it must have been a deliberate policy on my part. In fact, I did not plan it that way, but I think in retrospect there were reasons relating to both desire and opportunity. One of my urgent concerns was to dissociate myself from the It'aewon set who were my unwelcome neighbors, and from the exploitive tone of their relations with local women. At the same time, I was wary of entering into a relationship that would be defined from the outset as a path toward marriage, and this seemed to be the local norm.

But I have also to consider local perceptions of me as a romantic possibility. Malinowski (1989) wrote as if he had unbounded faith in his powers of seduction, and the only struggle was to keep himself from using them; but those of us who are less sure of our prospects have to ask why it is that certain people are romantically interested in us, while others are not. Compared to many of the foreign men in Seoul, I was a short, nerdy, bookworm type with glasses and a receding hairline – hardly the ideal of macho masculinity that is as ingrained in Korea as that of dainty, vulnerable femininity. A more serious drawback had to do, surprisingly, with cultural attitudes. Those Korean women who, for whatever reason, had decided to go with foreign men (a decision that was often made before becoming involved with a particular man) had a stake in being cosmopolitan and in being valued for their freedom from traditional cultural restraints. This made them willing to listen to groups of their boyfriends bad-mouthing Korea for hours on end, a tolerance that initially mystified me. But they had struggled hard to resist the coercion of those who told them to be good Koreans, and had little use for a foreign boyfriend who seemed to be telling them the same thing.

Korean-American women, on the other hand, have typically experienced great pressure to be American; to win acceptance from other Americans, and to succeed at their game, the alternative being to fall back on the safety net of a Korean immigrant community with which they only partly identify. They often have strong criticisms of that community themselves, but hate to hear condemnation of Korean culture from non-Koreans. It is a novelty for them to be valued for their Koreanness by someone who is not himself Korean; and I think this was something I had to offer to each of the Korean American women with whom I was involved. The pattern was established in Hawaii, and was to be repeated in Korea.

I had been continuing lessons in Korean music, but after some months my teacher left to continue her studies at a foreign university. She had introduced me to Professor Hwang Byung-ki, who is perhaps the most famous of all traditional Korean musicians as both a performer and a composer. He was the ideal person for me to study with, but I felt I was still at an elementary level, and hesitated to approach him. What finally made me pluck up courage was probably the desire to impress a third Korean-American woman to whom I was attracted at the time. The outcome was success all round: Professor Hwang proved a wonderful teacher and became my principal informant, asking only for English lessons in return; and the relationship with the woman turned the corner, though I think it would have done anyway. While it lasted, I was enthused about my work, and often discussed it with my new lover, who also provided helpful introductions and accompanied me to performance events such as plays which I would not have been able to appreciate alone. Because she was Korean, she helped me to gain access to the culture I was learning about; but because she was American, I did not have the misgivings I have described above. It eventually became apparent that we were not as compatible as we had at first thought, but indirectly the relationship had, to paraphrase Cesara, opened the gate to Korea for me.

One further experience may be worthy of reflection. Leaving the field is likely to be a time of emotional confusion and instability, when new attachments can seem like a good idea. I have observed this psychology in several expatriate friends as well as in myself. Towards the end of my third and most recent year in Korea I found myself in love with a Korean woman (not Korean-American this time) who, I felt sure, was fond of me too. The fact that I had not been involved with a local Korean woman before made the opportunity seem all the more unique, and my feelings were strong enough to overcome the qualms I had felt about dating Korean women in the past. But this was nearing the time when I was to leave, and I had to consider the likelihood of a long separation. I finally decided I was willing to commit to a long-distance relationship if she was – only to find that she was already in one. Until I stated my case, there had been no basis for her to tell me this; she had not shared it with other friends outside her immediate family. If my rational faculties had been operating at normal strength, I would have realized how impractical the romance would have been anyway; but at times of major transition, such as moving from one cultural context to another, reason can be overpowered by the longing for emotional security. The disappointment was severe enough to leave a sour taste about Korea, and to make me think for a while about changing my future research plans. It left me possibly a wiser but certainly a sadder man.

I do plan to return to Korea in 1995 to conduct research on the musical theatre genre *ch'angguk*; and it will be interesting to see how the difference in my age (always significant in Korea) will affect my experience. As a (presumably) single man in my thirties, I will present more of an anomaly in local terms than I did before. But then, anomalies are normal for foreigners: from an ethnographer's point of view, a possible advantage of a homogeneous culture that celebrates resistance to penetration is that locals do not expect outsiders to behave like locals. They do have other expectations, shaped by a history of previous interactions, and it is with these expectations that the ethnographer must come to terms in carving out an acceptable role that is appropriately differentiated from that of other outsiders.

Just as there is no single practice that is appropriate for all fieldwork situations, so there is no 'correct' policy on sex in the field. The untenability of generalizations should alert us to the dubiousness of the assumptions on which the concept of the field itself is founded. In my own case, the assumption that fieldwork is the relevant unit produces a marked distortion of my experience, since it misses the point that my love life in Korea continued a pattern established in Hawaii and reflected an unwillingness to conform to the prevailing modes of sexual interaction between locals and outsiders. These points would not emerge from a consideration of my field experience alone, which would appear much the same as anyone else's because of the homogenizing plot-structure of the preconceived fieldwork narrative. That structure, rooted as it is in the construction of sexual difference, should not go unquestioned when sex and the field are considered together.

Conclusions: rethinking the field

Despite some far-reaching efforts at reform, anthropology retains its powerful central myth of 'the field' as a place where ethnographers have a certain type of experience leading to revelation and full participation in the community of anthropologists. Just as people who have never travelled outside their own country are apt to speak of 'foreigners' and 'abroad' as unified concepts, so ethnographers, with much less excuse, have fallen into the habit of referring to 'the field' as a place with identifiable borders and homogeneous topography. Robert N. Bellah, in his foreword to Rabinow's *Reflections on Fieldwork in Morocco* (1977: xi), praises the author for an 'emotional honesty that anyone who has ever worked in the field at once recognizes' – as if someone, *anyone*, doing anthropological fieldwork in, say, Tibet, or among Australian Aboriginals, or for that matter in New York City could be assumed to have felt the same emotions as Rabinow did in Morocco. It appears that the field cannot be defined geographically, but rather by a frame of mind and a certain type of objective; nor can anyone be adequately prepared for a trip there: if you go to the field knowing what to expect, you will not be *in* the field. It is only after you have been there that you can recognize Rabinow's honesty in describing the 'same' experience.

Rabinow himself, citing Paul Ricouer, defines his goal in the interpretation of his fieldwork as 'the comprehension of the self by the detour of the comprehension of the other' (1977: 5). Having thus made his priorities clear, he later illustrates the lengths to which the fieldworker must go in order to make this detour. He describes how he overcame his informants' resistance to his enquiries into a sensitive historical matter by securing an account from an unpopular man whom he knew the others would want to correct. Rabinow was aware that this ploy 'would coerce, almost blackmail, the others into exposing aspects of their lives which they had thus far passionately shielded from me' (1977: 130). But he explains, 'To those who claim that some form of this symbolic violence was not part of their own field experience, I reply simply that I do not believe them. It is inherent in the structure of the situation' (ibid.). This is not a position with which one can argue; and there could be no clearer statement of the fieldwork plot-structure as one in which forcible penetration of the other is the means to an enhanced comprehension, and hence revitalization, of the self.

Stephen Tyler notes that the old anthropological subject, the 'savage', 'has become the instrument of the ethnographer's "experience"' (1986: 128); I would add that the 'field' which the 'savage' inhabits has become the locus of that experience. Tyler himself appears on the frontispiece of a book about 'the poetics and politics of ethnography' (Clifford and Marcus 1986), in a photograph that shows him busily writing with his back turned to a man and two children whose dark skins blend into the shadowy background of what appears to be a grass-roofed hut. The caption reads, 'Stephen Tyler in the Field. Photography by Martha G. Tyler'. A unique individual, Stephen Tyler, stands out in heroic personhood, his white shirt and manuscript almost the only light areas in the frame, his identity defining the subject; there is no need to say 'Stephen Tyler (left)'. The person behind the camera is likewise individually credited, and dignified with the term 'photography', which suggests an art form rather than mere documentation. But the other people and the location is simply 'the Field'.

Clifford's commentary points out how different this view is from the familiar fieldwork images of 'Margaret Mead exuberantly playing with children in Manus or questioning villagers in Bali' (1986: 1), but misses the irony of the reflexivist focus on the ethnographer as writer, a focus that makes of the field a homogeneous background to be sunk in shadows with its inhabitants, ultimately, ignored. The 'savage', whether we call her an informant, narrator, interlocutor, or whatever political correctness demands, has been reduced to a function of the plot-space traversed by the anthropologist-as-hero. That plot-space, the field, serves mainly to enable the narcissistic project of the ethnographer's encounter with himself, *his* renewal of *him*self through penetration of feminized, other space.

My own discipline, ethnomusicology, is distinguished from other kinds of musicology as much by fieldwork as by anything else; and though my experience of the field may have been marginal, I did undergo the dislocation of self that is supposed to be part of the ordeal. I also instantiated the classic fieldwork structure in that I went from a culture in which the core narratives are those of penetration to one in which they are of resistance to penetration, and one means to overcome that (real or imaginary) resistance was a sexual relationship that literalized the metaphor. My being white, straight, and male makes the structure obvious, though it is not necessary to my position in that structure.

My love affair in Korea may have conformed to the standard fieldwork narrative structure; but to isolate that affair from my pre-fieldwork experiences, as I have shown, would be to mask an important fact: the pattern of my love life did not change when I went to the field. On the contrary, I felt that to adopt the ready-made gender roles of either the expatriate or (with more difficulty) the local community would have been inimical to both my personal and professional goals. Though my encounter with the field was a significant experience, it need not define the frame of my story, and should not be equated with the experience of other fieldworkers in other fields. This is not to claim a special uniqueness for myself, but rather to argue that all fields are equally unique – a truism, perhaps, but one that is too often forgotten in the effort to create a community of anthropologists united by a common experience of 'fieldwork' that would otherwise contain very little that is shared. The 'field' is essentially a negative category, the place that is not ours, and whatever traits are attributed to it as a unified entity must be projections of an anthropological construct.

It is not only the WSM anthropologist who makes such projections. If, as I have argued, the plot-structure of fieldwork narratives as a genre automatically places the fieldworker in the heterosexual-masculine position of penetrating the feminized other, it is not enough to attribute that plot-structure (however justly) to the patriarchal and colonial foundations of the discipline. No fieldworker is exempted from the charge of replicating it on the strength of being female or homosexual. Nor am I: for all my evasions, my narrative remains one of penetration, and though I may, like Rabinow, be haunted by 'superego images of my anthropologist persona' (1977: 66), and even internalize those images to an extent at the ego level, in the last analysis I stand exposed by my id: it goes for Asians. Quite possibly this may spring from a subconscious desire to put myself in a heroic, masculine, dominating position over the Other; I am no authority on my subconscious desires. I do not, therefore, make an exception for myself when I speak of anthropologists who reproduce colonial narratives of penetration. But I would object equally to any claim that I should be either included in that category because of my gender, ethnicity, or sexual orientation, or excluded from it because of my class, regional background, or academic specialization. Marginality or its opposite is never intrinsic to individuals, but depends on the context; and the power of myths is not simply a question of who transmits them. The received myth of fieldwork, as self-renewal through penetration of other space, will not disappear when there are no more WSM ethnographers. It has become so powerful, its metaphor believed so literally, that we may now need to be reminded: there is no such place as the field.

Perhaps this will become clearer when someone edits a book of accounts by informants of their relationships with anthropologists; for the latter is surely the more cohesive of the two categories. Differences between fieldwork contexts are easily glossed over when our attention is on differences between ethnographers; but 'the field' is a unity only to the extent that it fulfills its prescribed role in ethnography's constitutive plot-structure. Thus, the question to be faced is one that encapsulates the current crisis of our *field* (in both senses of the word): if we find another plot-structure, will we still be doing anthropology? If not, where do our loyalties lie?

Acknowledgements

My warmest thanks go to the editors for leading me to introspect in new and rewarding ways; to Phyllis Laners for providing the introduction that led to my participation in this project; to David and Song-min Kosofsky for giving me a happy home during my last year in Korea and showing me just how successful a cross-cultural marriage can be; and to the anonymous women in my story, for enriching my life in ways that far exceed what I can here convey.

References

Angrosino, Michael V. (1986) 'Son and Lover: The Anthropologist as Non-threatening Male', in Tony Larry Whitehead and Mary Ellen Conaway (eds) *Self, Sex and Gender in Cross-Cultural Fieldwork*. Urbana and Chicago: University of Illinois Press.

Bell, Diane, Pat Caplan, and Wazir Jahan Karim (eds) (1993) *Gendered Fields: Women, Men and Ethnography*. London and New York: Routledge.

Burton, Richard Francis (1967) *The Erotic Traveller*. Ed. Edward Leigh. New York: Putnam.

Cesara, Manda (1982) *Reflections of a Woman Anthropologist: No Hiding Place*. London and New York: Academic Press.

Clark, Donald N. (1993) 'American Attitudes Toward Korea', in Donald N. Clark (ed.) *Korea Briefing 1993: Festival of Korea*. Boulder, Colo.: Westview Press.

Clifford, James (1986) 'Introduction: Partial Truths', in James Clifford and

George E. Marcus (eds) *Writing Culture: The Poetics and Politics of Ethnography.* Berkeley, Calif.: University of California Press.

Cormack, Mike (1992) *Ideology.* Ann Arbor: University of Michigan Press.

Crapanzano, Vincent (1986) 'Hermes' Dilemma: The Masking of Subversion in Ethnographic Description', in James Clifford and George E. Marcus (eds) *Writing Culture: The Poetics and Politics of Ethnography.* Berkeley, Calif.: University of California Press.

Cumings, Bruce (1992) 'Silent but Deadly: Sexual Subordination in the U.S.–Korean Relationship', in Saundra Pollock Sturdevant and Brenda Stoltzfus (eds) *Let the Good Times Roll: Prostitution and the U.S. Military in Asia.* New York: The New Press.

de Lauretis, Teresa (1984) 'Desire in Narrative', in *Alice Doesn't: Feminism, Semiotics, Cinema.* Bloomington: Indiana University Press.

Enloe, Cynthia (1992) 'It Takes Two', in Saundra Pollock Sturdevant and Brenda Stoltzfus (eds) *Let the Good Times Roll: Prostitution and the U.S. Military in Asia.* New York: The New Press.

Hansen, Christian, Catherine Needham, and Bill Nicols (1991) 'Pornography, Ethnography, and the Discourses of Power', in Bill Nichols (ed.) *Representing Reality: Issues and Concepts in Documentary.* Bloomington and Indianapolis: Indiana University Press.

Kabbani, Rana (1986) *Europe's Myths of Orient: Devise and Rule.* London: Macmillan.

Killick, Andrew (1991) 'Nationalism and Internationalism in New Music for Korean Instruments'. *Korea Journal.* Vol. 31, No. 3, pp. 104–16.

Kim, Kyong-dong (1993) 'Korean Perceptions of America', in Donald N. Clark (ed.) *Korea Briefing 1993: Festival of Korea.* Boulder, Colo.: Westview Press.

Lee, Daniel (1991) 'Transculturally Married Korean Women in the U.S.: Their Contributions and Sufferings', in Tae-hwan Kwak and Seong-hyong Lee (eds) *The Korean-American Community: Present and Future.* Seoul: Kyungnam University Press.

Lotman, Jurij M. (1979) 'The Origin of Plot in the Light of Typology'. *Poetics Today.* Vol. 1, Nos. 1–2, pp. 161–84.

Malinowski, Bronislaw (1955) *Sex and Repression in Savage Society.* Cleveland, Ohio: The World Publishing Company.

——— (1989) *A Diary in the Strict Sense of the Term.* 2nd edn. Stanford: Stanford University Press.

Marcus, George E. (1986) 'Afterword: Ethnographic Writing and Anthropological Careers', in James Clifford and George E. Marcus (eds) *Writing Culture: The Poetics and Politics of Ethnography.* Berkeley, Calif.: University of California Press.

McLuhan, Marshall (1965) *Understanding Media: The Extensions of Man.* New York: McGraw-Hill Paperback Edition.

Newton, Esther (1993) 'My Best Informant's Dress: The Erotic Equation in Fieldwork'. *Cultural Anthropology.* Vol. 8, No. 1, pp. 3–23.

Rabinow, Paul (1977) *Reflections on Fieldwork in Morocco.* Berkeley, Calif.: University of California Press.

Said, Edward (1978) *Orientalism.* New York: Pantheon.

Sontag, Susan (1990) 'The Anthropologist as Hero', in *Against Interpretation and Other Essays.* Anchor Books edn. New York: Doubleday.

Stephens, Michael (1990) *Lost in Seoul, and Other Discoveries on the Korean Peninsula*. New York: Random House.
Sturdevant, Saundra Pollock and Brenda Stoltzfus (eds) (1992) *Let the Good Times Roll: Prostitution and the U.S. Military in Asia*. New York: The New Press.
Tyler, Stephen A. (1986) 'Post-Modern Ethnography: From Document of the Occult to Occult Document', in James Clifford and George E. Marcus (eds) *Writing Culture: The Poetics and Politics of Ethnography*. Berkeley, Calif.: University of California Press.
Wade, Peter (1993) 'Sexuality and Masculinity in Fieldwork among Colombian Blacks', in Diane Bell, Pat Caplan, and Wazir Jahan Karim (eds) *Gendered Fields: Women, Men and Ethnography*. London and New York: Routledge.
Whitehead, Tony Larry and Mary Ellen Conaway (eds) (1986) *Self, Sex and Gender in Cross-Cultural Fieldwork*. Urbana and Chicago: University of Illinois Press.
Whitehead, Tony Larry and Laurie Price (1986) 'Summary: Sex and the Fieldwork Experience', in Tony Larry Whitehead and Mary Ellen Conaway (eds) *Self, Sex and Gender in Cross-Cultural Fieldwork*. Urbana and Chicago: University of Illinois Press.
Winchester, Simon (1988) *Korea: A Walk through the Land of Miracles*. New York: Prentice Hall.

Chapter 4

Walking the fire line

The erotic dimension of the fieldwork experience

Kate Altork

His hands reach up to remove the camera from around my neck, the tape recorder from my shoulder. Then he solemnly undresses me, as if I were a small and very sweet child. I stand willful before him, and there is no fear. His face is smudged with smoke and dirt, as he reaches out to pull me down into the water. Fighting the forest fire for days has not worn him down but, rather, stimulated him in strange and unexpected ways. His strong hands move like small, pulsing animals as he wraps my legs around his hard body. Looking up, I see pine trees, smell pine trees, taste wildness. The forest seems to be leaping, blurred by smoke from the huge fire many miles away. But we are underwater now, away from the smoke and heat, rolling like smooth river rocks in the stream. And we are suffused in sunlight.

Suddenly, I hear the helicopter moving overhead. It awakens me only seconds before the alarm blasts from the bedside table. I swiftly leap from the bed, my back and belly drenched in sweat. 'I don't believe it!', I mutter to myself. 'This is the third erotic dream like that I've had in a week! My fieldwork seems to be permeating every aspect of my life. I can't get away from it!' Packing up my gear in the hallway – cameras, tape recorder, notebooks, blank tapes – I vacillate between disappointment that it was just a dream and a growing sense of ambivalence. This fieldwork project has a grip on me that I'm unable to break away from even when I want a good night's sleep. It feels like an invasion – and a sweet and sour one, at that.

I was eighteen months into a fieldwork project in a rural, mountain town in Idaho when forest fires began breaking out in record numbers in the summer of 1992. Seven consecutive years of drought had rendered the land dangerously dry and vulnerable to fires started, more often than not, by lightning. Previous records were shattered, and a total of nearly 300,000 acres had succumbed to fire since 1985, more than 10 per cent of the gross acreage of that particular national forest.

As I studied and wrote about this place and the vernacular language utilized by the region's inhabitants to articulate and claim it, huge sections of the landscape were burning. All summer long, I had watched the planes and helicopters come and go, the small, local airport bustling with U.S. Forest Service personnel and aircraft, the air buzzing with 'birds' on their firefighting missions. Each morning, the helicopters rose up and over the mountains behind the house where I lived, moving overhead for the first run of the day at exactly 6:45 a.m. – a noisy and highly functional wake-up call which seemed to jump-start my days. Writing in my office in town one morning, it suddenly occurred to me that I had been listening to the almost constant droning of aircraft overhead for days. Jumping up, I began stuffing tapes and notebooks into my daypack, quickly locking the office door behind me. I wanted to be out there, in the forest, talking to the fire people.

The smoke jumper building and loft, sitting at the edge of the town of 2500 inhabitants, is one of the northwest's regional headquarter stations for U.S. Forest Service firefighting personnel. Through a fortunate series of events and circumstances, I was given permission to enter and to witness the world of the firefighters. Arrangements were made for me to be taken out to the fires, where I watched teams of firefighters build fire lines. I attended briefings and press conferences where the logistics of planning strategy for 3700 firefighters, flown in from thirty-two states, were determined. In the process, I was able to study a phenomenon of particular interest to me, the construction of what I term an 'instant place'.

In this process, well-coordinated and highly trained teams of people rapidly construct and complete the building of fire camps. These self-sustaining small 'towns' are erected in a single day, providing a base camp for firefighters and support personnel until nearby fires are contained. They are then quickly dismantled, often in less than a day, leaving no trace of having met the basic needs of from 300 to 3000 adults, depending upon the size of the fire.

The highlight of that month came when I traveled to the Warm Springs fire camp, located in a remote wilderness area high in the mountains, approximately forty miles from my study site. There, in a camp of 1100 inhabitants, I interviewed firefighters and U.S. Forest

Service Overhead Team (administrative) personnel. Eating and sleeping in the camp, watching and talking to people as they came and went from the fires or provided the support system required to sustain firefighting activities, I immersed myself in another reality. And it is the sensual nature of that reality, along with an exploration of the erotic component in the fieldwork enterprise, that comprise the focal points of this chapter.

I shall pursue this by investigating elements of the erotic which I will contend have a profound impact on what the ethnographer selectively learns in the field. This selective perception process also influences the ways in which a given land and its inhabitants are represented textually – the ripened fruit of the fieldwork process. These erotic elements include opening to sensory possibilities, confronting sexual and emotional passion as elements of the field experience, and allowing a language of passion to permeate the construction of texts. By contextualizing sexuality in the fieldwork experience, anthropologists may add elegant tools to their scientific and intellectual tool boxes. This involves working from the body, as well as from the mind. By funneling data gathered in this way through the senses, fueled by access to the full range of human emotions, it is possible to create texts which I contend will better enhance our understanding of other cultures (or groups within them) and of ourselves.

The heat of the field

The seductive nature of the field has been alluded to frequently by ethnographers who, at times, seem to radiate intensity as they speak of – or write about – their field locations and experiences.[1] Yet, as the introduction to this volume points out, the issue of the anthropologist's sexuality in the field has rarely been confronted as a focus of scholarly enquiry.[2] Newton's recent article moves in that direction as she explores elements of the 'erotic subjectivity' and experience of the anthropologist (1993a: 4). Arguing for inclusion of the erotic dimension in fieldwork accounts, she boldly claims that working with informants can involve working with potential sexual partners, particularly if one works, as she does, in what she calls a 'medium of emotion' (1993a: 10).

This medium, on a continuum as she describes it, moves from lively interest to passionate (although not necessarily consummated) erotic attachment (1993a: 11) and facilitates the fieldwork endeavor. It does so, she asserts, by motivating informants to enter into a relationship, rather than feeling intruded upon by the anthropologist's presence or questions. Newton's unconsummated 'crush' on Kay, an elderly woman she interviewed extensively for her ethnohistory of the gay and lesbian community of Cherry Grove (Newton 1993b), appears to have been beneficial to both parties. Of critical importance to the present enquiry, however, is her statement that the relationship significantly inspired her intellectual and creative work. She argues that 'the most intense attractions have generated the most creative energy, as if the work were a form of courting and seduction' (1993a: 15).

This sentiment is reflected in the earlier writing of Manda Cesara.[3] It was while making love with an informant whom she calls Douglas that she experienced an epiphanic moment. It was at that precise moment, she claimed, that she grasped a basic truth about the Lenda[4] culture. 'Body and brain were one, as were mind and flesh, the past and present, life and death', she wrote. 'I experienced the cerebral in the flesh. In Lenda nothing ever is purely cerebral, it is always mingled with flesh' (1982: 55).

Cesara wrote openly about her consummated sexual encounters in the field, claiming that 'it was inevitable that some ethnographers in certain settings should experience such an encounter' (1982: 59). Predating Newton's article by nearly a decade, Cesara's work asserted that the emotion of loving one individual in a culture allows one to lay hold of the culture itself by way of that individual person (1982: 60). Whether the relationship is consummated or, as in Newton's case, is contained as what might be called an affair of the emotions may be secondary to the fact that both anthropologists felt themselves and their work to be enriched by their passionate (and, of critical importance, reciprocated) attachments in the field.

What is it about the fieldwork setting that might foster an opening to erotic possibilities? As Dubisch (in this volume) notes, it certainly isn't the academic preparation for the field, where the prevailing protocol still seems to involve the twist that one has to be in the field in order to learn about how to be in the field (p. 30). And, as she rightly points out, advice about sex is not a part of the preparatory package for one embarking upon field research. Yet, as many anthropologists know, the most compelling ethnographic writings inevitably contain rhapsodic and sensual descriptions of people and places. What happens, on a subjective level, when an anthropologist and an entirely new environment collide?

It has been my experience that any new locale sends all of my sensory modes into overdrive in the initial days and weeks of my stay. I can recall the particular smell of the earth in the western wilderness as the snow receded from the trees after a long winter. I remember the pungent smell of sargasso seaweed fermenting in the shore break during the height of summer at a sea-lion refuge in California. The mention of a place can often trigger a cacophony of sensory memories: the taste of Greece, the sounds of downtown Washington, D.C., the almost unearthly quality of the light surrounding the Sangria de Cristo mountain range near Santa Fe.

Unfortunately, perhaps, the adaptation process dulls the sharp sensory feedback we receive from our surroundings once we've been in a given locale for a time. And for the anthropologist, traditionally charged with the task of scientifically studying 'the Other' while dressed in the straitjacket of so-called objectivity, the insistent feedback of the senses has often been something to be denied, squelched, or, at very least, granted secondary status to the intellect. It's almost as if there was something not quite right about responding and writing from a reflexive stance – a personal place – unless one hastened to link an overarching cerebral tone to the affective to ensure credibility.

Even Van Maanen (1988), who has written eloquently about the writing of 'impressionistic tales' as a means through which to breathe life into the field experience, is reluctant to allow the neophyte to bypass the traditional ethnographic writing route to engage in such passionate writing. When it's all said and done, he states, 'On advice to students of fieldwork, my feelings are traditional. There is, alas, no better training than going out and trying one's hand at realist tales' (1988: 139). Earlier in the text, he defines the narrator of the realist tale as one who 'poses as an impersonal conduit who . . . passes on more-or-less objective data in a measured intellectual style . . . uncontaminated by personal bias . . . A studied neutrality characterizes the realist tale' (1988: 47). That he finds this 'studied neutrality' feasible, or the notion of 'posing' as 'an impersonal conduit' workable, I find curious in light of his extensive exploration into the ethnographic enterprise. Moreover, I detect in his writing a hint of uncertainty about the true validity of more evocative texts, in spite of the fact that he ostensibly champions such efforts, and perhaps a dash of the old boot-camp mentality. But the subtext says: 'I had to do the cerebral [read linear and grueling] work before I got to write from the heart [the fun part, and I paid my dues to earn the right to have fun], so you should do that, too.'

I would contend that a healthy blend of working from the mind and the heart is in order, and is the logical compromise here for the scholar negotiating the mind/heart dichotomy. The ongoing myth that one can separate the intellectual from the emotional is reminiscent of the mind–body split that the Western medical institution has traditionally embraced philosophically (and is just beginning to question and move beyond, I might add). To compartmentalize is to master, it seems to claim, in the face of compelling evidence to the contrary, evidence that it is the interconnectedness of bodily and emotional functions which shape the lives of both healthy and unhealthy individuals.

Anthropologist Catherine Lutz speaks eloquently to this issue in her recent (1986) article, which criticizes the Euro-American construction of emotion. The central tenet of this construct, which she flatly labels 'emotion against thought' (1986: 289), centers on the notion that the emotional is antithetical to rationality (1986: 290). As such, Lutz writes, the prevailing view holds that 'To be emotional is to fail to rationally process information and hence to undermine the possibilities for sensible or intelligent action' (1986: 291). The ramifications of this view have been taken to heart by anthropologists concerned with building a base of professional credibility and respect among their academic colleagues. This has strongly influenced many ethnographers, who have traditionally striven to excise the affective from their ethnographies in order that the work be viewed as 'scientific' and, therefore, valid.

The logic behind this choice has become chillingly justified by the recent backlash against so called 'reflexive' writings, in which those who bring their emotions and personal biases into the discourse for analysis and examination have been accused of being 'too personal'.[5] 'Self-indulgent', they sniff when a field account is particularly delicious – more like a chocolate mousse than a piece of dry toast – 'unprofessional', 'inappropriate'. Or, worse yet, some anthropologists are accused of 'going native', as if by immersing themselves in a culture they have been somehow caught with their anthropological pants down doing the wrong thing (getting involved to the point where they are enjoying their work, perhaps?) at the wrong time.

As for those critics, who perhaps have never had the nerve to skinny-dip in their own work (while trusting their brains to function simultaneously), or to write from the hip – or from any other body part below the brain, for that matter – those critics sharpen their No. 2 pencils and produce another barrage of unintelligible, but academically familiar, books and articles. Business as usual, they say. What a relief.

For when certain anthropologists began writing more self-reflexive and passionate ethnographies,[6] a brief reprieve from the mind–body split occurred. The tight corsets were loosened, the mouth was allowed to relax, and a veritable flood of feelings and decidedly subjective materials came pouring out, mixed nicely with objective, rational perceptions and ideas into a fragrant, new intellectual stew. As though a fire hydrant in an inner-city neighborhood had broken on a sweltering August afternoon, some got to run around for a few minutes getting wet and having a ball. They also reached their goal, which was to cool down.

But, as one might imagine, it didn't take long for the word cops to come in with their sirens blaring, and their lights flashing. Before long the water is turned off. The kids go back to playing desultory and predictable games of stick ball in the streets. The anthropologists go back to writing from the head, hiding their clamoring feelings under the heavy blanket of technical language comprehensible only to their own kind. The party is over. Is this what we want?

Some anthropologists appear to be caught in the trap, wanting to integrate the emotions and the intellect into the language of anthropology, but fearful of criticism, of not being taken seriously. Although we may subjectively know that our senses work together with our intellects to provide us with data in complex and elegant ways, we persist in asking fieldworkers to operate predominantly from their eyes and ears and – most certainly – from the waist up. Repressing or avoiding our own erotic and sensual responses, we work in a haze of sensory anesthesia of our own making.

Places penetrating people: opening to the senses

I sit between two men, in a crowded roomful of men, listening to fire talk. The room smells of aftershave and leather, and laughter punctuates the space as they take a break from logistics to share an inside joke. Fire experts from Washington, D.C., nod in agreement as local experts discuss their strategies for putting out four major blazes which have burned over 27,000 acres of forest in recent days. They talk a fire language that's rough and masculine. 'Most of the heat in the fire is out at the head, and it's running to the north', they say. 'We had another fire pop up down here at Cherry Creek and just bam! Right out of the clear blue sky. We pounced on this one down here with an engine and one crew that picked it up. I knew it would work. That guy's fire savvy. He knows fire and he knows his job.'

Glancing over at the man next to me – he smells like sunlight and oak – I startle when I realize he is studying me. For a moment we lock eyes. A man across the table says, 'Let's hope you have a wet year next year', and another responds, 'Yeah, let's hope it goes the way of the wet year!' As laughter fills the room, I feel my face flush. The man next to me smiles a wry, winning grin and I return the smile, turning my face away, flustered. He's in charge of one of the fires, an Incident Commander, as they call it. I enjoy listening to his husky, earnest voice as he talks about his firefighting strategies. His hands move in swift, confident arcs through the air as he speaks. He says, 'If this thing gets bigger, we may need a few more people, but we try to keep it lean and mean, so . . .' When I am not taking my own notes, I study the bold blond hairs running up and down his tanned arms, the other voices in the room entering and receding from my awareness.

I struggle to integrate the cognitive dissonance I am feeling: the part of me that is attracted to these men who are, as a group, earnest and intelligent, charming and attractive, with the part of me that is unnerved and irritated by their blatant use of macho sexual imagery to discuss forest fires. The privileged sense of entitlement and ownership over a natural force which they appropriate by way of an insider's language seems, at times, to be both insidious and morally incorrect. Yet, as Cohn courageously admits in her essay on the experience of studying nuclear strategic analysts (whom she calls defense intellectuals), there is something thrilling about 'entering the secret kingdom, being someone in the know' in a realm that is both powerful and hidden from the outside world (1987: 704). Even as I struggled to analyze their 'fire language', and to situate it as a language of power and appropriation, I felt myself to be seduced by it, and felt privileged to be privy to it as a temporary 'insider', an experience both uncomfortable and intriguing.

Spontaneously, I ask this man if he will let me interview him about firefighting. When he says he'd like that and gives me the directions to his place for us to meet, I find my mind moving swiftly in two directions. One of them plans a list of fieldwork questions. But the other one . . . the other one fantasizes. And it is those fantasies which find their way into my dreams, causing me to awaken sometimes in the middle of the night as I work the fire project.

Nader (1986: 111) claims that ambivalent feelings are always involved in fieldwork. She recalls anthropologist Hortense Powdermaker remarking that walking the line between detachment and involvement is a built-in part of a field relationship. Nader writes, 'The amount of nocturnal dreaming and the ability to remember dreams seems to have multiplied several times over my usual behavior.' Landes (1986: 121) echoed that theme when she noted that one cannot separate 'the sensuousness of life from its abstractions, nor the researcher's personality from his experience.' The fieldwork experience is, in other words, a highly subjective process, affected deeply by bringing to play all of the senses.

When I locked eyes with the fire fighter, I thought of Landes' essay on her fieldwork experience in Brazil. The Brazilians call that gaze '*jogo de olhos*' (the game of eyes), Landes wrote. Her mentor cautioned that this can be dangerous in the field, as it might signal 'love information'. He believed the direct gaze was improper in that particular culture (1986: 135). In my fieldwork experiences, however, it often seems to facilitate matters, enhancing the communication process between myself and others in an already highly charged environment. Opening to the sensual aspects in my field surroundings, I am able to feel the environment in multiple ways. This opening is not restricted to flirtatious interplay (which may or may not occur) but, rather, encompasses an expanded use of all of the senses and a willingness to allow myself to gaze openly at others.

What is it about the senses that make their synthesized integration into the fieldwork process so important for the anthropologist attempting to come to know a place and its people? The definitive writer on the power of the senses may be Diane Ackerman,[7] who has painstakingly explored each sensory mode for its unique qualities and who informs us that, 'Seventy per cent of the body's sense receptors cluster in the eyes, and it is mainly through seeing the world that we appraise and understand it' (1990: 230). She points out that lovers close their eyes when they kiss in order to shut out visual distractions. 'Lovers want to do serious touching and not be disturbed', she writes. 'So they close their eyes.' Such is the power of the gaze, and the explanation helps us to understand why intense encounters with people in the field can have, at times, a seductive quality to them. Fieldwork involves coming into contact with many different people for the first time, a process which typically includes visual appraisal of the Other. Thus, the work itself brings with it possibilities for intimate scrutiny and the resulting need to confront our feelings as we strive to understand the workings of other minds in other places.

Ackerman doesn't stop at vision, in her exploration into the nuances of the senses. About smell, for instance, she writes, 'Smells . . . rouse our dozy senses, pamper and indulge us . . . stir the cauldron of our seductiveness, warn us of danger, lead us into temptation' (1990: 36). We bring our nose to the task, too: 'Odor greatly affects our evaluation of things, and our evaluation of people' (1990: 39). And, as if that weren't enough to contend with, our ears also fight for equal access to the environment. Ackerman writes, 'Sounds thicken the sensory stew of our lives, and we depend on them to help us interpret, communicate with, and express the world around us' (1990: 175). Finally, she reminds us that we have another powerful tool through which to view the world because, 'as sages have long said, the sexiest part of the body and the best aphrodisiac in the world is the imagination' (1990: 131).

As anthropologists have traditionally struggled to maintain an objective, 'scientific' posture in the field, is it any wonder they have perhaps experienced stress and confusion? Instead of blocking out this wealth of sensory (and sensual) input, or relegating it to private field journals, we might consider making room for our sensual responses in our work. The senses that we are equipped with are powerful antennae through which to experience, providing us with full use of what Ackerman calls our synesthetic abilities (1990: 290).

This involves opening to input from all of the senses, which combine to provide us with an enhanced understanding of others, of our surroundings, and of ourselves. In synesthesia, there is an intermingling of the senses so that, for example, one can taste a starlit sky or hear it, rather than only seeing it. Ackerman writes of how Rimbaud understood the power of synesthesia, as evidenced by his remark that the only way one can truly experience life is to be prepared for 'a long immense planned disordering of all the senses' (1990: 291).

Is it any wonder that the social scientist might feel threatened by the rush of sensory input and emotions that floods in upon entry into a new culture? How are we supposed to collect data in the cool and rational fashion we have been taught to affect, when the senses are 'disordered'? It's no wonder that the erotic elements of the field are rarely discussed and often denied. Such a messy business, trying to tabulate data and cope with a barrage of smells and tastes and errant fantasies or desires at the same time! In a culture which tends to deny dissonance (and deify order) this sensory barrage can often be viewed as an unpredictable burden or liability. Yet one can only conjecture how the quality of ethnographic writings might be enhanced and refined if it were culturally sanctioned to write about the field from this vantage point, eliminating the need to repress or compartmentalize certain feelings and thoughts.

One has only to think of the infamous Malinowski *Diary* (1989)[8] to wonder how his view of the fieldwork experience might have been transformed if he had accepted his own passions. The academic community's dogged focus on his sexual fantasies bypasses an equally compelling fact: Malinowski was a true synesthete. Throughout the *Diary* are descriptions such as this one: 'Marvelous sunset. The whole world drenched in brick color – one could *hear* and *feel* that color in the air' (1989: 67; italics in original). His ability to experience and to write in such a sensually descriptive manner allows us to witness the ways in which he was permeated by his environment. Perhaps his sexual stirrings, in part, were simply a byproduct of his sensual awakening in this new and exotic place. 'I went alone to Wawala', he wrote. 'It was sultry, but I was energetic. The wilderness fascinated me . . . Kenoria is pretty and has a wonderful figure. Impulse to "pat her on the belly". I mastered it' (1989: 153). One can follow, in these sentences, the way his mind moved from the sensual to the sexual in an organic, complex way, impacted by his intense emotional reaction to the landscape. To focus selectively on his comments about the woman he watched, by lifting it out of its environmental context, is both unfair and reductionistic.

The *Diary* is fascinating, in part, for what it reveals about Malinowski's extreme struggle to avoid elements of his own sensory input in order to affect the mask of the neutral scientist. This struggle was undoubtedly complicated by his Polish Catholic upbringing, as well as by an academic background in physics and mathematics that is likely to have predisposed him (by training, as well as perhaps by natural predilection) to privilege the rational and logical over the emotional or passionate. Moreover, he was engaged in a meaningful relationship with the woman who would later become his wife. His guilt at harboring what he apparently interpreted to be sinful thoughts about the women he saw in the field (while his beloved was far away) probably further fueled his conflict.[9]

It is highly unlikely that his academic training in anthropology – influenced by the British school of anthropology with which he was associated – gave him any way of understanding what was happening to him emotionally in New Guinea. Thus, having no context in which to house his erotic and sensual reveries, his writings disclose the incredible tensions with which he wrestled: 'I realized once again how materialistic my sense reactions are: my desire for the bottle of ginger beer is acutely tempting', he wrote. Then he confesses: 'Finally I succumb to the temptation of smoking again.' He manages to justify his behavior in the end by claiming, 'There is nothing really bad in all this. Sensual enjoyment of the world is merely a lower form of artistic enjoyment' (1989: 171–2). How sad, it seems to me, that he squelched his abundant nature this way, torturing himself for what could be construed as his natural reactions to his milieu.

Malinowski's efforts to repent for what can be called his 'sensual sinning in the mind' was militaristic in its rigidity. He wrote, 'I must have a system of specific formal prohibitions: I must not smoke, I must not touch a woman with sub-erotic intentions, I must not betray E.R.M. [his beloved back home] mentally, i.e., recall my previous relations with women, or think about future ones . . . my main task now must be: work' (1989: 268). The emotional hardship and pain he experienced, generated by the struggle with his own complex mix of feelings, is a kind of human tragedy in the light of his obvious gifts of synesthetic awareness. Moved by the landscape, deeply responsive to both the place and its people, he was unable to utilize his sensual knowing without guilt, to unlock more fully the secrets of the culture he studied. His desire to leave the field as soon as possible can certainly be better understood when one comprehends the incredible tensions he wrestled with. Unable to reconcile his fantasies with his image of himself as a scientist, he suffered. One can only wonder about the ways in which his work suffered, as well.

Mariana Torgovnick, a writer and professor of English, has written compellingly about the Western discourse on the primitive, or 'Other', asserting that it has often been a rhetoric of domination and of control. She offers a penetrating critique of a kind of arrogance which creeps through the thinking of the Western academic, who looks at the world as if the Western way is central, with everything else being considered 'non-Western' or derivative. Torgovnick argues that this rhetoric often hides what lies underneath: our more 'obscure desires: of sexual desires or fears . . . masking the controller's fear of losing control and power' (1990: 192). This, she asserts, allows the Western scholar 'to document the intimate lives of primitive peoples so that we can learn the truth about us – safely, as observers' (1990: 8).

Regarding Malinowski, Torgovnick states that 'the need to forget bodies – his own included – is part and parcel of the kind of scientific objectivity [he] sought' (1990: 230).[10] His disgust with the field (with himself?) emerged blatantly when he wrote, 'The life of the natives is utterly devoid of interest or importance, something as remote from me as the life of a dog' (1989: 167). This statement becomes even more disconcerting when one considers how moved he was by the field earlier in his stay, writing from a sophisticated level of synesthetic awareness. Yet, because he was denied a way to cope with his sexual fantasies, he censored rigorously, corseting himself into a narrow view of the place and its inhabitants. It is my belief that this could not help but weaken both his work, and himself, in the process; a high price to pay for being 'objective'.

Torgovnick vigorously defends Malinowski's passions, boldly stating that 'We should savor his unprofessional desires' (1990: 227), and calls for a 'rhetoric of desire, ultimately more interesting, which implicates "us" in the "them" we try to conceive as the Other' (1990: 245). This progressive viewpoint makes good sense when one considers that we are biologically wired to operate on multiple levels, possessing the capacity to use our bodies, hearts, and minds together to funnel and to interpret massive amounts of stimulus. By contextualizing our erotic responses and channeling them into the ethnographic endeavor, we might better represent those we study and claim to know. We would do this by fleshing out our accounts of people and places, openly bringing our own passions and insights to the task and articulating them in our textual representations.[11]

What is particularly interesting to me about the Malinowski debate is not the fact that he lusted for the women he studied at certain very human moments, but the fact that the revelation that he did so triggered such an uproar in the anthropological community. This speaks clearly to the somewhat unbelievably repressed state the discipline (and its inhabitants) existed in and, I would contend, continue to exist in. What were they thinking? That Malinowski would be far from home, steeped in a foreign and exotic culture for a long period of time, and be dead as a sensual being? The fact that his private journals were seized upon – as if they, too, should have been strictly scholarly and scientific in their contents – attests to the denial that the field operates in, its residents sublimated in the ubiquitous voyeuristic frenzy of uncovering someone else's secrets while affecting an emotional distance from their experience.

Defining sex in the field: what is it, anyway?

This brings us to another problem, which involves the defining of sex in the field. The traditional stance in American culture holds that sex has occurred when penetration – preferably leading to male orgasm – has happened. Do we, as anthropologists, want to restrict ourselves to that notion? If one becomes infatuated with someone in the field, or has a flirtatious fling with them that stops at deep kissing or intense longing, does that mean that sex didn't occur? Further, does that mean that it did?

The analogy of sex in the 1950s and early 1960s might be useful here.

It is a well-known fact that in those years 'good girls' didn't go 'all the way'. While it was commonly understood that many 'good girls' were, in fact, 'doing it', the etiquette of the day called for energetic denial. Thus, the 'good girls' who were 'doing it' were lying about it, which made them apparently morally and socially superior to the 'bad girls' who were both 'doing it' and telling the truth. The irony here is obvious. And for the girls who didn't go 'all the way', but went 'almost all the way', one could argue that by privileging such a small part of the sex act (penetration), we bypass the obvious fact that the ones who went 'all the way' at least weren't pretending that they weren't 'doing anything'.

An anthropologist I met once told me about a 'flirtation' she had with a male informant, hastening to add that 'We never actually had intercourse, but it certainly got intense there for a while!' When pressed, she admitted that the encounter was 'certainly sexual', but pointed out that she had later reminded the man of her role as an anthropologist and his as the 'informant', as if somehow by so doing she could erase what had transpired between them. Her inability to contextualize her own feelings resulted, I would contend, in a messy situation in which she attempted to justify her actions, while struggling to find a logical way out of a mess she hadn't yet been able to acknowledge to herself, a difficult state of affairs to unravel, to say the least. Pressed further, she confessed that the man had been both confused and angry with her, prompting her to blurt out, 'I guess I didn't know what I was doing, did I? I thought I was being a good professional by calling a halt to it.'

This particular anthropologist was concerned that if anyone were to find out she had developed a sexual interest in an informant, her work would be discredited. She felt forced to hide her experience in order to protect herself and, in so doing, became unable to analyze or to understand her own experience. An accomplished professional with a long list of publications to her credit, she will admit privately to 'involvements' with people in the field, while protecting herself publicly by claiming that her work is objective and unaffected by her personal feelings.

What are we afraid of? Do we make the assumption that an anthropologist who becomes sensually or sexually involved in the field can no longer think straight? I would contend that all relationships and events with which we are involved in the field change us in subtle ways and affect the way we perceive, and write about, the field. Does the anthropologist who plays at being 'objective' really create superior work to the one who immerses himself or herself in the field wholeheartedly? I am not advocating random and meaningless sexual encounters here, nor am I talking about situations where issues of colonialism and power imbalance enter into the discourse, which may be, in fact, most of the time.

But anthropologists today increasingly work in field situations where they operate collaboratively with so-called 'informants' (often called collaborators, in recent years) who are not inferior in terms of status or power. To hold on to the shield of 'neutral objectivity' in such situations, protecting oneself from being 'touched' by the field, might be unnessary in certain circumstances. The validity and sanctioning of relationships which are not abusive and which are mutually desired need to be explored as possibilities, for what they might teach us about ourselves and our ethnographic endeavors. In order to engage in such a dialogue, as a discipline, it is critical that we step out from our hiding places and explore our feelings and beliefs.

The point is not to encourage sensationalistic, *National Enquirer*-type confessionals from the field, replete with descriptive close-ups and minute details about how a given anthropologist had sex in the field. But we might at least acknowledge that we 'did it' if we did (or that we wanted to 'do it', even if we didn't) and be open to the fertile possibilities for dialogue about the ways in which 'it' changed, enhanced, or detracted from what we felt, witnessed, and interpreted in the field. In a discipline where such encounters have taken place, and have been kept, for the most part, in the realm of 'underground' stories or anecdotes, it is striking to consider how long the consideration of such relationships has been avoided and repressed by the discipline.

It may be that the pose of objectivity in the field is no more than another version of the folk tale about the emperor with no clothes. As anthropologists, we would do well to remember that we are all naked at times in the field – if not physically, then certainly emotionally. Therefore, despite our intellectual armor, we are inevitably somewhat open and vulnerable. And if it is true that the emperor really has no clothes on, then perhaps we should just stare openly at him, in the way of children, and see what he looks like. After all, it's just a body. And we might learn something.

Sexy business: immersion in the field

The Warm Springs fire camp, an instant community constructed to meet the basic needs of 1100 firefighters and support personnel, existed for sixteen days in August of 1992. Operating smoothly through hot, dry days and cold, sometimes snowy nights, it moved to its own rhythms under glaring sun or dangling stars, wrapped in the smells of pine and smoke. Huge generators provided electricity for light and cooking fuel in the camp, while semi-trucks housing portable showers gave weary firefighters a means to rid themselves of soot and sweat. Kitchens turned out hot, full-course meals three times a day and snack stations were located throughout the camp. The telephone company was brought in to hook up telephones, enabling those on site to connect with the outside world – to phone home. Portable sinks stood near the showers, equipped with mirrors and toiletry stands. While there were only approximately thirty females in the camp (and they were given separate showering and sleeping facilities), male and female firefighters and support personnel mingled socially with one another, moving from the showers to the sinks where the men shaved and men and women alike combed hair and engaged in friendly banter.

Under large, portable canopies, meals were taken and an ambience of warmth and camaraderie prevailed. At the long tables, it was not uncommon to see the sports pages handed from man to man[12] as each finished reading it, a gesture both friendly and surprisingly intimate, infusing the space with a quality of homelike domesticity. Throughout the camp, quonset huts provided sheltered stations for weather forecasting and map making, tool and equipment cleaning and dispersal, first aid assistance, strategy planning meetings, and the filing of disability insurance claims. A portable commissary dispensed razor blades and long johns, toothbrushes and shampoo, and T-shirts which proclaimed, 'Warm Springs Fire Camp – 1992'. At one end of the camp were the sleeping grounds, where large tents housed as many as twenty sleepers and small tents served those who preferred privacy.[13] Paths between tents were lit with ground lights, which gave the area a glowing, dreamlike quality at night. Men and women stood around smudge pots after dark when the temperatures plunged, talking and warming their hands over an electrical, high-tech version of the traditional campfire.

During the day, the sounds of heavy machinery filled the air as helicopters, buses, trucks, and cars brought firefighters on and off the fire lines some fifteen miles away from camp. Competing with that of the generators for airspace, the noise was intense and omnipresent. This was in sharp contrast to the late evenings when, after nightfall, people sat in groups telling stories and laughing, walked the paths in the sleeping areas, or slept noiselessly in their tents after long, grueling days on the line.

My response to this environment was immediate and clear. Intense and complex, it was one of the most engaging environments I had ever worked in and I couldn't get enough of it. My senses were hit with a constant onslaught of sounds and sights, smells and tastes. Sparks flew off shovels being sharpened for use on the line the next day. The smell of chicken and potatoes drifted from the cooking quarters. Machinery and voices, mixed with the rapid pace of motion in a place where the mission is the reason for its very existence – it was an intoxicating little world within the world, far from the realities of day-to-day life away from fires.

Unlike Malinowski's, my more progressive training for the field allowed me to relish the life of the senses while there. My graduate training, as well as my readings and writings on the anthropology of place, gave me a suitable context in which to house my own experiences.[14] Consequently, I was able to immerse myself sensually in this new environment, feeling my way into a growing understanding.

In the Warm Springs fire camp, I found myself in a very sensual world where the body meets one of the most powerful natural elements known to humankind – fire. In attempting to analyze what it was about this particular place that made it so sensual and intriguing, despite the military-like uniforms and the ubiquitous heat and dust, I turned to some of the fire personnel for answers. Regarding the most direct displays of sexuality, one woman had this to say:

> I'll tell you, after five days men get horny as hell and they will proposition anything they think they can bed. We call them fireline romances. You're very tight with people and shut off from the outside world.

It was this woman's opinion that such encounters were to be expected in situations where people are working closely with one another and are far from home. This is not to say that sexual activity is either condoned or commonplace in the firecamp setting. Indeed, official U.S. Forest Service policy dictates that firefighters and support personnel refrain from engaging in sexual activity with one another. Further, policies are set in place which are designed to deal with accusations of sexual harassment, and the people I spoke with seemed to feel that little, if any (depending upon whom one asked), outright sexual contact took place in the fire camps.

As for the males, there were a number of men with whom I spoke who alluded to the fact that women 'came on' to them after days of working together. If men were 'coming on' to other men (or women propositioning other women) in that environment, such activities remained resolutely hidden in the recesses of an institution which reflects the military's strong homophobic predisposition.[15]

What is critical here, however, is the fact that men and women were working together for long periods of time, engaged in activities which they found meaningful in a way that was defined by their collective goal – in this case, putting out fires – and that these kinds of human engagement are sexy by definition. I often saw small clusters of people laughing or talking together with a kind of intensity and mutual affection that is born out of such settings, where life revolves around a clear purpose and people know that they are equipped to get the job done.[16] By their nature, then, these types of setting are erotically charged. The issue is not one of men and women, but one of human and human, working together in a setting where everyone matters and each action signifies. There are few activities engaged in by people in more ordinary environments which have the kind of stark coherence and clarity of mission that one witnesses in the fire camps.

The similarities between people in a fire camp and anthropologists, who develop bonds with the people they study when immersed in a community far from home, can be teased out here quite readily. Moreover, in the case of the fire camps one can add to the mix the element of danger. One officer put it succinctly when he said, 'It's hazardous country, they're hazardous trees. It's hard to fight fire here. Fire fighters can get hurt. And, in the worst case scenario, they can die.' Therefore, these people work in an almost continual state of heightened physiological arousal. One woman said:

> You're on a constant adrenaline high because you have something important to do and you have to do it right away and then you go back to the camp and you crash. But it's a nice crash, because it's all encompassing. When I get bored on my regular job, I tell my boss, 'I need a fire to go to!'

Firefighters, who often refer to themselves proudly as 'fire bums' (in reference to their willingness to drop everything to 'go to a fire'), seem to thrive on an adrenaline-induced state of vigilance and energy that the fire situation fosters. This arousal state was palpable and I found myself responding to it by bringing a different quality of intensity to my own work in the camp.

There is also a quality of ownership regarding the forest environment and the fire that is sexy in its expression. Firefighters often refer, almost possessively, to 'my fire', or 'my baby' (in reference to the fire itself), using a language of passionate attachment when they describe their commitment to the work they are doing. For me, this unremitting and focused attention to the task at hand had an extremely erotic quality to it, like a lover whose eyes remain fixed on my face during the act of lovemaking. And this attachment is not just a solitary connection between an individual and the land. There is a collaborative, interdependent quality about the firefighters' activities which is moving to witness. One man articulated it this way:

> There's only us to take care of us here. And so people, being the creatures we are, tend to stick together and while we can be extremely independent, we also need, I think, that other human contact . . . and that reassurance that there are other people there working toward the same thing. So we go to other people for support even though they are relative strangers.

The vulnerability and need to connect with others expressed here add to the elements which come together to create a sense of place that is warm and inviting, yet crackling with excitement and potential danger. While there were occasions when I witnessed what appeared to be active flirting – three men laughingly throwing a cream pie on the shirt of a beautiful, blonde-haired woman (a cohort from the same management team), for instance, and her teasing, easy response[17] – some of the most sensual behavior in the camp took place between the lines. One could witness it in the silent sharing of tasks, the looks of respect and admiration that passed from one person to another when progress was made, the way in which camp inhabitants shared small spaces in the easy manner of those who feel safe and familiar with their companions because they all know what they're doing and share the same goals.

Nor is this dynamic confined to cross-gender interactions. The warmth and connectedness fostered by common purpose in a charged environment operated palpably between men, as well as between women. Back-patting, the tousling of hair, an arm thrown casually around a shoulder – these means of physical contact bespoke camaraderie, mutual respect, and friendliness in a setting where teamwork is the name of the game. Like the butt-slapping of football players in the NFL, these small physical acts which transpire between team mates signify 'insiderness' and connectedness in unique circumstances comprehended fully only by those on the 'inside'.[18]

For an anthropologist to enter such an environment and operate solely by asking questions and recording them on tape would be to miss the point. Some of my clearest insights into camp dynamics came while walking the paths in the sleeping areas at night, listening to the 'feel' of the place. Despite the codified and prescribed external structure of the U.S. Forest Service fire system, there was a sense of expansiveness and softness that seemed to permeate the overall experience. In other words, the subtleties about what makes a given environment tick often go on in the spaces between the work and the words. By opening to the senses, I was able to move closer to the nuances of the place, and to sense its meaning to those who inhabited it. By immersing myself in the field, I began to understand this small subculture from the inside out, rather than from the outside (by way of the intellect) in, 'feeling the field' with my body and heart, as well as with my brain.

Perhaps it was in this frame of mind that anthropologist Paul Rabinow had one of his most sensual encounters during his early fieldwork in Morocco. His account of making love to a woman from another village during a day off from fieldwork has been written about and scrutinized for years by other anthropologists.[19] This account is fascinating to me, not for what it reveals about his sexual behavior, but for his description of what led up to the sexual event itself. For it is here in his account that he describes how he left his fieldsite for a couple of days, let his guard down, and began to respond openly to his surroundings with the sensibility of the synesthete. He wrote, 'It was a beautiful, cloudless day, and we drove joyously away from Sefrou [the fieldwork site] into the mountain areas' (1977: 63). He goes on to say, 'As we left the highway, town, and society behind, I felt a mounting excitement, as if personal inhibitions and social conventions were also being left behind.' He admitted then: 'I had never before had this kind of sensual interaction in Morocco' (1977: 65).

The heart of his problem as a self-defined objective 'scientist' is then revealed, as he continues: 'Although it was incredibly welcome it seemed too good to be true. Haunting super-ego images of my anthropologist persona thickened my consciousness as the air became purer and the play freer . . . I felt wondrously happy – it was the best single day I was to spend in Morocco' (1977: 65). This is a remarkable statement, in the sense that it leads one to question how he was recording his notions about the people and place he studied *before* he opened to the fuller use of his own senses. Shut off from the deeper part of himself, restricted – as Malinowski perceived himself to be – to the role of voyeur and recorder, he deprived himself of aspects of his own sensual awareness as a potent data source.

This is all the more interesting in the light of his confession that the sexual event itself was anticlimactic for him. What really moved him was his ability to let his guard down and open up to the sensuality of the weather and his female companions. 'Here we were, after an absolutely splendid romp through the mountains, sitting down next to some sulphur springs, and they were going swimming', he exults (1977: 67). Of the sex itself, he wrote somberly, 'Aside from the few pillows and charcoal burner for tea, there was only the bed. The warmth and non-verbal communication of the afternoon were fast disappearing. This woman was not impersonal, but she was not that affectionate or open either. The afternoon had left a much deeper impression on me' (1977: 69). In other words, when the visual and sensual elements were altered, and he was face to face with a woman with whom he had no true emotional connection – in a meager environment far removed from the sensual joy he had experienced earlier that day – the act of lovemaking was internalized as a diminishing act by comparison.

This statement is courageous, in my view, in that it not only breaks down the myth that sensual pleasure must culminate in sexual intercourse, but also highlights emphatically the idea that the anthropologists can make a conscious choice about how to conduct themselves if they understand their own sensual experiences and can put them in perspective. Perhaps Rabinow might not have chosen to make love with the woman if he had understood the nature of his own intense experience that day. Having no way to contextualize his feelings and responses, he carried through to the logical – although perhaps unnecessary – conclusion. Having sex while in the field is not something one can decide clearly upon if one is unaware of the sources of desire and alternative ways of handling those desires.

Words melting on the page: writing the erotic into the text

My own fieldnotes from the firecamp days are peppered with sensual and sexual references:

> 8/16/92 The sounds of helicopters and heavy machinery move in me in a rhythmic way. I wonder what it would be like to make love in a helicopter. One man, one woman, and one engine . . . an intriguing triangle.
>
> 8/19/92 These people live in a world so elemental – in the grip of fickle weather patterns, at the mercy of the wind. Everything is about basic needs here: food, water, sleeping place, work. They work on the edge, reduced to focusing on the moment at hand as they

> confront fire. It seems to give them a directness and the ability to listen cannily and acutely – like forest animals – that is almost primitive. It's very seductive.
>
> 8/22/92 No one here is distracted by furniture or decor, by superficial tasks or by social niceties. It's pared down and lean, a world where words and acts are measured and channeled directly into the work. The quality of silence is intensely erotic, as if anything you say – any sound you might make – carries with it deep meaning. They listen with the rapt attention of the lover who doesn't want to miss anything, who is tuned to the nuanced. It's almost overwhelming at times.

In attempting to translate the field experience onto the virginal, blank, white page, I am filled with ambivalence. What will my colleagues think if I put sexual fantasies in a chapter like this? I visualize myself reading a professional paper, standing in front of a large room full of anthropologists. Suddenly, someone shouts out, 'So, do you really think it's OK to have sex when you're working?' Another voice rings out aggressively, 'So, you're condoning sex in the field? How unprofessional. How could you?' And the feminists . . . all this talk about men and erotic attractions. Where is the evidence of my twenty years of feminist self-identification here, hidden behind talk of macho machinery and locking eyes with male strangers?

If I'm going to write about sex, I tell myself, perhaps I'd better at least protect myself with some scholarly armor. Maybe I should retreat behind the cool, gray wall of academic language, haul out some big words. I could throw in a few of the top-ten favorites of the earnest anthropologist, for instance – problematize . . . metacommunication . . . de con struct ion.

Margaret Mead (1972) once wrote of how troublesome Reo Fortune's (1963) passionately written account of the Dobuans became over time, fostering suspicion from many of his anthropological colleagues about the validity of his work. His immersion in the world of the sorcerer, and his choice of writing about it in a lively and subjective way, weren't considered appropriate by those who expected work produced solely from the precisely analytical part of his mind (Mead 1972: 184; cf. Cesara 1982: 136). As Cesara accurately points out, 'He [the practicing anthropologist] cannot escape passion, and yet he is not able to claim it as central to his knowledge' (1982: 100). Therefore, one is left with the impression that it's bad enough he had to feel it (passion, the heat of the field), but even worse that he couldn't keep it out of his writing (poor boundaries, bad judgment).

But there are others in recent years who see it differently. Paul Stoller (1989), for instance, speaks movingly about his long-time commitment to one particular place and its people, in one of his writings about the Songhay of Niger. 'In 1969 my senses were tuned to otherness . . . my senses of taste, smell, hearing, and sight entered into Nigerian settings', he wrote. 'Now I let the sights, sounds, smells, and tastes of Niger flow into me' (1989: 5). By not restricting himself to the Western 'gaze', which he refers to as the 'privileged sense of the West' (1989: 5), he was able to produce a representation of a people and their lives that is vital, rich, and alive.

Stoller calls on the anthropologist to move beyond the dry and impoverished language of traditional academic writing, in order to give the reader what he calls 'the taste of ethnographic things'. This, he contends, can be done by writing ethnographies which attend to the sensual aspects of the field, ethnographies that 'will render our accounts of others more faithful to the realities of the field – accounts which will then be more, rather than less, scientific' (1989: 9). By allowing ourselves to be penetrated by the field, with all of the dissonance that may elicit, we might 'walk along our solitary paths in the field, exposing our hearts so full of excitement, fear, and doubt' (1989: 54–5).

It is important to note that Stoller is not suggesting that we relinquish the 'objective' data at our disposal, nor that we lapse into experimental forms of representation that render understanding difficult, if not impossible.[20] Rather, he contends that the anthropologist can choose to work from a place of vulnerability and acceptance of the emotional and intellectual dissonance which is part and parcel of the process of trying to come to 'know' a place and its people. It was the understanding of this dissonance which allowed me to integrate and to interpret my sexual fantasies and sensual reveries as a normal part of the fieldwork process, and therefore to set the limits that kept me from acting on them, particularly when tempted by the golden arms of a handsome firefighter.

Working from this place of vulnerability and acceptance can give the reader 'the taste of ethnographic things', Stoller asserts, with 'filmic or narrative images: the smells, the tastes, the sounds, the colors – lyrical and unsettling – of the land' (1989: 156). By so doing, we might enable the reader to sense what it is like to live in a certain place without having to pretend that we have mastered a culture intellectually while maintaining a detachment from it emotionally.

Outside of the academy, it is a well-known fact that there are those who accuse academic writers of 'linguistic constipation'[21] or of being 'out of touch' with the 'real' world. The phrase 'out of touch' is particularly apt here, as it reflects the sentiment that there are those who cannot 'feel' the writing of academics who stay hidden behind a language form that, by its nature, is inaccessible to many.

This is a double-edged issue, it seems. We need to ask, first of all, whether we want to study a culture in a calculating, solely intellectual way, and then – when we turn to the task of bringing the culture to others – whether those whom we study would want to be represented in that way. Finally, if I dared, I would ask: who would want to read such an account? How many papers and articles have anthropologists read or listened to over the years from which every ounce of sensual and emotional content had previously been bled in the name of credibility?[22] Do we really have to avoid lyrical description, subjectivity, and the personal voice in order to hold our place in the line-up of respected social scientists? Cesara, in a letter to a loved one, articulated her view clearly:

> Deep inside of me something tells me that art and science are one . . . What happens to a man who sits outside his cage of rats and experiments on them? Does the interaction between these men and rats not affect the scientist? I think it does. I think such a scientist's view of the human condition becomes simplified, often deterministic: in some instances he loses all sense of the individual's wholesomeness, freedom, responsibility, and dignity.
>
> (1982: 193)

When it's all said and done, it seems to come down to a question of whether we work and write from the head or from the heart. And it is here where the logical compromise emerges. Is it not possible to forge an amalgam of the two, in which we allow ourselves to be immersed as sensual beings in each phase of the ethnographic endeavor, from project planning to final textual representation, while simultaneously employing our capacities to analyze and to reason? I believe that this is not only realistic, but is a highly beneficial way to conduct the anthropological enterprise. By accepting ourselves as sensual – and yes, sexual – beings, we might harness all of our collective intellectual and sensory capacities for use in both the work itself and the written product created from it.

Erotics and the field: making love to one's self

So, where does this leave us? Do we make love in the field or don't we? And, if we do, how far do we go? How can we untangle the web of moral and ethical issues involved and explore, as well, the dissonance between the unspoken rules of the academy and our own personal beliefs and actions? When I say, for instance, that some of the best lovemaking I have yet experienced with my husband took place on my return home between forays into the world of the firefighters, does that trivialize or cheapen what we shared together? I would contend that the opening of my senses, in an environment which was passionately compelling, created a heightened level of awareness in me which served to bring me closer to myself. And it is that connection to self which allowed me to blend the images of smoke and helicopters, hard work and attachment to others, and which I then brought most advantageously to the marital bed.

Looking at field photos from that time, I notice that my face looks radiant, as women (and, sometimes, men) often look when they fall in love or become passionate about their work. My powerful attraction to the firefighters and to the world they dwell in excited me in a way that seems to have attached me more firmly not only to them, but to myself. In the way that the act of masturbation is a self-absorbed act which forms a closed circle between the individual and her or his own body, so the field experience can function in similar fashion. When the anthropologist works with an open heart and mind, allowing the senses to operate freely, an erotic place is created between the anthropologist and the place she or he studies. Undisrupted by the complexities of the 'outside world', the anthropologist has a rare opportunity to learn about the so-called 'Other' by learning to know more about the self, with few expectations or distractions from the 'outside'.

In the fire camp, my very presence as a solitary female from the 'outside' was provocative, inducing specific sensual verbal and non-verbal responses from certain men. Golde (1986: 6) states that the very accessibility of the woman fieldworker can be considered provocative. In my particular situation, I came and went freely in the field, a fact that was widely registered by those whom I studied. Striding around the grounds, eating meals with the firefighters, I moved in and out of their living and sleeping environment in an obvious way. With so few women on site, I was a highly visible presence. As a result, I became more visible to myself – as a female – over time. Having my gender reflected so consistently by those with whom I came in contact brought me ultimately to a point where I became more aware of myself as a gendered being. This may be one of the most distinct and unnoticed advantages of the fieldwork endeavor: the opportunity to know the self better, particularly in terms of gender considerations, by seeing oneself reflected in the eyes of others.

Steeped in one's own senses, the boundary between self and other might slowly blur at times (see Geertz 1983). And while noticing difference, we might be able to feel – from the innermost part of ourselves – the power of similarity. For while the use of the word 'other' serves to separate us from other people, it is also likely that it separates us, in subtle ways, from ourselves. If it is true that our senses work synesthetically, in what Hiss calls 'simultaneous perception' (1990: 4), is it not possible that we are more connected to those we study than we might sometimes like to admit? Perhaps, by repressing our sensual feelings or sexual urges, we maintain a distance that – in the end – does a disservice to the sensitive work we claim to do as cultural recorders and interpreters.

Perhaps by acknowledging our own feelings and desires, we might actually look at other people and places more objectively, by being able to ferret out our own biases and distortions as we do our work. Hiss suggests that those who attempt to come to know a place should utilize simultaneous perception for just that reason. Bringing all of the senses to the task in this way 'helps us experience our surroundings and our reactions to them, and not just our own thoughts and desires' (1990: 4). Unlike Malinowski, who was forced perhaps to dislike those whom he studied in a sturdy effort to propel himself away from his own overwhelming sensual feelings, we might then be open to interpreting from a more centered, stable vantage point. With the energy conserved by not having to fight our hormones or our fantasies, we could perhaps better grasp an inhabited landscape in a sensual, but more fully accurate, way.

To be permeated by a place – truly to feel its heart beat – is both a gift and the primary fringe benefit of the work that we do. To respond to that place and its inhabitants without holding back, and to represent them fully in the spirit of generosity and abundance, is the way we might return the favor.

On the last day of the fire project, I stand under a large ponderosa pine with two firefighters, protected from the direct glare of the midday sun. They express gratitude that I thought enough about what they do for a living to have given over a chunk of my own time to come and 'check it out'. Thanking them for their feedback, I ask if I might take a picture of the two of them under the tree. 'You know, end of fire – exhausted, but victorious firefighters prepare to return home', I intone in the voice of the television newscaster. Laughing, one of the men amiably throws an arm over his companion's shoulder, preparing to pose. But the other one objects, 'Hey, wait! I'm covered with soot, and my clothes are filthy. Wouldn't you rather get your shot after I clean up, so you can see how handsome I really am?' He sticks an elbow into his buddy's ribs for emphasis.

But the other man shakes his head and, turning to his friend, says this: 'What do you mean? This is how we look out there, man! This is what it's all about – men and machines, sweat and grit. Why wash it off?' Turning to me, his face opening into the grin of the heartbreaker, he adds, 'Hey, Katie, this is the way it really is, right? It's hot and heavy work. But, what the heck, it's kind of sexy, don't you think?' And then, looking me full in the face, he winked. And I winked back.

Acknowledgements

I extend my gratitude and respect to Don Kulick and Margaret Willson for their editorial guidance and unstinting support as I shaped and reshaped this essay to please their exacting eyes. In addition, I am indebted to the work of Paul Stoller, whose writings about the use of the senses in fieldwork validated my own developing notions about that connection. Diane Ackerman's writings on the senses have been critical to the development of a language with which both to understand and to articulate the complexities of sensual awareness and expression. I sincerely thank my mentor, Mary Catherine Bateson, for her incisive questions, editorial eye, and steady encouragement. I am grateful to composer, songwriter, and musician Michael King for several fertile dialogues which contributed greatly to the writing of this chapter. I also owe a dept of gratitude to the representatives of the U.S. Forest Service, who opened all of the right doors for me and who gave unstintingly of their time to support my project and to enhance my understanding of the fire culture. In particular, I thank Gene Benedict, John Humphries, Heidi Bigler-Cole, Susan Reinhard, Sue Exline, Brenda Graham, and John Williams for teaching me about the workings of the U.S. Forest Service firefighting system. I also sincerely thank Terri Cundy Aihoshi for her careful reading of and commentary on the text, as well as Kathleen Taylor and Gloria King for their helpful editorial comments. Finally, I want to acknowledge the writings of humanistic anthropologists such as Miles Richardson, Barbara Tedlock, Stanley

Diamond, Dan Rose, Dennis Tedlock, Bruce Grindal, and Barbara Myerhoff. The humanistic influence on ethnographic writings has continued to grow in recent years and will continue to be important to those who appreciate lively anthropological writing and believe it is not diminished by evocative language, written from both the head and the heart.

Notes

1 See, for instance, Malinowski (1961) [1922]; Levi-Strauss (1955) [1984]; Turnbull (1968); Chernoff (1979); and, in more recent years, Trawick (1990).

2 Notable exceptions include Cesara (1982); Read (1986); and Schneebaum (1969, 1979, 1988).

3 A pseudonym. It is unfortunate that her fascinating, reflexive account of her fieldwork experiences in 'Lenda' is so difficult to obtain. It has long been out of print, but can sometimes be found tucked away in second-hand bookstores in university towns.

4 A pseudonym.

5 See, for example, Whitehead and Conaway (1986).

6 See, for example, Myerhoff (1978); Fernandez (1982); and, in more recent years, Rose (1987); Stoller and Olkes (1987); Brown (1991); Behar (1993).

7 Her book *A Natural History of the Senses* (Ackerman 1990) is an extraordinary exploration of the pleasures of sensory experiences and should be required reading for anthropologists embarking upon journeys into the field. A poet and professor of literature, she has much to offer to social scientists wishing to expand and develop their sensibilities, and the written expression of those sensibilities, in any given locale.

8 This *Diary* (first published in 1967), and its impact on the anthropological community, have been written about extensively. For an excellent analysis of the *Diary* in regard to sexuality and Malinowski's sometimes drastic attempts to 'contain' his feelings and urges, see Torgovnick (1990).

9 As Raymond Firth points out, in the introduction to Malinowski's *Diary*, Malinowski's sincere love and respect for the woman he would marry has been well documented (Firth 1989: xviii) However, it is also noted that he had failed to break off his emotional link with another woman with whom he had formerly been involved, which would certainly have added to his self-recriminations, remorse, and abject discomfort with himself during his stay in New Guinea (p. xix).

10 Anthropologists Whitehead and Conaway (1986) write about the traditional ethnographic endeavor, in which the anthropologist attempts to achieve objectivity. They note accurately that the more personalized accounts of field experiences were often considered to be 'an unmitigated self-indulgence'. They claim that the prevailing sentiment in the profession held that 'confessional narratives' were considered to be appropriate for travel writers, but not for them (p. 2). This is fascinating, especially when we consider that the anthropologist invariably travels to other places. In some respects, we *are* travel writers. This rejection of the

personal response to the field began to yield a bit with the advent of more reflexive accounts, exemplified by the work of Myerhoff and Ruby (1982) and, more recently, Behar (1993) and Brown (1991).

11 Torgovnick offers an excellent example of this approach in practice when she discusses the writings of anthropologist Tobias Schneebaum, who entered into the rituals of a men's group which went on a mission involving the killing of enemies, male homosexual rituals, and the cannibalizing of dead enemies. Torgovnick writes that Schneebaum was stunned by his encounter with 'the primitive within himself' (1990: 182). She notes that his book *The Wild Man* (Schneebaum 1979) has been out of print since its first edition was released, due to what Torgovnick describes as its 'aggressive endorsement of homosexuality among primitives as the "natural" thing to do' (1990: 182).

Schneebaum himself writes freely and openly about his experiences, according to Torgovnick. One can't help but wonder if his writings would have caused more of an uproar if they had not been homosexually contextualized, i.e. if he had had passionate affairs with women 'natives' and written about it as candidly as he wrote about his homoerotic experiences. It's almost as though he could be written off – the marginal writing about the marginalized – since his behavior didn't involve a cross-gender interaction. This is a sad indictment of one of the ways in which our culture compartmentalizes and privileges certain kinds of experience as being more meaningful and, perhaps, more worthy of being entered into the academic discourse.

12 I do not mean to imply that women do not read the sports page, although I did not witness any women doing so during my stay in the fire camp. Rather, I point to the casual act of sharing the sports page as an example of a way in which the camp took on many of the characteristics of a family setting, where members might typically pass a section of the paper on to one another after reading it.

13 Several women in the camp informed me that the women tend to stick together when it comes to sleeping arrangements, either putting their one-person tents up in close proximity to one another or sharing a large tent. They do this in order to 'feel safer', as one woman put it, as well as to 'be with our own kind' after long days of working in a situation where they are greatly outnumbered by males.

14 A volume of essays written by anthropologists on the anthropology of place, edited by Margaret Rodman and Terri Aihoshi, is currently under review for publication. That volume, entitled *Spacializing Narratives: The Anthropology of Place*, stands on the cutting edge of the scholarly discourse on the meanings of place. For other writings by anthropologists, one can turn to Altman and Low (1992); Rodman (1992); Basso (1988); Appadurai (1988). However, writings on place have traditionally been undertaken by those working in other disciplines, including architects and landscape architects, historians, geographers, and sociologists. Some of the best include Agnew and Duncan (1989); Appleton (1975); Entrikin (1991); Fitchen (1991); Hiss (1990); Hough (1990); Jackson (1984); Pred (1990); Tuan (1974, 1977); Walter (1988).

My doctoral work was done through the Union Graduate School in Cincinnati. Dedicated to interdisciplinary enquiry and a student-structured program of study, the university values work that marries rigorous, scientific research with the humanistic and creative. The publication rate for Union graduates is high, a tribute to scholarly work that tends to be both academically solid and pleasurable to read.

15 In fairness, it must be pointed out that I did not enquire into the topic of same-sex sexual relationships while in the camp, the subject being outside of the scope of my original project. Therefore, such relationships may well exist, just as 'fireline romances' exist between men and women. Clearly, this indicates a direction for needed future research.

16 Other 'instant communities' often have this erotic dimension and dynamic operative within them, including those in which racing-car drivers and racing sailors ply their trades. These activities, highly collaborative by nature, seem to foster an atmosphere of sensuality amidst a tense and gritty environment of competition.

17 I would point out here that this behavior, while considered socially appropriate between 'equals' (in terms of rank and power), does not seem to go on between, for instance, members of the management team and the firefighters themselves. The acts of playful flirting that I witnessed took place inevitably between social equals within that particular system, when they took place at all. Further, they were contextualized as 'fooling around' and not typically construed to be 'sexual' in connotation.

18 I am indebted to Mary Catherine Bateson for reminding me of the erotic element of heterosexual male bonding in certain settings, and the importance of that notion in this context.

19 See Newton's commentary (1993a: 7) for an elaboration on this.

20 There are sometimes problems with experimental writing forms. Birth (1990: 556), for instance, cautions against the simplistic discarding of the frame of referentiality, to be replaced by an ethereal poetics which can be indecipherable to a reading audience. Other critics of such writings (e.g. Caplan 1988; Mascia-Lees *et al*. 1989; Sangren 1988) remind us of what should be obvious; namely, that we have a responsibility to the reading audience. As Margery Wolf points out (1992: 138), 'The message of exclusion that attaches to some of these [experimental] texts contradicts the ostensible purpose of experimental ethnography, [which is] to find better ways of conveying some aspect of the experiences of another community.'

21 This acutely pointed phrase was used by two well-respected professionals I have spoken to, one a writer of fiction and the other a corporate executive working in a setting where a premium of respect is paid to those who can get rapidly to 'the bottom line' without going around the linguistic merry-go-round.

22 The humanists in the field of anthropology are a welcome exception here, dedicated to the exploration of different writing genres and styles in their writings. Represented in the discipline by the Society for Humanistic Anthropology (a unit of the American Anthropological Association), they continue to advocate the inclusion of poetics, fiction, and other forms of evocative expression in ethnographic writings. Many wonderfully written books, filled with sensual imagery and reflexivity, have been (and continue to be) the fruit of these efforts.

References

Ackerman, Diane (1990) *A Natural History of the Senses*. New York: Vintage Books.

Agnew, John A. and James S. Duncan (eds) (1989) *The Power of Place: Bringing Together Geographical and Sociological Imaginations*. Boston and London: Unwin Hyman.

Altman, Irwin and Setha M. Low (eds) (1992) *Place Attachment: Human Behavior and Environment*. Advances in Theory and Research Vol. 12. New York: Plenum.

Appadurai, Arjun (1988) 'Introduction: Place and Voice in Anthropological Theory'. *Cultural Anthropology*. Vol. 3, No. 1, pp. 16–20.

Appleton, Jay (1975) *The Experience of Landscape*. London and New York: John Wiley.

Basso, Keith H. (1988) 'Speaking with Names: Language and Landscape among the Western Apache'. *Cultural Anthropology*. Vol. 3, No. 2, pp. 99–129.

Behar, Ruth (1993) *Translated Woman: Crossing the Border with Esperanza's Story*. Boston, Mass.: Beacon Press.

Birth, Kevin (1990) 'Reading and the Righting of Writing Ethnographies'. *American Ethnologist*. Vol. 17, No. 3, pp. 549–57.

Brown, Karen McCarthy (1991) *Mama Lola: A Vodou Priestess in Brooklyn*. Berkeley, Calif.: University of California Press.

Caplan, Pat (1988) 'Engendering Knowledge: The Politics of Ethnography'. *Anthropology Today*. Vol. 4, No. 5, pp. 8–12, and Vol. 4, No. 6, pp. 14–17.

Cesara, Manda (1982) *Reflections of a Woman Anthropologist: No Hiding Place*. London and New York: Academic Press.

Chernoff, J.M. (1979) *African Rhythm and African Sensibility*. Chicago: University of Chicago Press.

Cohn, Carol (1987) 'Sex and Death in the Rational World of Defense Intellectuals'. *Signs: Journal of Women in Culture and Society*. Vol. 12, No. 4, pp. 687–718.

Entrikin, J. Nicholas (1991) *The Betweeness of Place*. Basingstoke: Macmillan.

Fernandez, J.W. (1982) *Bwiti*. Princetown, N.J.: Princeton University Press.

Firth, Raymond (1989) 'Introduction', in Bronislaw Malinowski, *A Diary in the Strict Sense of the Term*. Stanford: Stanford University Press. (Original edn. Routledge and Kegan Paul, 1967.)

Fitchen, Janet M. (1991) *Endangered Spaces, Enduring Places: Change, Identity, and Survival in Rural America*. Boulder, Colo.: Westview Press.

Fortune, Reo (1963) *Sorcerers of Dobu: The Social Anthropology of the Dobu Islanders of the Western Pacific*. New York: E.P. Dutton.

Geertz, Clifford (1983) *Local Knowledge: Further Essays in Interpretive Anthropology*. New York: Basic Books.

Golde, Peggy (ed.) (1986) *Women in the Field: Anthropological Experiences*. 2nd edn. Berkeley, Calif.: University of California Press.

Hiss, Tony (1990) *The Experience of Place*. New York: Alfred Knopf.

Hough, Michael (1990) *Out of Place: Restoring Identity to the Regional Landscape*. New Haven and London: Yale University Press.

Jackson, John Brinckerhoff (1984) *Discovering the Vernacular Landscape*. New Haven and London: Yale University Press.

Landes, Ruth (1986) 'A Woman Anthropologist in Brazil', in Peggy Golde (ed.) *Women in the Field: Anthropological Experiences*. Berkeley, Calif.: University of California Press.

Levi-Strauss, Claude (1955) [1984] *Tristes Tropiques*. New York: Atheneum.

Lutz, Catherine (1986) 'Emotion, Thought and Estrangement: Emotion as a Cultural Category'. *Cultural Anthropology*. Vol 3, No. 1, pp. 287–309.

Malinowski, Bronislaw (1961) [1922] *Argonauts of the Western Pacific*. New York: Dutton.

——— (1989) *A Diary in the Strict Sense of the Term*. Stanford: Stanford University Press. (Original edn. Routledge and Kegan Paul, 1967.)

Mascia-Lees, Frances E., Patricia Sharpe, and Colleen Balleriono Cohen (1989) 'The Postmodernist Turn in Anthropology: Cautions From A Feminist Perspective'. *Signs: Journal of Women in Cultural and Society*. Vol. 15, No. 11, pp. 7–33.

Mead, Margaret (1972) *Blackberry Winter: My Earlier Years*. New York: Simon and Schuster.

Myerhoff, Barbara (1978) *Number Our Days*. New York: Simon and Schuster.

——— and Jay Ruby (1982) 'Introduction', in Jay Ruby (ed.) *A Crack in the Mirror: Reflexive Perspectives in Anthropology* Philadelphia: University of Pennsylvania Press.

Nader, Laura (1986) 'From Anguish to Exultation', in Peggy Golde (ed.) *Women in the Field: Anthropological Experiences*. Berkeley, Calif.: University of California Press.

Newton, Esther (1993a) 'My Best Informant's Dress: The Erotic Equation in Fieldwork'. *Cultural Anthropology*. Vol. 8, No. 1, pp. 3–23.

——— (1993b) *Cherry Grove, Fire Island: Sixty Years in America's First Gay and Lesbian Town*. Boston, Mass.: Beacon Press.

Pred, Allan (1990) *Making Histories and Constructing Human Geographies*. Boulder, Colo.: Westview Press.

Rabinow, Paul (1977) *Reflections on Fieldwork in Morocco*. Berkeley, Calif.: University of California Press.

Read, H. (1972) *Surrealism*. New York: Praeger.

Rodman, Margaret (1992) 'Empowering Place: Multilocality and Multivocality'. *American Anthropologist*, Vol. 94, pp. 640–56.

Rose, Dan (1987) *Black American Street Life: South Philadelphia, 1969–1971*. Philadelphia: University of Pennsylvania Press.

Sangren, P. Steven (1988) 'Rhetoric and the Authority of Ethnography: "Postmodernism" and the Social Reproduction of Texts'. *Current Anthropology*. Vol. 29, No. 3, pp. 405–35.

Schneebaum, Tobias (1969) *Keep the River on Your Right*. New York: Grove Press.

——— (1979) *The Wild Man*. New York: Viking Press.

——— (1988) *Where the Spirits Dwell*. New York: Grove Press.

Stoller, Paul (1989) *The Taste of Ethnographic Things: The Senses in Anthropology*. Philadelphia: University of Pennsylvania Press.

——— and Cheryl Olkes (1987) *In Sorcery's Shadow*. Chicago: University of Chicago Press.

Torgovnick, Marianna (1990) *Gone Primitive: Savage Intellects, Modern Lives*. Chicago: University of Chicago Press.

Trawick, Margaret (1990) *Notes on Love in a Tamil Family.* Berkeley, Calif.: University of California Press.

Tuan, Yi-Fu (1974) *Topophilia: A Study of Environmental Perception, Attitudes, and Values.* Englewood Cliffs, N.J.: Prentice Hall.

——— (1977) *Space and Place: The Perspective of Experience.* Minneapolis: University of Minnesota.

Turnbull, Colin M. (1968) *The Forest People.* New York: Simon and Schuster.

Van Maanen, John (1988) *Tales of the Field: On Writing Ethnography.* Chicago: University of Chicago Press.

Walter, E.V. (1988) *Placeways: A Theory of the Human Environment.* Chapel Hill: University of North Carolina Press.

Whitehead, Tony Larry and Mary Ellen Conaway (eds) (1986) *Self, Sex and Gender in Cross-Cultural Fieldwork.* Urbana and Chicago: University of Illinois Press.

Wolf, Margery (1992) *A Thrice Told Tale: Feminism, Postmodernism and Ethnographic Responsibilty.* Stanford: Stanford University Press.

Chapter 5

Tricks, friends, and lovers

Erotic encounters in the field

Ralph Bolton

Whether or not an ethnographer engages in sex in the field is first and foremost a purely personal matter, but the traditional taboo on such behavior strikes at the very core of the discipline. Consequently, the taboo itself merits serious critical consideration. Its existence raises significant and unsettling questions about how anthropologists conceptualize the people they study and how their own views on sexuality are shaped by unexamined cultural premises and biases. The taboo on sexual involvement in the field serves to maintain a basic boundary between ourselves and the Other in a situation in which our goal as ethnographers is to diminish the distance between us. Sex is arguably the ultimate dissolution of boundaries between individuals. Indeed, good sex creates a physical and emotional connection in which it may be difficult to determine where 'I' stop and 'the other' begins.

But it should be noted that it is precisely the maintenance of a distinction between 'self' and 'other', between 'us' and 'them', and of cultural boundaries (as if cultures actually existed other than as a construct), that is at once central in anthropology and also profoundly problematic and responsible for an anthropological contribution to the perpetuation rather than the resolution of human problems. By emphasizing – indeed quite often exaggerating – human differences, we strengthen what divides us and weaken our sense of our common humanity. Contrary to our hopes and claims, our enterprise may actually increase, rather than reduce, ethnocentrism, racism, homophobia, religious intolerance, and sexism. Refusing to share in sexuality across cultural boundaries helps to perpetuate the false dichotomy between 'us' and 'the natives'. The anthropological agenda of studying what is conceptualized as Other carries with it the implication that we view the people we study not as individuals or fellow humans but as specimens of a reified cultural entity that we have labelled and put under the microscope. Without abandoning our quest to understand human differences, the anthropological emphasis on cultural differences needs to be rethought.

As a young anthropologist, the field for me was the Andes, where I spent six years between 1962 and 1974, primarily investigating aggression, social conflict, and related topics in rural Peruvian villages. Then, in the late 1970s, I turned my attention to Norway, intending to approach problems of violence and aggression by focusing on a society noted for its peacefulness (Gullestad 1992), the society which Naroll (1983) labelled 'the model country'. During my second year in Norway, 1982–3, my research agenda was derailed when I found myself attempting to cope with suppressed aspects of my sexuality, specifically with the transition from denial to acceptance of my homosexuality (Bolton in press, b).

One winter evening, I went to the municipal swimming pool in the city where I was teaching. The municipal baths, I quickly discovered, was a place where same-sex erotic encounters occurred, particularly in the changing booths. While dressing, I noticed that I was being watched by a man who was also preparing to leave. Our eyes met from time to time, but we didn't speak. When I left the baths I walked to the nearby waterfront. A few minutes later he followed me, and standing on a snow-laden pier, we struck up a conversation. I learned that his name was Bjørn. He was a professional dancer from Oslo currently performing in a local theater. After a few minutes, he invited me home for the night. We hit it off, and Bjørn, the first gay man I knew, and I became lovers. Shortly after we met, Bjørn and I spent a Sunday afternoon cross-country skiing in the forest outside the city. During a breath-catching pause in our tour, he asked if I'd heard of the new disease that had been discovered among gay men in America, then called GRID, or gay-related immune deficiency. I confessed my ignorance. That conversation marked the beginning of the end of my innocence. Bjørn and the AIDS crisis radically transformed both my personal and my professional life. Our intimate relationship lasted a year; our friendship endured until his untimely death from AIDS a decade later following a long, heroic struggle.

Bjørn is gone, but the epidemic rages on. Gay male sexuality, which was a complex and difficult issue for me before knowing Bjørn, is no longer personally problematic. Instead, it is a source of profound meaning and fulfillment. But gay male sexuality in the age of AIDS is politically, socially, and medically charged, more so than ever. Pleasure and danger co-exist, now in a heightened state of tension (Vance 1984), and gay communities around the world are challenged and threatened by the powerful forces of death and heterosexist oppression. My engagement with the epidemic, on an intellectual level as an anthropologist doing research on gay culture and AIDS and on a personal level as a member of a community devastated by the tragedy, deals with the questions, 'How to have sex in an epidemic – and survive' (Callen and Berkowitz 1983; Crimp 1988; Kyle 1992) and 'How to protect gay communities from attacks on their rights to exist and thrive'. In this chapter, I shall discuss the interplay of the personal and the professional as I have attempted, through ethnographic research, to contribute to our knowledge of the problems of gay men faced with the crisis caused by AIDS.

Sex research in a time of crisis

Sex is the most prominent and symbolically significant domain in gay culture. Same-sex erotic desire is what undergirds gay identity and community.[1] To the dismay of gay assimilationists and non-gay erotophobes alike, gay culture celebrates the erotic, the foundation of its being (Bronski 1984; Holleran 1988). Before HIV entered the scene, communitas was enhanced by the free flow of body fluids among gay men. Once those body fluids became infected with a deadly virus, this joyous sharing of self contributed to a rapid acceleration of the epidemic. What happens, then, to community when the erotic communitas on which it is based is broken? How can the bonds of community be maintained when the sexual communitas which created it threatens the physical survival of its members as well as the cultural forms it has elaborated? Observers of gay communities have acknowledged that a remarkable process of adaptation to the new situation has occurred, including the widespread adoption of safe-sex practices which permit the continuation of communitas. But playing safely is not universal among gay men, and this fact calls for basic research on the conditions which foster risk reduction.[2]

It has been a longstanding belief of mine that when studying a culture, one should pay particular attention to the problems it confronts and to those aspects of the culture that are salient to its members. In gay culture, sex is where the action is. What is needed, especially in the context of AIDS, is intensive, extended ethnographic research that addresses the processes of adaptation and change surrounding sexuality. Unfortunately, the work of most anthropologists (certainly those studying AIDS issues) rarely involves traditional ethnography. Real ethnography, under the pressures for quick-and-dirty results, has been replaced by one-month consultancies, phone surveys (farmed out to marketing firms), focus group interviews (contracted out to social marketeers), and rapid assessment procedures.[3] For me the value of fieldwork has always been in the close encounter with people whose lives I am trying to understand. The prolonged and intimate contact we associate with traditional fieldwork has always been the greatest source of anthropological insights and knowledge and the surest route to understanding a culture. During the AIDS crisis, the ethnographic vision has largely been lost (Bolton 1992, in press, a; Carrier and Bolton 1991).

My research on gay male sexuality in the United States has been supported almost exclusively by small grants from my own institution. Applications to outside agencies (e.g. to the Wenner-Gren Foundation, for research on gay bathhouses, and to the American Foundation for AIDS Research, for an analysis of gay male sexual cognition) have been singularly unsuccessful. Given the odds, I did not bother to apply for a grant to analyze gay male erotica (Bolton in press, c). The paucity of publications on the subject and conversations with other scholars lead me to believe that my inability to get grants for ethnographic work on gay men is due less to personal deficiencies and poor grantsmanship than to a pervasive bias against ethnographic research on AIDS in general and on gay men in particular. Over the past decade, I learned what other gay and lesbian scholars have learned in the past: to do any research on gay cultures one must disguise one's intentions or piggyback the work onto another project (Society of Lesbian and Gay Anthropologists 1992; Williams 1993).

My luck changed when I applied to the Fulbright Program to do research on the social and cultural responses to AIDS in Belgium, without mentioning my interest in the gay community and certainly without mentioning gay male sexuality. I had spent the summer of 1985 exploring the societal responses to AIDS in Norway (Bolton 1986), and an argument in favor of a comparison with another culture, I surmised, might work. I got the grant and used the opportunity it provided to explore gay male sexuality.[4]

But why Belgium?

The seduction of Brussels

For me, Brussels is a magical place, a fascinating city to which I return whenever I can. But it was not by choice that I fell in love with Brussels. I was a victim of Cupid's Arrow. Though Brussels has its unique charms – such as the Grand Palace, an exquisite cuisine, and an almost small-town ambience for a city that fancies itself the Capital of Europe – it is set on a flat plain with a cold, rainy climate that I don't find appealing. Since my first taste of Brussels in 1985, however, it is there that I have returned time and again, hopelessly seduced by the friendliness of its people and, above all, by the sex appeal of its men.

It began by accident. I never intended to do research in Belgium. En route from Amsterdam to Luxembourg, I had stopped over in Brussels to visit a colleague from home who was staying with a friend there. He had reserved a room for me at the Mykonos Hotel, a small establishment with little to recommend it except its modest price and central location not far from the Grand Place. Preparing for my stopover, I'd consulted a copy of *Spartacus*, the international gay guide, for the names and addresses of bars to check out while in town. But the maze of crooked streets was confusing, and on my first try I couldn't find one. I was returning to my hotel room when it happened. As I approached the entrance to my hotel, a young man passed me going in the opposite direction. Our eyes met – lust at first sight. His pace slowed, but he continued walking. Our eyes unlocked. I paused in the hotel doorway and watched him cross the street, glance back, and then turn into a bar which I was planning to look up in *Spartacus* to see if it was a gay bar.

I dashed up to my hotel room and pulled out my *Spartacus* guide. A quick glance confirmed my suspicion and raised my hopes: yes, the Kaktus was gay. I inserted my contact lenses (no point in taking a chance that no one would make passes at a man wearing glasses) and left for the Kaktus.[5] The small bar was packed with a jovial crowd of men, mostly older. I managed to snag a stool at the bar, and from where I sat I was happy to notice that the man I'd seen in the street earlier was talking with a group of friends at the other end of the bar. I ordered a beer, and then another. How long I sat there observing the proceedings, I don't recall. From time to time, my eyes and his would catch, but he was occupied.

Too shy to approach him myself in this context and finally concluding that he would not make the first move, I departed, but glancing back as I crossed the street, I noticed that he had followed me out. I slowed down and waited on the corner. He came up and introduced himself as Philippe. He accepted without pausing when I invited him to my room, conveniently at hand. With both of us obviously horny, we stripped and had sex without further formalities. He was a hot man, in his late twenties or early thirties, tall, with dark hair, a moustache, and a 'body to die for' as the old saying went. We made love twice over the next two hours, with an interlude of conversation. On leaving, he expressed the hope that we'd meet again if I ever returned to Brussels. I left Brussels the next day, but before I left Europe that summer I returned to Brussels for my last three days on the continent. On that return visit, to my regret, I didn't run into Philippe. Since then, however, I have seen him often while there, usually in a bar where we chat and joke around. We have mutual friends. But, alas, we never had sex again.

On my second visit to Brussels, I decided to check out the sauna scene, spending several hours at the Olympus bathhouse. Before leaving the sauna, I stopped at the bar for a Coke to replenish fluids lost in the steamroom. The owners of the Olympus were fooling around, dancing and bantering with an extremely handsome man who was fully clothed and flirting with me with his eyes. For me, this was more than lust – upon seeing this man I had an overwhelming feeling of 'love at first sight'. I didn't need it. I'd been that route before, leaving Europe on the cusp of a Great Love. So I left the sauna and returned to my hotel. Later that evening, I decided to go to the Kaktus on the off-chance that I might run into Philippe. Instead, to my surprise, I noticed the mystery man from the Olympus. Because it was the only available space in the packed bar, I ended up standing near him. He smiled when he saw me and soon asked me to dance.

After a while, he told me he wanted to go to another bar, and I was welcome to come along if I wished. With some confusion caused by his English (my French at the time was still deficient, so we were speaking English), it was not clear to me what he wanted. He went to the door, stopped and looked back to see if I was coming along. I joined him and we had drinks in another bar. Suddenly, he asked if I wanted to go for a swim. 'Sure, but where at this time of night?' I asked. It turned out that he had in mind a gay sauna on the same block as the bar we were in. We went there, and he paid my entrance fee. We jumped into the pool; he swam – it was too cold for me. Then we entered the jacuzzi, which we had to ourselves, and engaged in kissing, hugging, caressing. He invited me to spend what remained of the night at his place. With both of us exhausted, the sex was anticlimactic, but I fell asleep in love. The next two days we spent together, sharing the stories of our lives. We had a lot in common: he was only five years younger than me, both of us had been married and had children, and we'd come out later in life. Unlike me, he was in the process of a difficult divorce and still struggling with his homosexuality. Our conversations, he said, were therapeutic for him. There was a strong bond of empathy between us, but, as I was to discover, from his side it wasn't love.

We maintained contact over the years, letters from me, an occasional card from him when he was on vacation. And when I was in Brussels, we would dance, and talk, and flirt when we saw each other in the bars, until the time I returned one winter and was told by the owners of the Olympus, who knew about our affair, that he had died a few weeks earlier. A heart attack, they claimed, but I was left to wonder about the possibility that he'd died a self-inflicted death. He'd confided in me how between my visits to Brussels, unable to cope with his sexuality, he'd made several suicide attempts. Perhaps he'd succeeded. When I returned from that month in Brussels, I found a death notice and a note from his ex-wife. My Christmas card to him had ended up in her hands.

And that's how I came to apply for a grant to do research in Belgium, to return to Brussels where I'd left my heart. Over the years, I've been romantically involved with numerous Belgian men. Sometimes the affairs were brief, a month or two (affairettes, I sometimes call these); other relationships lasted longer, one of them two years. In all cases, the emotional involvement was strong, and while the sexual intimacy did not endure, these lovers became friends – with one exception, an instance in which the breakup left me feeling that I'd been used. Some of these relationships were ended by me, others by my partners. Pain resulted for one or both of us when things didn't work out, but I don't believe that any of us regretted what had existed, the mutual pleasure and sharing, no matter how transient. Each relationship produced personal growth and had its rewards. I maintain contact with most of the men with whom the sexual contact was not merely a one-night stand. But even with many of those with whom the encounter was brief, there remains a bond which is renewed when I'm back in Belgium and we run into each other on the social circuit.

In 1993, my American partner and I visited Brussels together; we lodged in the apartment of a former lover and dined repeatedly with two other friends, one of them a young man with whom I'd had a brief, torrid affair. The bonds of love and affection we'd forged through sexual intimacy are enduring.

Sexual ethnography

> It is generally assumed that what we may call homosexual 'scattering' – the fact that homosexuals have a multitude of love affairs, each of which may last only a moment – expresses the fundamental instability of the homosexual condition, the search for a dream partner through a series of brief unsatisfactory affairs. The homosexual pick-up scene may well be experienced in such a way, at least at the level of what 'queers' tell each other or what they have found out about themselves. But instead of translating this scattering of love-energy as the inability to find a centre, we could see it as a system in action, the system in which polyvocal desire is plugged in on a non-exclusive basis.
>
> (Hocquenghem 1993: 131)

My Fulbright fieldwork was loosely structured. As defined for purposes of the grant, I was to address the question of how Belgian society was responding to the AIDS pandemic, which for me translated largely into how the gay community was handling the crisis. To gather information, I conducted interviews arranged by the Ministry of Public Health with leaders in AIDS and gay organizations and with AIDS researchers throughout Belgium, and collected written materials from both official sources and gay publications. Mostly, however, I hung out in gay venues, observing and engaging the men who frequented these places in conversations about their lives.[6] There is no true gay ghetto in Brussels, although many of the bars and other gay-oriented businesses are located within a few blocks of the Grand Place. My *modus operandi* was to spend the evening (many times until dawn) in the bars and discos talking to people. Sometimes, when I 'got lucky,' I would spend the remainder of the night in bed with someone. The next day I would sleep until late morning, then get up to write fieldnotes for several hours about the previous evening. Some afternoons I went to the baths, where I could observe and participate in daytime gay life, since the bars were usually sparsely populated during working hours. Then I would go home and prepare to go downtown again for another night in the scene.

Fieldwork, as I understand it, is not a nine-to-five job. It's twenty-four hours a day on call. Fieldwork in Peruvian villages meant being surrounded day and night by the people we were studying, late-night storytelling events or sorcery sessions, participation in three-day wedding ceremonies or religious holidays, daytime interviewing or observing men and women at work. It is easy for lab scientists working with animals, or even for those in the human sciences gathering data by administering questionnaires or conducting focus groups, to segregate their professional and personal time and to separate their roles as scientists and as individuals. But for ethnographers, life is not so simple. All perceptions and experiences are potentially data.

From my graduate-school days, I can clearly recall the recommendation that the ethnographer keep two sets of notes, one, fieldnotes proper which contain observations, interviews, and so forth, and two, a diary in which one records one's own thoughts and experiences. I have never been able to follow this advice since it seems more natural to me to relate both simultaneously during the process of writing down information. What I am seeing, feeling, hearing, and thinking all affect how I, as the data-processing instrument, interpret the world I'm experiencing.

In my life in Brussels, the line between the personal and professional was blurred as I entered fully into the life of the community I was studying. As a gay man studying the erotic culture of gay men, I was drawn to them for both personal and professional reasons, and my interactions simultaneously affected my work and my private life. As someone they got to know as sympathetic and willing to participate in some of the most meaningful aspects of their lives, I was offered friendship and acceptance as a member of the community. Participation provided entrée into people's homes, which in some cultures is not easy. It pulled me into friendship networks and provided access to social events (meals, parties, meetings) from which I otherwise would have been excluded. In short, I became a player in the scene, reciprocating by introducing my tricks, friends, and lovers to others in my network. Being open to the possibilities of sexual adventures made me more aware of how the system of 'homosexual scattering' described by Hocquenghem functioned in the Belgian context. By experiencing them, I came to learn of blow jobs from bartenders when the door was locked at closing time, of jacking off in cruising spots in a park near the Grand Place in partially public view, of sexual encounters in alleyways between someone headed home from the bars and someone on his way to work at dawn, of sexual action in the dunes along the coast and on the piers in Ostende and in the backrooms of discos and in the bathrooms of ordinary bars.

Sexual behavior is not easily observed, and I learned more through participation than by simple observation or direct interviewing. Moreover, information obtained post-coitally (except in quickie encounters in public places), when people tend to relax and open up about their lives, was always richer, more from the heart, and more revealing than the data gathered in a more detached manner. Once one has shared physical and emotional intimacy, sharing other knowledge about oneself seems easier. By remaining aloof from the sexual interaction system, what I would have learned through other means – unobtrusive naturalistic observation or the examination of erotic texts – would have been superficial at best and inaccurate at worst. How people talk about sex, perhaps even how they think about sex, is influenced by the context in which the talk takes place. And it differs, too, by the extent of mutuality in the sharing of intimate information, meaningful experiences, and profoundly personal knowledge between the people involved in the interaction. Just as sex creates community among gay men, it is also the route to intimacy. Sex itself, as Holleran (1988) has noted, is not the ultimate indicator of intimacy; it is a means to that end.

I cannot imagine doing fieldwork without sex, perhaps from a feeling that life is too short and one must enjoy it while one can. We don't get younger. Perhaps it's because I came out late and am 'catching up'. In truth, it's probably because I enjoy sex too much to remain voluntarily abstinent. It is most definitely not a sacrifice I would make for my profession. But the question of identity is implicated as well. In the hierarchy of components of my personal identity, gayness ranks higher than ethnicity, nationality, and profession. And that aspect of my being is expressed and celebrated through sex. Certainly, I could never again engage in fieldwork in a society where I would have to disguise an essential part of myself in order to be accepted and effective, to subject myself to the hypocrisy that is forced on gays and lesbians so much at home as well (Dickemann 1990).

My American friends insisted that on my last sabbatical I stay closer to home; they were bemused by my returning from each trip to Brussels deeply enamored of someone, by my pangs of desire or anguish over a long-distance affair, and by my deep attraction to European men, which they did not hesitate to diagnose as a sign of fear of commitment. But the phenomenon is much more complex than that. I was always open to the possibility of moving to Europe, where I enjoy living, or of having a lover move to America, and in a couple of instances we were on the verge of this before I got cold feet about the responsibility for inducing such a cisatlantic relocation. There's no accounting for taste, and intense infatuations (love?) have been my lot whether in the United States or abroad. In large measure, my relationships in the field resulted from the response of Belgian men to me. For some reason, I enjoyed a popularity in Brussels greater than at home. I suspect it is because for me being 'in the field' is real life. It's where I become more fully alive, in part because 'at home' the press of obligations and routine work tends to become all-consuming of energies, whereas the field represents freedom from the tyranny of schedules and duties.

The gay community in Brussels was a welcoming one in which I felt at home and at ease. Among many gay men, sex is the cement that holds the building blocks of community together. To have remained aloof would have kept me outside that community, and I suspect that refusing to participate, denying my sexuality, would have made me seem strange indeed, as other anthropologists have reported (Williams 1993; Proschan 1990). The shared sexual experiences established a warmth and intimacy that is difficult to achieve otherwise. Being open and personally interested in the men I met also brought me access to subcommunities which I otherwise might have missed. Thus, for example, I was drawn by friends and lovers into the local leather scene, a subset of gay men who form an international fraternity of those with an interest in an eroticism based on various combinations of fetishism, sadomasochism, and dominance/submission role playing, which previously I had known about only from reading. There are definite gaps in my data on sexual venues in Brussels because I was not comfortable observing or participating in some scenes, such as tearooms (Humphreys 1970). But some sex venues, such as the saunas, I came to know well.

Research on the baths could have been conducted through simple observation, supplemented by informal interviews. Some sites in the sauna where sex takes place are relatively public, such as the steamroom and the orgy room, but the presence of non-participants in those settings alters the flow of interaction, and in some settings lighting and other impediments to observation preclude visual monitoring, though not necessarily exposure to auditory stimuli. Interviewing could have been done in the normally non-sexual settings in the sauna (the bar area or the television lounge) – talking is discouraged by custom in other areas. But most conversation between bathhouse clients occurs as post-coital sharing in the private sex rooms or in the bar area.

It would be difficult for a gay man to investigate such a highly charged erotic environment and not be tempted to participate. In a pioneering study of the baths by Styles (1979), the ethnographer began his study by declining to participate. He reports how his understandings of the interactions in this setting had to be revamped completely after he altered his decision to abstain and became a participant observer instead of a mere observer.

The results of my participant observations in the baths were complemented by survey data from a sample of Flemish gay men (Bolton *et al.* 1994). This analysis, one of only two or three that have been done on gay baths despite the prominence of political controversies over the closure of bathhouses in the United States, showing that men who attended the baths were more knowledgeable about AIDS, had changed their behavior more in the direction of safe sex, and were less likely to engage in unsafe sex, has important policy implications. The results have been used by community leaders in other countries to support their efforts to prevent the closure of these institutions, which have a key position in the history and symbolic structure of gay culture. This is not the place to go into a history of the debate between social control and educational approaches to saunas, but it should be noted that this work, so strongly influenced by my participant observation in the baths, contributes to the empowerment of gay communities instead of to the destruction of their institutions. The intent is to preserve sexual rights, within the parameters set by a deadly virus and with the least possible intervention, and to protect against the unwarranted destruction of gay institutions, by homophobia camouflaged as public health, at a time when the forces of repression insist that gay men become celibate or settle down, become monogamous and have 2.1 pets.

Ethical issues in sexual participant observation: the Belgian case

Sex research, regardless of the methodology, is always controversial, and sex researchers historically have invariably been scrutinized and criticized as immoral (Allgeier and Allgeier 1991; Brecher 1971; Humphreys 1970; Nardi 1994; Pomeroy 1972). My own work in Belgium is not exceptional in this regard, although sexual participant observation raises some additional issues which need to be addressed. In this section, I shall review these issues.

At the outset, I must emphasize two points: (1) that I *never* engaged in sex for the purpose of collecting data, and (2) that I never engaged in unsafe sex, defined as unprotected anal intercourse.[7] I was always interested in my partner as a person, not as an informant. Indeed, I find it impossible to refer to any of my friends, lovers, or tricks as 'informants'. Certainly I learned much from them. They expanded the horizons of my knowledge and awareness on many levels in ways that are difficult to articulate, and I came away from each encounter and relationship richer in understanding, about them and about myself. Though self-knowledge (navel-gazing) was not the goal of the research, the two are intimately linked. Indeed, self-awareness may be a precondition for understanding others, but the process is a continual one of mutual discovery. Although one of the goals of my research was to understand gay male sexuality in Belgium, my personal, intimate interactions were not conducted with that goal in mind. Still, as Davis (1983: xxi), who advocates a phenomenological approach to the study of sexuality, has noted, 'The most direct resource available to the sex researcher is his own sexual experience.' Agreeing with Davis's conclusion that 'the intellectual benefits derived from drawing on direct subjective resources in the study of sex far outweigh the personal risks involved', I have decided not to exclude that resource.

Another point worth underscoring is that my sexual life in the field was not qualitatively different from my sexual life at home, except to the extent that in the field I had more unencumbered time in which to pursue this dimension of my life (and, thanks to the great abundance of time, I was more conscientious about keeping a record of my encounters). In addition, my sexual life was not qualitatively different from that of the men who were my partners. All of them were participants in the 'system of scattering of love-energy' (Hocquenghem 1993: 131); they engaged in anonymous encounters and so-called casual sex (a misnomer).

Research ethicists generally utilize four fundamental principles when assessing ethical issues (Allgeier and Allgeier 1991; Marshall 1991, 1992a, 1992b). I shall discuss each of these principles as they apply to the Belgian case.

Freedom from coercion

In no instance were any of my partners coerced into having sex with me. Each encounter involved a voluntary decision based on mutual erotic attraction. This is not to deny that some of my partners may have had other motivations as well, since the determinants of sexual decision making are rarely simple (Bolton 1992, 1994; Hoffman and Bolton 1993). One hustler with whom I had sex didn't do so for money (I didn't even know when we went home together one night that he was a hustler), but he may have done so out of loneliness, or even for a place to spend the night. Another, I eventually figured out, entered into a relationship with me because he needed a secure haven from an abusive relationship which he was just coming out of; he was genuinely fond of me, but it was not a case of love. However, power was not a factor in this context, except to the degree that erotic power, the primary factor in most gay encounters, is involved (Davis 1983), and on that score I would rate myself as average at best (though this is both age-related and highly subjective, of course). Moreover, my style of cruising tends to be subtle and hesitant rather than persistent and aggressive. I tend not to be a persistent suitor. Status differentials based on class, wealth, education, or profession, which might be important in other field situations, gave me no advantage over my partners. Indeed in anonymous sex venues, such as the baths, those factors would be considered totally irrelevant even if they did exist. In gay society, eroticism cancels out the advantages of everyday life.

By the same token, I never allowed myself to be bullied or pressured into having sex with someone to whom I was not genuinely attracted. That is not to say that I never accepted overtures from someone below the usual cut-off point on my personal scale of erotic desirability. Because of extraordinary horniness or as an act of kindness, many gay men do this, in part because others have been similarly generous to them or because of a sense of communal reciprocity – which is often misinterpreted and labeled by the term 'indiscriminate coupling'. At other times, one puts off those who are not one's type, and over the years I refused some persistent men whom I did not find attractive. Rejecting and being rejected, accepting and being accepted, are all part of the sexual dance. Coercion, in this community, is not.

Protection from psychological or physical harm

It is incumbent on all researchers to refrain from engaging in activities which could harm the people with whom they work. And, indeed, some research on sexuality cannot or should not be done because dissemination of the results might prove detrimental. Since my fieldnotes contain intimate details about the lives of my partners, the potential for social psychological harm (embarrassment, conflict) is theoretically present. To safeguard against this possibility, however, names and information that might lead to the identification of individuals have been altered to ensure anonymity. An ethnographer's fieldnotes are not privileged by the courts, however; thus the ultimate protection for my partners must rest in my willingness to destroy these materials and suffer the consequences rather than turn them over to legal authorities.

None of my partners suffered any physical harm from our encounters.

Given my seronegative status and consistent adherence to the safe-sex guidelines used in Belgium, the possibility of a risk of transmission of HIV can certainly be ruled out. Nor did my partners suffer psychological harm. While some of the relationships did undeniably lead to some emotional pain when they ended, in no instance did that pain outweigh the psychological benefits derived from the relationship – except in the case where I was the one harmed.

The risk–benefit principle: beneficence

Research that entails risk to the well-being of the participant must be justified by a clear rationale in which the potential benefits to be derived from the research outweigh the risks incurred. While the risks outlined above were minimal, the potential benefits from the fieldwork are significant. The lives of these men are at serious risk, not from research but from the existence of HIV; thus the potential for saving the lives of my partners and their loved ones, directly or indirectly, is real. In post-coital conversations I often raised the issue of safe sex and tried to convey its importance, especially to partners whose behavior or comments suggested that they did not always practice it. Moreover, among the latter, it could be argued that had they had sex with someone other than me on this occasion, someone not committed to safe sex, they could have become infected by that partner. They were safe with me.

The information that I gained from these encounters, that is, that safe sex was not normative in this community, was conveyed to public health authorities in a position to influence funding for more intensive prevention efforts in the community. Such efforts, if carried out, have the potential to save thousands of lives in this community, which is in a life-and-death situation. Without such action, there is no question but that great suffering and many unnecessary deaths will occur in this population, as they have in other gay communities. My primary goal was to help prevent this from happening. Similarly, our findings on sexual behavior in saunas provided important evidence in support of gay community institutions (Bolton *et al.* 1994).

Under this principle (Marshall 1991), the problems of control over the use of research data, as well as the investigator's competing allegiances to the research sponsor, communities, and study populations, must be assessed. In my fieldwork, I alone controlled my field data. Although during this research I was affiliated with a government institution, no one at that institution or at the granting agency had rights of access to my data. Moreover, there was no conflict of allegiance associated with this research. My sole allegiance was to the community of gay men with whom I participated in daily life. While I did voluntarily give a brief oral summary of my conclusions to Ministry officials, I did so only because of the importance to the community of informing the Ministry of its erroneous conclusions and the dangers of not providing more support for AIDS prevention programs for gay men.

Respect for persons and informed consent

This principle is the most problematic for my research, as it is for most ethnographic work. I did not get signed informed-consent forms from my sexual partners. Some of them, particularly the totally anonymous partners, did not know prior to the encounter that I was doing research on sex and AIDS. I never refrained from indicating what I was studying when asked. Was I obligated to get signed informed consent before bedding a partner? I don't think so. While I subsequently used what I learned in my encounters to inform my assessment of gay male sexual behavior in Brussels, those encounters were engaged in for personal, not professional, reasons. A broad interpretation of the informed-consent principle would require its implementation in all research involving humans. A narrow interpretation suggests informed consent is required whenever the research involves the risk of harm to the individual or community. Under such conditions, the purpose of informed consent is to prevent harm to the individual, or if harm could occur, then to obtain permission and acceptance of that risk by those who would incur it. In my judgment, no risk was involved in the Belgian fieldwork.

It goes without saying that preserving absolute confidentiality and the privacy rights of participants is a *sine qua non* for any research on sensitive subjects. Within the Brussels gay community itself, gossip spreads rapidly about who has slept with whom, including the American anthropologist. While I did not reveal to others private information about my sexual partners, whom I had sex with did become common knowledge in some instances in this community, where such information is a major topic of conversation.

Patricia Marshall (1991, 1992a, 1992b), the leading ethicist in medical anthropology, has discussed the problems associated with the application of informed-consent requirements in various forms of anthropological research. In her review of my Belgian research

(Marshall 1992a), she agrees that there existed a compelling argument for participation. However, she refers to my 'methodology' as one of 'passive deception' because of the absence of informed consent. I would reject this characterization on the grounds that I did not engage in sexual encounters for purposes of research. If I had gone to bed with someone in order to obtain data, passive deception would have been involved and this would be ethically suspect, in my view.

Informed consent, while important in cases of potential harm, is not the ultimate guarantor of protection for human subjects. As a research subject in a major AIDS project, I have signed informed-consent forms, all done quite properly. And still I have felt violated – and my community harmed – when the analyses I read coming from that project are flawed by both lack of understanding of the cultural context of my life and homophobic interpretations of the data.[8] In the final analysis, the protection of participants in research depends much more on the integrity, intentions, and intelligence of investigators and on their primary allegiance to the well-being of the population being studied than on formal, bureaucratic instruments.

It is interesting to compare my form of participant observation to the observational studies on gay saunas conducted by private investigators on behalf of the state in various cities in the United States over the past decade (Bolton 1994). The latter, while they did not involve sexual participation, also did not obtain informed consent. Nor were they carried out with the interests of the participants and the gay community in mind. Rather, they were carried out as elements in the system of state control of gay men's sexuality by unsympathetic, hired outsiders. That work deserves condemnation, yet I have seen no outcries from ethicists about such activities. My research, in contrast, was empowering for both individuals and the community.

Finally, I would note that the Belgian case is in full compliance with the ethical code of the American Anthropological Association. In Section I of the Principles of Professional Responsibility it is noted that 'anthropologists' first responsibility is to those whose lives and cultures they study'. I viewed that as my *only* responsibility.[9]

Writing sexual ethnography

As a sexual ethnographer who has learned most of what he knows from personal participation in erotic encounters, the problem I face is how to prepare that information for professional dissemination, either to the anthropological community or, more importantly, to men and women on the front lines of AIDS prevention who might find the information useful. Sexual ethnographers whose work does not include participation, or who do not disclose their participation as a source of data, do not have this problem. Still, few sexual ethnographies have been published (Gregor 1985; Parker 1991), and the few that do exist tend to focus on the publicly visible and readily articulated aspects of sexuality, on ritual and symbolism rather than on the down-and-dirty details of sexual encounters. In short, by emphasizing the public aspects of sex and slighting the personal, they tend to miss the essence of sexuality – meanings and emotions.

Through intensive immersion in the life of one community, I learned about how gay men conduct and think about their sexual lives – or at least some of them, presumably those most at risk for HIV because of their life in the fast lane. The difficulty lies in writing up my fieldnotes; it's a problem I have not resolved. Despite postmodernist and reflexive pretensions, no non-fictional genre exists within anthropology in which the encounter with the ethnographer is clearly portrayed as the primary source of data and understanding. The difficulties of writing such accounts are magnified when the topic is sexuality because of the zones of privacy which the ethnographer may feel constrained to protect. To reveal how we know what we know, anthropologists working with sexuality may have to disclose more about ourselves than is customary – thereby risking job discrimination, the closing off of future grant opportunities, and just plain small-minded gossip and moralistic tongue-wagging.

Gilbert Herdt, whose work has focused on sexuality, has noted: 'It is astounding but understandable that in the whole ethnographic literature I know best – Melanesia – there is not one sentence on an ethnographer's sexual feelings for (let alone involvements with) the natives' (Herdt and Stoller 1990: 392). Thus, I appear not to be alone in not knowing how to present such information. I am certainly not the only ethnographer who has not only had but acted upon sexual feelings for 'the natives'.[10] But uncertainty about how to write about personal sexual encounters is probably not the major deterrent to openness. As Newton (1993: 8) has pointed out: 'It is just because silence regarding the unwritten rules of the sex and gender systems makes changing the rules impossible that hardly any of the powerful, or those who hope to be, are willing to break them.' It is ironic, of course, that as a gay man, I am in many ways freer than my straight counterparts when it comes to talking about sex, because frankness and honesty about sexuality are more widespread in my subculture and because, being already stigmatized for my sexuality, it is not a great step to be open about eroticism in the field. The few who have written most explicitly about such matters are precisely those on the margins who, not by choice but because of discrimination, have been excluded from academically respectable positions in major universities – in other words, individuals with nothing to lose by being honest and forthcoming.

In the age of AIDS, however, there is a lot to lose by the failure to disclose what we know. Silence in this situation is tantamount to death in communities to which I owe my allegiance, not as an anthropologist but as a gay man. One basic conclusion from my participation in community life in Brussels was that unsafe sex was still widespread among these gay men. This finding ran counter to a conclusion arrived at by the Ministry of Public Health. I reported orally on my findings to my superior in the Ministry. Originally, I did not intend to use what I had learned in any professional way, and the decision to discuss this personal material was not easy, because the potential for misinterpretation, misrepresentation, and disapproval is high. The reputational costs, too, may be high. But these costs must be weighed against the costs of remaining silent, of not doing whatever is necessary to save the lives of men at risk.

Conclusion

My knowledge about gay male sexuality arises out of the processes of intimate interaction. My objective, however, has not been to comprehend some abstract Other, but to understand the behavior of individual gay men, a category that includes me. The emotional connections were essential to the pursuit of this goal; they resulted in often prolonged, sometimes agonizing contemplation and the 'testing' of hypotheses about why my partners behaved the way they did in specific contexts, and about my own behavior as well. The relationships were important and meaningful. The process is no different at home.

It could be argued that since gay culture involves a diaspora of sorts, I was not dealing with the Other. Gay men, in metropolitan areas of

Western societies at least, do share elements of a common culture across ethnic and national boundaries.

The gay milieu in Brussels included – in addition to Walloons and Flemings – Turks, Moroccans, Egyptians, Israelis, Spaniards, Brazilians, Canadians, Germans, Irishmen, Portuguese, Americans, Russians, Frenchmen and Japanese, to mention just some of the nationalities I encountered during my time there. In this setting, identities and Otherness based on ethnicity were real, to be sure, but so was a sense of Oneness grounded in sexual orientation. Heterosexuals, for whom sexual identity is not as problematic and not the basis of community, are more likely to emphasize divisions based on ethnicity and nationality. For gay men in Brussels, communitas, created by shared sexual interests and experiences, was extended across cultural and ethnic boundaries.

Wengle (1988: 25) writes: 'The celibate anthropologist is, if nothing else, secure in his sense of identity.' Abstinence, in essence, serves to maintain the ethnographer's cultural identity, which sexual involvement would threaten. But I would argue that, in the interest of promoting a more inclusive identity and a deeper understanding of the people being studied, the ethnographer's cultural identity *should* be called into question. The individual who feels a need to reserve his or her sexuality for members of his or her own culture of origin exhibits cultural insecurity, and perhaps sexual insecurity as well. The secure ethnographer will not be threatened by the potentially powerful effects of intimate encounters with people in the field. To be sure, each field situation is different, and whether or not an ethnographer decides to become sexually involved with members of the host culture depends on the specific context, including the risks associated with involvement, as well as his or her own values and needs. The dangers of sexual involvement may be significantly more pronounced for women than for men, especially gay men, except in societies where male homosexuality is severely penalized.

Ethnographic work, at its best, enmeshes us in the lives of the people we study. For better or for worse, we have a mutual impact. As anthropologists we generally recognize that our personal lives as well as our professional work are enriched by our experiences in the field, and we gain immeasurably from the attachments we develop with the people we study. Indeed, the very philosophy behind the emphasis on extended periods of fieldwork is that we should be transformed by the experience of seeing and experiencing the world in unaccustomed ways. The exclusion of sexual bonding, despite the importance of the erotic in our lives as transformative experiences, requires explaining. It is due, I would suggest, to our unexamined, ethnocentric adherence to traditional sexual values. Monogamous ideals place sexual encounters in the field off limits to married colleagues, who, if such encounters occur, are not free to discuss them. But many young ethnographers going into the field for the first time are single, and norms against premarital sex have long since been abandoned within our culture. Perhaps what is off limits to their professors, then, is made taboo for everyone on the principle that what's prohibited for the powerful must be prohibited for all.

The taboo on sex in the field reflects a disciplinary stance consistent with a long tradition in Western thought on the relationships between sex, knowledge, and morality, which can be summarized as follows:

1 *Plato*: spiritualized love, not physical intimacy, is the pathway to wisdom.
2 *St. Augustine*: sexual abstinence is the pathway to knowledge of God.
3 *Judeo-Christian doctrine*: a faithful, monogamous heterosexual relationship is the only morally acceptable context for sexual expression.
4 *Freud*: sexual repression is the pathway to civilization.
5 *Evolutionists*: the Victorian nuclear family structure is the pinnacle of human social evolution, at the opposite end of the evolutionary scale from 'primitive promiscuity'.
6 *Anthropologists*: denial of sex with 'the natives' is the pathway to knowledge of the Other.

A perspective which considers all sexual activity between consenting adults as moral challenges each of these axioms, proclaiming instead that sexual expression (1) may be intensely spiritual, (2) may lead to more civilized behavior through a reduction in destructive competitive striving, (3) may result in more complex and varied forms of social organization not based on the companionate heterosexual model, (4) may lead to wisdom through a reduction in the hypocrisy and ignorance surrounding one of the most important domains of human life and pleasure, and (5) may produce greater knowledge through a reduction in the imaginary and artificial barriers of Otherness which are sustained by rules of sexual exclusion. This perspective, widely held among gay men in Western cultures, is profoundly disturbing to many people, precisely because it presents a revolutionary alternative to the prevailing erotophobic and heterosexist assessments of sexuality that prevail in many societies.

This chapter is not intended as the 'confessions' of an American in Brussels. Nor is it intended as a Foucauldian exercise in speaking about sex in relation to power, much less as a discourse on the love that dare not speak its name or a contribution to an epistemological breakthrough in anthropology. Rather, it is a simple plea for sexual openness and honesty as a way of exorcising the pernicious effects that silence has on sexual well-being in our own and many other cultures. 'Silence = Death' is not just an ACT-UP slogan; it is much broader than that. Power-dictated discourse on sex needs to be countered by a liberating discourse that is freely generated from within. Silencing discourse on sex, including discourse on the eroticism of ethnographers in the field, is a form of repression which must be confronted by an insistence on such discourse from below, on discourse that is not tied to the courts, to confirmation hearings for high officials, to reporters dealing with the sexual peccadilloes of political candidates, to sermons and papal edicts, or to the realms of medicine and psychiatry. What is needed is discourse from those for whom sex is positive and empowering; not dirty, deplorable, and dangerous.

We must learn to talk about sex, including our own sexuality, if we are to penetrate beneath the surface and demystify this phenomenon. In an era when sexual expression carries with it not only the most profound human pleasure but also the risk of the most devastating consequences, talking about sex honestly, unabashedly, and without shame is crucial (Reiss with Reiss 1990). And we must ask ourselves: What right do we have to enquire into the sex lives of Others, whether in our own culture or in some exotic distant realm, if we insist on our right to privacy, to remain silent about our own intimate lives?

Sexual secrecy undergirds and perpetuates sexual hypocrisy, in anthropology as well as in the larger culture of which we are a part. Sexuality, as an important component of our identities, is not something to leave unexamined, even though the risks of exposing such basic aspects of our being may be considerable. It is easier, of course, to deny the realities of sexuality and its place in our lives. Being open invites attacks from those who are ashamed or embarrassed about their own sexual 'secrets' and those who profit from the sexual status quo; witness televangelists railing against sex from the pulpit while also hiring prostitutes and having sex driving along the freeway. Sexual secrecy perpetuates interpretations of sex as dirty, degrading, and immoral. Openness is required because so many real problems, from

AIDS and other STDs to rape, sexual abuse, sexual harassment, teen pregnancies, and sexual dysfunctions of all kinds, are the unfortunate by-products of secrecy and sex-negativism. Talking about sex in the field is not just something we must do in order to get our own disciplinary house in order; it's something we need to do throughout our culture. If people can learn to talk about sex, they might learn how to have safer and more satisfying sex lives. We would all be better off. The issue of the sexuality of ethnographers in the field should force us to think about the larger questions – how we as individuals and as a discipline construct our sexual lives and our understandings of sexuality – and to rethink our fundamental assumptions about sexuality.

A rallying cry of the feminist movement has been the slogan, 'The personal is political'. To that notion should be added the acknowledgement that 'the personal is also professional'. With the survival of millions of gay men at stake and with gay culture – my culture – under siege, the boundaries between 'the personal', 'the political', and 'the professional' are necessarily obliterated. My primary identity is that of a gay man living in a time of crisis whose aim is to do what he can to make a contribution to ending the plague which afflicts his own community. My identity as an anthropologist depends heavily on the extent to which my training, knowledge, and experience in this discipline can assist me in this endeavor.

Notes

1 Honoring the widespread preference among women who have sex with women not to be included in a general category of 'gay', but instead to be called lesbian, I use the term 'gay' throughout this paper to refer to men who have sex with men, and 'gay community' to refer to the community of gay men. In the Brussels context, the gay and lesbian communities are quite separate, and women were not part of the community I studied, even though individual gay men may have counted some lesbians among their friends. The case is not always the same in other places. For example, in small towns such as Ostende, there is considerable interaction between gays and lesbians in public settings. But this was not the situation in Brussels, where lesbians were almost never present in the public scenes that I studied. Since I did not study the lesbian community, I am in no position to comment on lesbian life in Belgium.

In addition, I do not discuss the risks of contracting HIV that Belgian women face. I can note here, though, that in Belgium, women's risk of contacting HIV during heterosexual intercourse is incurred mainly in contacts with heterosexual males who are from Africa or who have lived in Africa, not from having sex with a man who has sex with men. I am not aware of any cases reported in the literature of any Belgian lesbian becoming infected as a result of sex with another woman.

2 Research suggests that the practice of safer sex has increased in recent years in Belgium, but risky sex, there as well as in many other gay communities, is still occurring at disappointing levels (Vincke and Bolton n.d.)

3 The dangers of relying on quantitative methodologies divorced from in-depth qualitative research have been discussed at length by Carrier and Bolton (1991), Parker and Carballo (1990) and Schoepf (1991).

4 My application was undoubtedly helped by a personal factor; the director was personally affected by the epidemic because a long-time family friend had been diagnosed with AIDS. How big a part this played in the approval of the application, I'll never know, but personal impact has been a major factor in taking the epidemic seriously. While in Belgium I managed to develop a partnership with two Belgian scientists, a sociologist (John Vincke) and a physician (Rudolf Mak), who were able to get Belgian government support for an ongoing research effort in the gay community (Bolton *et al.* 1992; Bolton and Vincke n.d.; Vincke *et al.* 1991, 1993a, 1993b).

5 The names of individuals (tricks, friends, and lovers) in Belgium as well as the names of bars, saunas, and hotels have been changed to ensure anonymity.

6 My sexual participation activities were not funded by the grant awarded to my Belgian colleagues for a survey of gay life; even though my qualitative data were useful in connection with studies produced under that grant, the two projects must be considered as separate. Nor was the Ministry of Public Health, with which I was affiliated during my Fulbright grant, nor any of its officials, nor the Fulbright Commission or any of its personnel privy in advance to the participatory aspects of my fieldwork. The Ministry did give me free rein to conduct investigations as I saw fit, with no oversight other than knowing that I was engaged in AIDs-related research while under their sponsorship.

7 Reports have reached me of ill-intentioned or badly informed colleagues spreading rumors that I engaged in unsafe sex in the field. Such allegations are categorically false. Not even with my long-term lovers in Belgium did I ever engage in risky sex. To do so would have violated my personal code of conduct and vitiated the goal of my research. I am aware of AIDS educators and researchers who fail to uphold this standard; it's how one fucks, not whom, that matters.

8 The texts of the observational investigations commissioned by Los Angeles public health authorities were used in judicial proceedings aimed at regulating or closing the bathhouses in that city. These documents have not been published, but I have obtained copies of these depositions.

9 Space limitations prevent me from discussing the methodological issues which might be raised concerning the interpretation of my data, particularly representativeness of the 'sample' and the 'objectivity' of an investigator who is sexually involved with the people he is studying.

10 In addition to the better known instances, referred to and discussed elsewhere in this volume, of anthropologists writing about sex in the field (e.g. Rabinow 1977; Cesara 1982), oblique references or coded allusions can be found in Wafer (1991), Williams (1986), and Read

(1986). More recently, Williams (1993) has written an article that is more forthcoming. Newton's (1993) remarkable account of love and erotic attraction does not include sex. Gay anthropologists often do not even disclose their sexual orientation, let alone hints about sexual contact, even when they are studying homosexual topics. The writings of Taylor (1993) and Murrray (in press; see also 1991) are exceptional in their frank acknowledgement of sexual involvement.

References

Allgeier, Elizabeth R. and Albert Richard Allgeier (1991) *Sexual Interactions*. 3rd edn. Lexington, Mass.: D.C. Heath.

Bolton, Ralph (1986) 'AIDS and Culture: The Case of Norway'. Paper presented at the annual meeting of the American Anthropological Association, Philadelphia.

——— (1992) 'Mapping Terra Incognita: Sex Research for AIDS Prevention – An Urgent Agenda for the 1990s', in Gilbert Herdt and Shirley Lindenbaum (eds) *The Time of AIDS: Social Analysis, Theory, and Method*. Newbury Park, Calif.: Sage.

——— (1994) 'Erotic Communitas: Sexual Encounters in Gay Saunas'. Paper presented at the Annual Meeting of the Society for Cross-Cultural Research, Santa Fe, February.

——— (in press, a) 'Rethinking Anthropology: The Study of AIDS', in Han Ten Brummelhuis and Gilbert Herdt (eds) *Culture and Sexual Risk*. New York: Gordon and Breach.

——— (in press, b) 'Coming Home: The Journey of a Gay Ethnographer in the Years of the Plague', in E. Lewin and W. Leap (eds) *Doing Lesbian and Gay Anthropology: Issues in Fieldwork and Ethnography.* Champaign: University of Illinois Press.

——— (in press, c) 'Sex Talk: Bodies and Behaviors in Gay Erotica', in William Leap (ed.) *Beyond the Lavender Lexicon: Authenticity, Imagination and Appropriation in Lesbian and Gay Languages*. New York: Gordon and Breach.

——— and John Vincke (n.d.) 'Risky Sex and Sexual Cognition: The Cartography of Eros among Flemish Gay Men. Unpublished manuscript.

———, John Vincke, and Rudolf Mak (1994) 'Gay Baths Revisited: An Empirical Analysis'. *GLQ: A Journal of Lesbian and Gay Studies*. Vol. 1, No. 3, pp. 255–73.

———, John Vincke, Rudolf Mak, and Ellen Dennehy (1992) 'Alcohol and Risky Sex: In Search of an Elusive Connection', in Ralph Bolton and Merrill Singer (eds) *Rethinking AIDS Prevention: Cultural Approaches*. New York: Gordon and Breach.

Brecher, Edward M. (1971) *The Sex Researchers*. New York: New American Library.

Bronski, Michael (1984) *Culture Clash: The Making of Gay Sensibility.* Boston, Mass.: South End Press.

Callen, Michael and Richard Berkowitz (1983) *How to Have Sex in an Epidemic: One Approach*. New York: News from the Front Publications.

Carrier, Joseph and Ralph Bolton (1991) 'Anthropological Perspectives on

Sexuality and HIV Prevention'. *Annual Review of Sex Research*. Vol. 2, pp. 49–75.

Cesara, Manda (1982) *Reflections of a Woman Anthropologist: No Hiding Place*. London and New York: Academic Press.

Crimp, Douglas (1988) 'How to Have Promiscuity in an Epidemic', in Douglas Crimp (ed.) *AIDS: Cultural Analysis/Cultural Activism*. Cambridge, Mass.: MIT Press.

Davis, Murray (1983) *Smut: Erotic Reality/Obscene Ideology*. Chicago: University of Chicago Press.

Dickemann, Mildred (1990) 'The Imperatives of Fieldwork: Impact on Non-Heterosexual Fieldworkers'. Paper presented at the Annual Meeting of the American Anthropological Association, New Orleans.

Gregor, Thomas (1985) *Anxious Pleasures: The Sexual Lives of an Amazonian People*. Chicago: Univeristy of Chicago Press.

Gullestad, Marianne (1992) *The Art of Social Relations: Essays on Culture, Social Action and Everyday Life in Modern Norway*. Oslo: Universitetsforlaget.

Herdt, Gilbert and Robert J. Stoller (1990) *Intimate Communications: Erotics and the Study of Culture*. New York: Columbia University Press.

Hocquenghem, Guy (1993) *Homosexual Desire*. Durham: Duke University Press (Original edn 1972.)

Hoffman, Valerie and Ralph Bolton (1993) 'Motivations for Sex Among Heterosexual Men'. *Abstracts of the IX International Conference on AIDS & HIV STD World Congress*, Berlin, Abstract No. PO C20-30681.

Holleran, Andrew (1988) *Ground Zero*. New York: New American Library.

Humphreys, Laud (1970). *Tearoom Trade: Impersonal Sex in Public Places*. Chicago: Aldine.

Kyle, Garland Richard (1992) *Whatever Happened to Passion? Writings from the Epidemic Years*. San Francisco: Modern Words.

Marshall, Patricia A. (1991) 'Research Ethics in Applied Medical Anthropology', in Carole E. Hill (ed.) *Training Manual in Applied Medical Anthropology*. Washington, D.C., American Anthropological Association.

——— (1992a) 'Ethical Issues in Anthropological Research on HIV Risk Behavior'. Paper presented at the Conference on Culture and Sexual Risk, Amsterdam, July.

——— (1992b) 'Research Ethics in Applied Anthropology'. *IRB: A Review of Human Subjects Research*. Vol. 14, No. 6, pp. 1–5.

Murray, Stephen O. (1991) 'Sleeping with the Natives as a Source of Data'. *Society of Lesbian and Gay Anthropologists Newsletter*. Vol. 13, No. 3, pp. 49–51.

——— (in press) 'Male Homosexuality in Guatemala: Possible Insights and Certain Confusions from Sleeping with the Natives', in E. Lewin and W. Leap (eds) *Doing Lesbian and Gay Anthropology: Issues in Fieldwork and Ethnography*. Champaign: University of Illinois Press.

Nardi, Peter, M. (1994) 'The Breastplate of Righteousness: 25 Years after *Tearoom Trade*'. Paper presented at the Annual Meeting of the Society for Cross-Cultural Research, Santa Fe, February.

Naroll, Raoul (1983) *The Moral Order: An Introduction to the Human Situation*. Beverly Hills, Calif.: Sage.

Newton, Esther (1993) 'My Best Informant's Dress: The Erotic Equation in Fieldwork'. *Cultural Anthropology*. Vol. 8, No. 1, pp. 3–23.

Parker, Richard (1991) *Bodies, Pleasures and Passions: Sexual Culture in Contemporary Brazil*. Boston, Mass.: Beacon Press.

——— and Manuel Carballo (1990) 'Qualitative Research on Homosexual and Bisexual Behavior Relevant to HIV/AIDS'. *The Journal of Sex Research*. Vol. 27, No. 4, pp. 497–525.

Pomeroy, Wardell B. (1972) *Dr Kinsey and the Institute for Sex Research*. New York: Harper and Row.

Proschan, Frank (1990) 'How is a Folklorist Like a Riddle?' *Southern Folklore*. Vol. 47, pp. 57–66.

Rabinow, Paul (1977) *Reflections on Fieldwork in Morocco*. Berkeley, Calif.: University of California Press.

Read, Kenneth (1986) *Return to the High Valley*. Berkeley, Calif.: University of California Press.

Reiss, Ira with H.M. Reiss (1990) *An End to Shame: Shaping Our Next Sexual Revolution*. Buffalo: Prometheus Books.

Schoepf, Brooke Grundfest (1991) 'Ethical, Methodological and Political Issues of AIDS Research in Central Africa'. *Social Science and Medicine*. Vol. 33, No. 7, pp. 749–63.

Society of Lesbian and Gay Anthropologists (1992) *Proposal to the American Anthropological Association for the Creation of a Task Force on Discrimination Against Lesbians and Gay Men in Anthropology*. Prepared by the Committee on Discrimination, E. Blackwood, chair.

Styles, J. (1979) 'Outsider/Insider: Researching Gay Baths'. *Urban Life*. Vol. 8, pp. 135–52.

Taylor, Clark L. (1993) 'Sex in the Mexican Baths', in Winston Leyland (ed.) *Gay Roots: An Anthology of Gay History, Sex, Politics and Culture*. Vol. 2. San Francisco: Gay Sunshine Press. (Originally published in *Gay Sunshine Journal*, Nos 29/30, 1976.)

——— and David Lourea (1992) 'HIV Prevention: A Dramaturgical Analysis and Guide to Creating Safer Sex Interventions', in Ralph Bolton and Merrill Singer (eds) *Rethinking AIDS Prevention: Cultural Approaches*. Philadelphia: Gordon and Breach.

Vance, Carole S. (ed.) (1984) *Pleasure and Danger: Exploring Female Sexuality*. Boston, Mass.: Routledge and Kegan Paul.

Vincke, John and Ralph Bolton (n.d.) 'Sexual Behavior Changes Among Gay Men in Flanders, Belgium, 1989–1993'. Unpublished manuscript.

———, Rudolf Mak, and Ralph Bolton (1991) *Mannen met Mannen: Welzijn, Relaties en Seksualiteit*. Ghent, Belgium: CGSO/AIDS Referentie Centrum Universiteit Gent.

———, Ralph Bolton, Rudolf Mak, and Susan Blank (1993a) 'Coming Out and AIDS-Related High-Risk Sexual Behavior'. *Archives of Sexual Behavior*. Vol. 22, No 6, pp. 559–86.

———, Rudolf Mak, Ralph Bolton, and Paul Jurica (1993b) 'Factors Affecting AIDS-Related Sexual Behavior Change among Flemish Gay Men'. *Human Organization*. Vol. 53, No. 3, pp. 260–8.

Wafer, J. (1991) *The Taste of Blood: Spirit Possession in Brazilian Candomble*. Philadelphia: University of Pennsylvania Press.

Wengle, John L. (1988) *Ethnographers in the Field: The Psychology of Research*. Tuscaloosa, Ala.: University of Alabama Press.

Williams, Walter, L. (1986) *The Spirit and the Flesh: Sexual Diversity in American Indian Culture*. Boston, Mass.: Beacon Press.

——— (1993) 'Being Gay and Doing Research on Homosexuality in Non-Western Cultures'. *The Journal of Sex Research*. Vol. 30, No. 2, pp. 115–20.

Chapter 6

My 'chastity belt'

Avoiding seduction in Tonga

Helen Morton

I was seven weeks pregnant when I began fieldwork for my doctorate. My family thought I was mad, and I hadn't dared tell my supervisors or anyone else in my university department. I chose to fall pregnant at that time for several reasons, but I think my subconscious wish was that the pregnancy, and the relationship with my Australian partner that it embodied, would anchor me to my life in Australia. My fieldsite was Tonga, a chain of tiny islands in the South Pacific. This chapter explores the ways in which my previous experiences in Tonga had made me need such an anchor, and examines the effects of my pregnancy on my fieldwork.

In this era of reflexivity in anthropology there is much talk of the 'cultural baggage' that fieldworkers take along with their notebooks, pens, and enthusiasm. Packed within this baggage are the preconceptions the anthropologist brings of the people to be studied.[1] These preconceptions have a significant impact on fieldwork, especially when they have been formed by prior associations with the society involved. Indeed, the extent and type of previous contact influence the entire process of fieldwork, including the preconceptions held about the anthropologist by her or his 'subjects', and therefore the treatment she or he receives. Working in a foreign yet familiar fieldsite can entail many of the same hazards and advantages experienced by 'indigenous anthropologists' returning to their own societies to carry out fieldwork.

In this, my own reflexive exercise, I hope to show why I needed to wear my pregnancy as a symbolic chastity belt to prevent myself from being seduced by this 'exotic' culture – as I had been nearly a decade before. To do so, I need to examine not only my experiences during fieldwork, but also my earlier times in Tonga, when the possiblity of doing a Ph.D. in anthropology had not yet entered my mind. Throughout all these experiences, sexuality was an ever-present element, even in its absence, just as in Tongan culture itself.

Embracing Tonga

My first visit to Tonga early in 1979 was a month-long holiday. I was dazzled and thrilled by the attention paid to me by the young Tongan men I encountered. At 18, blissfully ignorant of such matters as colonialism and neocolonialism, the struggles of Third World countries, and even sexual politics, I simply enjoyed the feeling that I was special, beautiful, and desirable to these immensely desirable young men.

Tongans, having never been formally colonized, have no colonial chip on their shoulders; indeed, they are intensely proud of their country's independence. They are quite ambivalent about 'Western' culture, desiring the 'development' (*fakalakalaka*) it brings yet wary of its effect on Tongan values and culture. Young males, however, are the least ambivalent and the most willing to embrace Westernization – increasingly so, in the context of land shortages and rising unemployment. For many of these young men, *pālangi* (white) women not only represent the desired culture but also a potential passport to a Western country. As well, they are seen as the antithesis of Tongan women, who are ideally modest, dignified, restrained, and sexually unavailable outside wedlock.

Four months after my holiday I returned to Tonga, having abruptly resigned my position as a cadet journalist and abandoned my belongings and the turmoil of my life. Like so many others, I had been seduced by a naive vision of an idyllic tropical paradise. In Nuku'alofa, capital of the main island, I found work and accommodation at a girls' college. When I remember that time, I cringe at the memory of my insensitivity to the significance of 'cultural difference'. I befriended a couple of other *pālangi* teachers and we behaved much as we would have done at home, personifying the negative Tongan stereotype of '*pālangi* women'. We drank, smoked, and swore, went out late at night, wore 'immodest' clothes, joined in male activities such as *kava* drinking, and generally behaved in a manner that was perceived as undignified and improper. In other words, we were everything that Tongan women were not supposed to be. We were not unaware of this, nor of the fact that our very difference made us desirable to many of the young men we met.

Not long after returning to Tonga I met a young man, a teacher at another high school, who had spent some time in Australia. We became lovers, and almost immediately he asked me to marry him. Later, when I was a little less naive, my friends and I would joke about the standard questions that we were asked on the dance floors of the local hotels: 'What is your name? . . . Where are you from? . . . Will you marry me?' When Siale asked me to marry him, I did not know that proposals of marriage would be so common: I thought it was True Love and accepted. One night I attended a party held by some Peace Corps men and my fiancé came and dragged me out and along the road to my house at the college. When he told me angrily that he would beat me if I went out drinking like that after we were married, I hastily called off our engagement.

At that time, there were two main venues in Nuku'alofa for night-time entertainment: the conservative International Dateline Hotel, and the down-market Joe's Hotel. We seldom went to dances at the Dateline, which were popular with tourists and elite and upwardly mobile Tongans. We preferred the dingy but lively Joe's, with its regular crowd of *fokisi* (female 'prostitutes'), *fakaleitī* (male transvestites), young Tongan men, American Peace Corps men, and a smattering of tourists, usually backpackers.[2] I don't think I even noticed the absence of ordinary Tongan women. Sometimes fights erupted that sent bottles and chairs flying, and customers scurrying out of the way. There was an undercurrent of sexual violence, too. One of my friends narrowly escaped being raped when she was attacked in the outside toilet, and I was manhandled and punched on the dance floor by a man I had earlier refused to dance with.

Some time after my relationship with Siale ended, I fell for Sione, bass guitarist in Joe's resident band. My physical attraction to him outweighed the fact that his English was not good and therefore we could not communicate well. Indeed, he was the epitome of all I found desirable in Tongan men – tall, muscular, handsome, and extremely charming.

The attraction to 'difference' that I mentioned above was not one-sided: for me, Tongan men were 'different' not only physically but in many other ways, such as their apparent self-assurance, their cheeky charm. I feel quite uncomfortable about that attraction now, with its possible overtones of racism. If 'sex in the field' has been a taboo topic, the intersecting questions of racial difference and racism have been even more rigorously avoided. The kinds of joke I heard later as a student – puns such as 'a bit of the Other', or humorous comments about the number of male anthropologists who returned from the field with 'native' wives – suggest that anthropologists are uneasy about these issues. One could take a hard line and argue that part of the colonialist heritage of anthropology is the desire to (sexually) possess the Other. Such desire is most commonly (or more openly) attributed to males, and it does seem far more common for men to 'take' women during fieldwork than vice versa (but cf. Cesara 1982).

The notion of 'otherness' in the ethnographic project is complicated by considerations of gender. As a woman I was effectively the Other in my own culture; moreover, 'Other' culturally constituted as inferior and subordinate. To the Tongan men I met, especially before I married, I was 'Other' as both woman and *pālangi*, but our relationships were far less overtly hierarchical: perhaps my dual statuses cancelled each other out. It seems to me that often the sexual relationships of white women in the field can less readily be dismissed as exploitive or conventionally racist than those of white men, whose position within patriarchal colonialism was and is less ambiguous. Yet the issue is surely more complex: after all, male and female anthropologists frequently choose their fieldsites out of an attraction to many aspects of another culture and out of a partial rejection of their own culture. If my attraction to some Tongan men can be construed as racism, then so can my strongly negative feelings at that time toward *pālangi* men.

My unease about my attraction to 'Tongan men' stems also from an awareness of the bias *against* them that I developed when my relationship with Sione broke down. My experience with Sione and my knowledge of some other Tongan men led me to feel cynical and distrustful of *all* Tongan men. When I returned to Tonga for fieldwork, time had considerably mellowed my views, but I retained a cautiousness that did impede my fieldwork in some respects, as I will show. However, this caution also served a purpose, as it was a mechanism that supported my wish to remain celibate at that time.

So, when Sione and I met we were both attracted to one another's 'difference'. Although I did not realize it at the time, Sione also saw me as a passport out of Tonga. I cannot begrudge him that, since for me he was a means of *staying in* Tonga. By this time I had begun to dread returning to Australia, where my life seemed so much more complicated and unhappy. At 19, I was at the tail end of an adolescence marked by rather extreme *Sturm und Drang*, and Tonga held the promise of a new life. I stopped using birth control, in a kind of superstitious challenge to fate, and soon fell pregnant. Sione and I were both delighted, and 'eloped' as soon as my pregnancy was confirmed.[3]

Our relationship until then had been fairly secretive, since my position at the girls' school necessitated discretion. I had only met Sione's family once, briefly, so they were shocked when we announced our marriage. His father's sister immediately locked herself in her room, weeping and praying.[4] It was not that I was a *pālangi* (Sione's sister had married an Australian), but the impropriety of our hasty nuptials that concerned them. As often happens after elopements, we attended church the following week in full Tongan wedding outfits, so that the family could acknowledge our marriage publicly. Unfortunately for me, the church nearest our home in Nuku'alofa was that used by the girls' college. I had to totter to the front of the church, wrapped in yards of fine mats, with the wide eyes of every girl upon me.

Sione's family also showed their acceptance of me in an unexpected way. When I returned home from teaching one afternoon only days after our wedding, I found our bedroom transformed. The walls were papered, a *tapa* cloth ceiling had been constructed, and even glass louvre windows and an iron four-poster bed had been installed. Before, the tiny room had been filthy, dark, and empty but for piles of Sione's clothing. The room was in a ramshackle hut that we shared with Sione's brother and his wife, and their two small children. On the same land was a large house, occupied by my husband's father, paternal aunt, sisters, and a sister-in-law and her five children.[5]

I gradually adapted to the physical conditions in which we lived: the poor diet, lack of electricity and running water, a hole-in-the-ground toilet, pigs sleeping under the hut, and assorted pests living in it. However, suddenly becoming an affinal member of a Tongan extended family, let alone a wife and mother-to-be, was tremendously difficult and I could not, would not, fully adjust. Many of the problems I faced are familiar to most fieldworkers – a complete lack of privacy, language problems, sudden acute longings for things familiar, and resentment at having to 'share' all one's belongings and income.[6] For the most part I muddled along, learning by trial and error, since my new family rarely offered advice or information and I (unlike a fieldworker!) was reticent about asking direct questions. The only direct advice I received concerned my pregnancy: the older women would occasionally tell me of food or behavioral restrictions that I should observe.[7]

As the wife of the youngest son I was at the bottom of the adult hierarchy. I was therefore expected to contribute my labor to the household, but my incompetence at many tasks made my load lighter than if I had been Tongan. Although I ate with the whole family and was obliged by my father-in-law to attend family worship on Sunday evenings, I did not develop more than a polite and mostly amicable relationship with them. I did befriend my husband's sister-in-law – our mutual status as outsiders drew us together – and I became very fond of her children. (The other sister-in-law returned to her natal village shortly after I moved in, while her husband was working as a ship's cook.)

My poor knowledge of Tongan was one of the greatest obstacles I faced, and it was very isolating and frustrating. I struggled through a book of language lessons but seldom put them into practice due to my shyness, and the tendency of all the Tongans I knew to laugh uproariously at my mistakes. I was never allowed to live down my use, on one occasion, of *falemalolo* (toilet) instead of *fakamolemole* (please).

My relationship with Sione was rocky, to say the least. I soon learned that Tongan men generally have a great deal more freedom of movement outside the home than do women, and that they frequently socialize separately from their spouses.[8] Sione did not want me to go to Joe's Hotel once I was a respectable married woman, and since he worked and socialized there all night, and slept or rehearsed during the day, we seldom saw each other. I also realized that the sexual double standards I was familiar with in Australia were far more marked in Tonga. Many men, especially younger men, have extramarital relationships, but wives are expected to remain chastely at home. Sione's infidelities were hard for me to accept. It was also difficult to accept that his first loyalty would always be with his own kin and that, like all Tongan men, his loyalty and obligations to his sisters outweighed those to his wife. Because he never explained such things, I continued to feel perplexed when he did not support me in the many covert battles I waged with one of my sisters-in-law. They were nearly always over trivial matters, such as use-rights of a kerosene stove I bought, but I sensed the deeper power struggle long before I knew that I represented a threat to her rights over her brother's 'goods and services'. Fortunately, Sione did support me on one crucial occasion, when she wanted to adopt our child and I refused.[9]

It was my advancing pregnancy that retained a strong bond between us despite our problems, and we were both delighted by the birth of our son. Giving birth to a child who was (and still is) accepted as 'a real Tongan' also helped me, for a while, to maintain my illusion of becoming more Tongan myself. When our baby was two months old, at the end of 1980, we moved to Australia. Sione told me that we would work for a couple of years to earn money to build a house in Tonga, but this plan was soon abandoned and he made it clear that we would not be returning. We lived, for the most part, with members of Sione's family and socialized almost exclusively with Tongan migrants. Many of the problems I had experienced in Tonga worsened, both in my marriage and in my attempts to adapt to *anga fakatonga* ('the Tongan way'). Personal and cultural differences are of course interrelated, but it was the latter that I largely blamed for the breakdown of our marriage.[10] With hindsight I place more emphasis on personal factors such as the brevity of our courtship, our immaturity, and, for me, the strain of living in a large, close family, having grown up in a two-person household. I expect that from the perspective of Sione and his family I was introverted, unfriendly and ungenerous. After eighteen months in Australia I left Sione, feeling deeply disillusioned, and took our son to live in another city. Not long afterwards I enrolled at university and commenced my degree in anthropology. I began studying academically the phenomenon of 'cultural difference' that had so fascinated and frustrated me during my marriage.

Return to 'paradise'

At the end of my undergraduate training in 1986 I returned to Tonga with my son for a two-month holiday, this time with a more anthropological eye. I also had a considerably more cynical view of Tongan men, and when I was the object of any amorous attention I no longer felt 'special'.[11] Contact had virtually ceased between myself and Sione and his family after our bitter separation. For several years my son had not seen his father, who had remarried. However, I had remained in contact with friends in a small village some twelve miles from Nuku'alofa, and we stayed with them while on holiday, and during my fieldwork in 1988. Apart from a brief formal visit we did not see my former affines during our holiday, but during fieldwork we stayed with them for two weeks, very amicably.

It was widely known in the village that I was now divorced, so it was assumed that I was there to find another Tongan husband. Despite my denials, the two main groups of unattached males in the village often hung around the house in which I was staying. One group was the village youths, aged around 16–18, on school holidays and thoroughly bored. One boy was related to the family I was staying with, and he often helped me with Tongan language lessons. His friends would join us and spend hours on mats under the trees in a giggling group, mock-fighting, joking, and generally vying for my attention. Their youth did not prevent them from flirting with me, and constantly putting on macho displays to impress me. One of them even boasted to me that they spent a lot of time in their 'gang house' watching European pornographic videos.[12] Since the other videos they watched tended to be martial arts films, I wondered what sort of image they had developed of *pālangi* women – and how they saw me.

The second group was made up of older men, in their twenties and thirties, who were un- or underemployed and spent much of their time drinking alcohol or *kava*. Many had worked overseas for periods, and some had been deported as overstayers. Early in our stay I acceded to my hosts' request to hold a *kava* evening, and most of the men who attended were from this group. In Tonga, *kava* drinking evenings are often an arena for courtship, with the unmarried men present courting the young woman chosen to mix and serve the *kava*. I knew this and was quite reluctant to take on the role, but felt I could not refuse without causing offense. It was a long night, listening to their ribald jokes and lengthy courting songs. They rarely addressed me directly, and when they did they were mildly flirtatious but polite. Yet as the only female present and as the subject of their jokes, comments, and songs, and the focus of their gazes, I felt for most of the night as uncomfortable as if I had been sitting there naked.

These men became a frequent, slightly menacing presence. On the bus to town two or three would sit behind me, touching my shoulders and hair and whispering in my ear – usually lines from American songs of the 'Ooh baby I love you', 'Trust me, baby' genre. Or they would make loud jokes and comments, to the amusement of the other passengers. They were undeterred by my female companions scolding them, or, as on one occasion, hitting them with an umbrella. At home they would linger outside at night, calling to me to come out. One persistent fellow stood at the open front door to 'chat me up' one night, and when I went to my bedroom to escape him he simply moved to the bedroom window and continued to talk.

Much of their speech to me took the form of jocular comments, so it was hard to justify my annoyance and, at times, fear of these men. However, in all of my encounters with the single young men of the village I felt helpless in my inability to deal with the situation appropriately. I was always worried that if I expressed my irritation I would offend one of my hosts or friends, since many of the men were their relatives. I was also afraid of what could happen if I made the men hostile, as I had often witnessed the violence induced by alcohol and sexual jealousy. I knew that sexual assaults were not uncommon, despite the fact that women seldom go about alone at night, and unmarried women are 'chaperoned' at all times by children or other women. Occasionally the feeling that I was being watched grew oppressive enough for me to escape into town.

I never felt comfortable engaging in the kind of banter that occurred between Tongan men and women, which was frequently sexual. Such banter occurs in many contexts and the participants may be acquaintences or strangers.[13] I felt particularly uneasy with 'street remarks' (Gardner 1984), public comments by men I did not know, since my own socialization led me to interpret them as expressions of male power to which my 'appropriate' response was silence and restraint. Apart from my own inhibitions, knowing that I was perceived as fundamentally different to Tongan women made me unsure how my attempts to respond would be construed. Not that I was not encouraged by my friends: on one occasion during fieldwork, for example, when I was talking about how the young men in town sometimes called out comments to me, my female friend laughed and advised me to poke my backside towards them and retort, 'Speak to me here!'[14] I never quite worked up the courage to do so! There was also the language problem, as I never felt that my Tongan was fluent enough to engage in the complex punning and double-entendre that so much joking entailed. The most I would do was smile and laugh, look uncomfortable or cross, or pretend not to understand. What really annoyed me was my own reluctance to handle the situation as would a Tongan woman.

Tongan women deal with men's joking by returning the banter and often by being quite aggressive: hitting, punching, or pushing the men, laughing all the while. I have shown elsewhere that a great deal of Tongan discourse is humorous, with joking, teasing, and banter being frequently employed in everyday conversation (Morton forthcoming; and see Bernstein 1983). Since in most contexts it is regarded as improper to express strong emotions openly, except joy and happiness, humor is a useful device for maintaining a light and pleasant tone in social relations. It is used as an alternative to expressing anger directly (though it may entail mock-aggression, as above), or as a means of diluting or deflecting the effects of anger that has already been expressed. Angry speech is typically followed by joking and laughter, restoring the all-important social harmony. Much of the humor employed is sexual or scatalogical, so that there is a pervasive element of sexuality that contrasts sharply with the absence of public displays of heterosexual intimacy.[15]

In spite of the unwanted attentions of some of the men of the village, I enjoyed my holiday. We had beach picnics, we joined the village's

Christmas and New Year celebrations, and my son became an expert tree climber, pig-chaser, and mischief-maker. By the end of the two months part of me had fallen back in love with Tonga, and I was fantasizing about a more permanent return. As with all holiday romances, however, returning home brought me down to earth. I felt unsure of my ability to cope with actually living in Tonga – a legacy of my failed marriage. Besides, I was happy in Australia and enjoying life as a university student. I continued my studies and after my Honors year moved to the Australian National University in Canberra to begin my doctorate.

Inevitably, perhaps, I chose to carry out my fieldwork in Tonga. There were the practical advantages of familiarity with the country and language, and established contacts. More important was my sense of continuing connection to Tonga through my son, and my desire to try to comprehend the culture that had previously both seduced and confounded me. I am sure this desire has been shared by many an ethnographer: it makes even more cogent the anthropological maxim that in knowing the Other we come to know ourselves.[16]

Fieldwork: completing the cycle

Which brings me back, at last, to my 'need' to be pregnant when I left for the field in 1988. On reflection, I think that as well as my great desire to have another child, I wanted the pregnancy to be a statement of my unavailability to Tongan men, and a reminder to myself of my ties to Australia. Wengle has argued:

> An anthropologist's self-imposed celibacy can help him [*sic*] preserve his sense of identity by forcing him to direct his probably acute sexual needs and fantasies outside of the field environment and back to his home culture.
>
> (1988: 25)

This seems a particularly masculine account, placing sexual needs foremost. Apart from 'sexual needs and fantasies', there are many aspects of emotional attachment that celibacy functions to channel homeward. From a female perspective, celibacy, when translated into a local reputation of sexual unavailability, can also be a powerful distancing mechanism that *may* help prevent sexual assault. The decision to remain celibate may also be simply pragmatic, since it is the only certain form of birth control.

Nevertheless, it does seem clear that if sex is seen as the ultimate intimacy, and therefore as a loss of self, celibacy does function to retain a private part of the self. This self-imposed celibacy may be less difficult to maintain when the fieldworker has a partner (husband/wife/lover) in the 'home culture'. Although this was the case for me, I knew only too well how easily I could be seduced by the Tongan lifestyle. Time had mellowed my bitter feelings about my marriage, enough for me to have had a brief relationship with a Tongan man in Australia not long after my Tongan holiday in 1986. I retained my cynicism and distrust but I was aware that I still found some Tongan men physically attractive. Although I never consciously thought of it as such, being pregnant in the field was an effective means of preventing a double seduction.

As it happened, my pregnancy did keep me bound to my life in Australia. A few days after I arrived in Tonga, I wrote in my journal: 'I wonder how John [my partner in Australia] is? Is he missing me too? It already all seems so unreal – I'm so glad I'm pregnant, to tie me to reality.' Three months later, after moving in with my former in-laws for a brief stay, I wrote: 'I'm really not very brave, or good at adapting, but I'm not falling apart yet! It feels so reassuring to have Paul [my son] beside me, baby in my belly, and John loving me, from afar.' My pregnancy gave me a tangible and powerful tie to my partner; perhaps too strong a tie. Keeping myself connected to home in this way meant that I never immersed myself as fully as I might have in life in Tonga. This increased the 'distancing' that is generally part of the ethnographic project and which I found balanced the intense but confused engagement I had previously experienced. Knowing that I was observing, in order to interpret and analyze, also prevented me from being entirely egocentric. During my marriage even the ubiquitous question '*Alu ki fe*?' (Where are you going?), a simple greeting equivalent to our 'How are you?', had become an infuriating invasion of privacy.

Although having a partner waiting at home can make it easier to remain celibate in the field, the intense focusing of sexual and other fantasies onto that person can lead to an idealization that creates problems during and after fieldwork. I argued earlier that celibacy enables the fieldworker to avoid the loss of self that sexuality entails. Yet I would argue further that in focusing one's fantasies onto a specific person 'at home', there is a corresponding or even greater loss of self, at least potentially. A sexual relationship with someone 'in the field' may entail a temporary 'loss of self', but it is real and immediate. The idealized, increasingly imaginary relationship with the partner at home can even involve a feeling that part of oneself is absent. ('My heart is with John in Australia.') Tangible tokens of that relationship, such as letters, assume enormous significance and are relied upon to reaffirm one's identity. For example, if there is any problem with communication – the letters are not frequent enough, or they lead to misunderstandings – it can have a profound effect on the fieldworker's functioning on all levels. When the only communication I had from John for many weeks was a brief note that led me to believe (wrongly) that we would not be able to live together immediately after my return, I wrote in my journal that his note had 'turned everything upside down . . . I feel so much less secure and sure . . . I really need to know where I stand.'

Idealization of one's partner and fantasies about life with him or her after fieldwork can also exacerbate the 'reverse culture-shock' experienced on returning home. Wengle has claimed that 'to experience reverse culture-shock, a person must have experienced some degree of secondary identification with the foreign culture' (1988: 32). However, if what Wengle would call one's 'primary identity', that associated with the home culture, has been radically altered and distorted by the fantasies centered on the partner, then 'reverse culture-shock' can occur even without such 'secondary identification' having developed. Indeed, the imagined future life can in itself become a kind of 'secondary identification'. Anecdotal evidence from colleagues suggests that such reverse culture-shock has often contributed to the breakdown of relationships.

When John came to Tonga for our daughter's birth, the shock began the moment he stepped off the aircraft and did not even seem to *look* like the man I had been fantasizing about. He returned to Australia a week after the birth, and in the two weeks before the children and I joined him I eagerly revived my fantasies, telling myself the past few unhappy weeks had been an aberration caused by hormones and the strain of finishing off my fieldwork. Sadly, I was wrong. When our daughter was seven months old we finally separated.

My pregnancy had also produced some unanticipated effects on my research. For my fieldwork, I returned to the village in which I had stayed in 1986–7, and again people assumed that, pregnant or not, I was on the look-out for a Tongan husband. Because I was pregnant and unmarried, it was also assumed that I had 'run away' to Tonga in shame. To my dismay, no one in the village ever really believed that I was there as a serious researcher. I was already too deeply embedded in their own social categories – as a Tongan man's ex-wife, as mother of a 'real Tongan boy', as ex-teacher, as friend, and so on. This was also the case in Nuku'alofa, where Sione's family lived, and where it sometimes seemed that every second person knew of our divorce and wanted to offer an opinion.[17] People still allowed me to interview them, compile genealogies, do household surveys, etc., but I could not help feeling they were just humoring me. Of course, this familiarity also had a great many advantages in terms of 'participant observation', but either way, it profoundly influenced my fieldwork. Being pregnant also lent a sense of urgency to my fieldwork, as I knew I could not (or would not) continue after the baby was born.

As my pregnancy became visible, and word spread that I did indeed have a *de facto* husband in Australia, I was increasingly accepted as a married woman. The single men of the village did not court me and I was not asked to host *kava* evenings or go to dances. I found that my pregnancy made me feel safer and more confident around men, even though it did not render me entirely 'off limits'. I felt no fear of sexual assault when I lived in Nuku'alofa toward the end of my pregnancy, and I often walked alone along the sea-front in the cool of the evenings. The groups of young men who sometimes gathered there to talk and drink beer still called out jokes and comments to me even when I was hugely pregnant ('Hey, baby, come over with us!'), but I did not feel embarrassed or threatened as I would have done ordinarily.

The women of the village acknowledged my social repositioning by treating me more as their equal. Because my 'husband' was not Tongan, my status as an outsider was more fully restored. During my fieldwork, my relationships with the Tongan women I encountered were quite different from before, since my perception of them had also been transformed. When I was married I had seen 'Tongan women' as generally threatening, either as sexual rivals or as superiors within the family hierarchy. The politics of family and school had kept me wary of most women who could have been friends and allies. Fieldwork was therefore very rewarding in terms of my associations with other women. Contributing to my changing perception was, of course, my own development, and I was certainly a far less inhibited, more confident woman in 1988 than I had been when I first 'ran away' to Tonga. I found I was able to engage more openly with the women I met and did not baulk at intimacy as before, as when women touched my belly, or held my hand when out walking.

I did experience problems dealing with some Tongan men, to the detriment of my fieldwork, though this was largely unaffected by my pregnancy. I found that often, when I was accepted by males (young and old) as a serious researcher, they were nervous and reticent, but when I was perceived only as a *pālangi* woman they were flirtatious, jocular, and confident – but still unwilling to answer questions. Males on their own were more likely to take me seriously; with anyone else present this seemed impossible and the brash machismo would reappear as if to cover their embarrassment. One way in which I successfully circumvented this problem was by visiting high schools and administering questionnaires that enabled the students to write open-ended, anonymous comments.[18]

Speaking to males alone did not always prove successful, as when a couple of the married men I knew well unexpectedly switched from serious interviewing to flirting and overt sexual advances. In any case, I was wary of spending much time with men since it was likely to make their wives jealous and resentful. I had learned during my previous visits to Tonga that some women resented me talking in depth with their husbands. This was especially so when the man wanted to speak with me in English and his wife could not follow our conversations; in these cases the men had lived overseas for varying periods of time. This was not a major problem because I was more interested in associating with women anyway, as 'informants' – as childbearers and major caregivers – and as friends, but my limited work with men still represented a 'gap' in my work.

Conclusion: a structuralist's dream?

Carrying out fieldwork in a culture that was already so familiar to me made me very aware of the rapid changes it was undergoing. I felt that to a certain extent Tonga and I had moved closer together: I had learned to be more 'culturally sensitive' and was thus properly behaved, modestly dressed, and so on, and at the same time Tongan society had become more Westernized. Younger people, particularly, had begun to question many of the conservative attitudes toward dress, sexuality, and gender-appropriate behavior that had been prevalent a decade earlier.

Certainly, my previous familiarity with Tongan culture was a tremendous asset in my fieldwork, in many ways. Yet my experiences in Tonga and with Tongans in Australia had made me overly cautious. Instead of being open to all possibilities (the ideal fieldwork condition?) I approached my fieldwork warily, with ambivalent feelings and many preconceptions. My pregnancy – my pre-conception – helped me to deal with this to some extent, though it caused its own interesting problems, as I have shown. My concern to avoid seduction, by Tongan culture and/or Tongan men, stemmed from my wish to retain my 'self' as it was just before I left for the field. Fieldwork was a means to an end, not the intense and all-absorbing experience that it is often claimed to be. I had already undergone the painful identity crisis, 'cognitive clashing', and 'death of self' that involvement with another culture can precipitate (see Wengle 1988), and had no desire to repeat the process. I will never know what would have happened during my fieldwork if I had not previously been to Tonga and married a Tongan, or if I had not had a partner in Australia and been pregnant in the field. As with most other ethnographers, I suspect, my reflections on fieldwork are filled with 'what ifs'.

All of my experiences in Tonga obviously have been greatly affected by my gender. Personal circumstances are crucial too: my decision to arrive in the field already pregnant is not one that many women would choose to make. However, the fact that most women *could* choose to become pregnant, or that they may avoid sexual relations in the field for fear of pregnancy, means that we share a particular, gendered perspective on fieldwork. Similarly, women are far more vulnerable to threatened or actual sexual violence, and this may have a profound influence on their work and personal life in the field. Another 'what if' question I have often pondered is 'What if I had been male?' – a question I suspect many women have asked themselves in similar circumstances.

My story has a happy ending. Nearly two years after we separated, when I had finished writing my thesis, John and I married and I was soon, much to our surprise, pregnant with our second daughter. Finishing my thesis meant that I completed the cycle begun a decade earlier; it enabled me finally to accept my 'primary identity' and to forge a new, 'real' relationship with John. When I went to Tonga in 1979 my relationship with Sione, and my pregnancy, enabled me to avoid living in Australia and signalled a desire to lose myself in Tongan culture. Despite my willingness, cultural difference became something threatening and incomprehensible. Returning to Australia and realizing I could never *be* Tongan left me confused, with many unanswered questions. Later events can be interpreted as a neat structural reversal: my pregnancy tied me to Australia and *prevented* an identification with Tonga, and my fieldwork and subsequent thesis fulfilled my need to try more actively to comprehend the culture that I had failed to embrace.

It is interesting that it was in the process of obtaining anthropological knowledge that I felt, and, I think it is safe to say, many other anthropologists feel, that sexual relations seem inappropriate, taboo. There appears to be a dichotomy posed between lived experience in another society, when close identification with the culture allows for sexual relationships, and the distanced, academic process of understanding, with engagements with the culture determined largely by the agenda of the specific research project. This distinction inevitably becomes blurred, because anthropologists who have remained in the field for long periods often claim to become so personally immersed in the culture that they begin to understand in the 'real' sense of lived experience (see Hirschkind 1991; Jacobs 1991).

My own case upended this whole process, since I began by immersing myself in Tongan life, expecting my sexual relationship to facilitate my understanding (assuming, as in my own culture, that 'love conquers all'). Although I left my marriage feeling baffled by 'Tongan culture', I had unwittingly absorbed a great deal of knowledge that would later make sense. For example, it was not until I began to read anthropological accounts of Tongan kinship that the tense triangular relationship between myself, my husband, and his sisters became comprehensible. For me the supposedly distinct threads of knowledge attained through 'lived experience' and academic research have become woven together into a seamless personal narrative – my own 'partial truth'.

Acknowledgements

Warmest thanks to Don Kulick and Margaret Willson for their editorial support. Don's perceptive questions helped me to undergo the often painful but rewarding self-analysis that resulted in the final version of this chapter.

Notes

1 For a useful survey of relexive anthropology, see Tedlock (1991). Also see Clifford and Marcus (1986).

2 'Prostitute' is an innacurate gloss for *fokisi* (lit.: fox), as the category includes women of 'bad reputation', who do not receive payment for sexual services. *Fakaleitī* (lit.: like a lady) or *fakafāfine* (like a woman) openly dress and behave as women. They include hetero-, bi-, and homosexual men.

3 Elopement (*mali hola*) is a very common form of marriage in Tonga. Often, when the families have reconciled themselves to the marriage a proper ceremonial marriage is performed or, as in our case, the couple attends church in full Tongan wedding outfits to reveal their married state publicly.

4 The father's sister, or *mehekitanga*, commands respect and obedience, and can have considerable influence over her *fakafotu* (brother's children), including their choice of spouse.

5 In Tonga, cross-sex siblings (real and classificatory) have a respect/avoidance relationship, in which sisters and their children are 'chiefly' (of higher status) in relation to brothers and their children. A number of *tapu* (prohibitions) pertain to this relationship, which act to separate brothers spatially from sisters, and preclude too much familiarity between them. Although these *tapu* are weakening in modern Tonga,

one of the more persistent is that in which brothers should not sleep under the same roof as sisters after they reach about ten years of age. Boys have separate sleeping huts, or sleep in the hut used as a kitchen.

6 Accounts by Calkins (1971) and Varawa (1990) of their marriages to a Samoan and Fijian respectively reveal very similar difficulties. Although marred by a certain amount of 'noble savage' imagery (in Varawa's case juxtaposed with the image of Fijians as 'ex-cannibals'), both accounts make fascinating reading.

7 Tongan women observe a number of food taboos, based on principles of 'sympathetic magic': for example, eating octopus will cause the infant to be born with spots on its limbs. Minor behavioral restrictions are also followed, such as not cutting meat for fear of damaging the fetus. The number of such *tapu* and the care with which they are observed are diminishing today.

8 A great deal of gender socialization in Tonga centres on the notion that 'boys go, girls stay'. This extends to a perception of males as more independent.

9 It is quite common in Tonga for sisters to ask for a brother's child to raise. The mother's ability to refuse is influenced by her husband's wishes and the views of the parents' families. It is also common for other relatives to adopt or foster children.

10 One aspect of specifically cultural differences that I found troubling was notions of childrearing, especially discipline. I eventually wrote my doctoral dissertation on Tongan child socialization as a direct result of this early concern (Morton forthcoming).

11 See Cowling (1988) for some poems by another anthropologist who has worked in Tonga, which express something of the same cynicism.

12 In many villages there are huts used by adolescent boys for sleeping and socializing (see n. 5). Influenced by American movies these groups often style themselves as 'gangs', with names such as 'Revenge of the Black Power' ('RBP'). Videos have become extremely popular in recent years in Tonga.

13 When cross-sex siblings are present, conversations are more polite and restrained. If a man swears or makes improper jokes in front of another man's sister it can even lead to violence, as the brother defends his sister's honor. 'Men' and 'women' here include adolescents.

14 Presenting the buttocks (clothed, or, on rare occasions, naked) is a form of insult associated with anger, hostility, derision, or rivalry, but which is performed humorously.

15 Affection is publicly displayed between same-sex friends, and between people of all ages with young children. Physical contact between people of the opposite sex is in public usually restricted to the kind of mock-aggressive pushing, hitting, and so on mentioned above.

16 However problematic this notion has become (cf. Mascia-Lees *et al.* 1989), it continues to be a significant element of the anthropological endeavor.

17 This was also very difficult for my son, particularly since many of the comments offered about my ex-husband were very critical. The entire fieldwork experience was very trying for Paul, who had his own identity crisis to deal with. For some accounts of fieldwork with children see Butler and Turner (1987) and Whitehead and Conaway (1986).

18 I found that adolescent girls were either reticent or giggly, and again I had difficulty talking with any but those I came to know well. The questionnaire proved far more successful than I had anticipated; in a society in which children and youths are rarely able to voice their opinions and critical thinking is discouraged, most students eagerly took this opportunity to be open and forthcoming, with some most interesting results (see Morton forthcoming).

References

Bernstein, Louise (1983) '*Ko e Lau Pe* (It's Just Talk)': Ambiguity and Informal Social Control in a Tongan village. Ph.D. thesis, University of California, Berkeley.

Butler, Barbara and Diane Turner (eds) (1987) *Children and Anthropological Research*. New York: Plenum.

Calkins, Fay (1971) *My Samoan Chief*. Honolulu: University of Hawaii Press. (Original edn 1962.)

Cesara, M. (1982) *Reflections of a Woman Anthropologist: No Hiding Place*. London and New York: Academic Press.

Clifford, James and George E. Marcus (eds) (1986) *Writing Culture: The Poetics and Politics of Ethnography*. Berkeley, Calif.: University of California Press.

Cowling, Wendy (1988) 'Poems from a Tongan Sequence'. *Canberra Anthropology*. Vol. 11, No. 2, pp. 64–9.

Gardner, Carol Brooks (1984) 'Passing By: Street Remarks, Address Rights, and the Urban Female', in J. Baugh and J. Sherzer (eds) *Language in Use: Readings in Sociolinguistics*. Englewood Cliffs, N.J.: Prentice Hall.

Hirschkind, Lynn (1991) 'Redefining the "Field" in Fieldwork'. *Ethnology*. Vol. 30, No. 3, pp. 237–49.

Jacobs, S.-E. (1991) 'The Predicament of Sincerity: From Distance to Connection in Long-term Fieldwork'. *International Journal of Moral and Social Studies*. Vol. 6, No. 3, pp. 237–45.

Mascia-Lees, Frances E., Patricia Sharpe, and Colleen Ballerino Cohen (1989) 'The Postmodernist Turn in Anthropology: Cautions from a Feminist Perspective'. *Signs: Journal of Women in Culture and Society*. Vol. 15, No. 1, pp. 7–33.

Morton, Helen (forthcoming) *Becoming Tongan: an Ethnography of Childhood*. Honolulu: University of Hawaii Press.

Tedlock, Barbara (1991) 'From Participant Observation to the Observation of Participation: The Emergence of Narrative Ethnography'. *Journal of Anthropological Research*. Vol. 47, No. 1, pp. 69–93.

Varawa, Joanna McIntyre (1990) *Changes in Latitude: An Uncommon Anthropology*. London: Andre Deutsch.

Wengle, John (1988) *Ethnographers in the Field: The Psychology of Research*. Tuscaloosa, Ala: University of Alabama Press.

Whitehead, Tony Larry and Mary Ellen Conaway (eds) (1986) *Self, Sex and Gender in Cross-cultural Fieldwork*. Urbana and Chicago: University of Illinois Press.

Chapter 7

Fear and loving in the West Indies

Research from the heart (as well as the head)

Jean Gearing

Sociocultural anthropology is unique in requiring graduate students to conduct lengthy, qualitative research or 'fieldwork' in another culture.[1] Fieldwork is the prescribed rite of passage that must be successfully negotiated before the doctoral student is recognized as fully professional; fieldwork transforms the neophyte into a 'real' anthropologist (Johnson 1984; Tedlock 1991: 67–70). Because of its central place in the identity of the discipline, it is not surprising that the impact of fieldwork upon the identity of the fieldworker, and vice versa, is the subject of intense scrutiny at a time when anthropology is questioning its definition as a discipline. Nor, considering the secrecy which customarily surrounds all rites of passage, is it remarkable that it has taken anthropologists so long to examine their own identifying experiences critically and publicly (DeVita 1990; Tedlock 1991).

The introspective analysis of the anthropological endeavor has been prompted by critics from a variety of perspectives, including postmodernism, feminism, and postcolonialism.[2] While these perspectives overlap and influence each other, it is possible to isolate and discuss the salient themes of each. While all of these critics have mounted parallel arguments against the myth of the dispassionate, detached, scientific observer, the postmodernist perspective has focused more on ethnographies as written representations of culture that obscure authorial power (Clifford 1986; Clifford and Marcus 1986; Geertz 1988; Marcus and Cushman 1982). Postmodernist anthropologists adhere to the interpretivist model of cultural anthropology, and describe fieldwork as a dialogic process between ethnographer and those studied. The postmodern approach recommends new, experimental styles of writing ethnography that give voice to both the ethnographer and the interpreted in the text, and that therefore constitutes more accurate representations of cultural interpretations (Crapanzano 1980; Dwyer 1982; Favret-Saada 1980; Marcus and Fischer 1986). Postmodern writers have been criticized for leaping over the context of anthropological practice, the stages of fieldwork and analysis, to focus exclusively on writing and analyzing texts (D'Amico-Samuels 1991; Delany 1988; Mascia-Lees *et al.* 1989; Newton 1993; Spencer 1989). However, one of the postmoderns, Paul Stoller has argued forcefully and eloquently for 'the benefits of grounding our theoretical ruminations in descriptive ethnography' (1989: 9), an ethnography, moreover, that stresses the importance of sensual experience in observing, recording, and analyzing ethnographic information. (See also Altork's contribution to this volume.)

Feminist and postcolonialist anthropologists have taken a more holistic approach to the criticism and reconstruction of anthropology. They have addressed the issues of androcentric and Eurocentric biases in the choice of research topics and informants, in methods of conducting research, and in writing ethnographies. The feminist perspective has argued for deconstructing the researcher as a whole human being, complete with biases and prejudices, thoughts and feelings, perceptions and sensations, fears and ambitions; an historic person[3] who is engaged interactively with those being researched (Mascia-Lees *et al.* 1989). Feminist researchers have pioneered new methodologies and new forms of representation (Cesara 1982; Farganis 1989; Harding 1987; Myerhoff 1978; Shostak 1981).

The postcolonialist perspective stresses the importance of acknowledging the existence and the ethnographic effects of the disparities of power and status between ethnographers and the typically poor, disenfranchised, 'Third World' peoples that they study (Bourgois 1991; D'Amico-Samuels 1991; Harrison 1991a, b; Johnson 1984; Whitehead 1986). Postcolonialist, feminist, and postmodernist anthropologists all suggest that anthropological knowledge, or what we believe we know, emerges from interaction and our inevitably value-laden analysis of it, rather than existing independently of human agency. All of these perspectives encourage more reflexivity in our written representations, although feminist and postcolonialist researchers are more explicit about their political aims and the necessity of involving those studied in the research process (D'Amico-Samuels 1991; Delany 1988; Harrison 1991b; Farganis 1989; Mascia-Lees *et al.* 1989; Newton 1993). To understand the 'Other' better we must first understand our contribution to the fieldwork encounter better, and second, we must explore the context of the encounter in all its human intersubjectivity (Tedlock 1991: 71).

It is revealing that in our attempts to attain a deeper understanding, some domains of our own subjectivity, as well as some interactions with those we study, remain obscured. For most of us, sexuality plays an immensely important role in our sense of self-identity, and yet sex in the field remains a tabooed topic, addressed metaphorically if at all (Crapanzano 1980; Mascia-Lees *et al.* 1989; Newton 1993). Who we are, as gendered and sexual persons, affects how we respond and how others respond to us, even in non-sexual contexts (Whitehead and Conaway 1986). The issue of sexuality, and sexual involvement with the 'Other', raises troubling questions of partiality, of vulnerability, of loss of control, of loss even of the self, all of which make it difficult to maintain a position of authority, and thus power, vis-à-vis one's research (Newton 1993). But if we are serious about examining ourselves as researchers, we must grapple with the impact of our sexuality on our fieldwork.

Esther Newton recently posed a question: 'Is all this [romantic yearning to know the Other] totally sublimated in field notes and language learning only to emerge in texts as a metaphor for the "heroic quest by the single anthropologist," or does the erotic ever make a human gesture?' (1993: 4). In my case, the erotic dimension was much more than a mere gesture, it was the most significant aspect of my fieldwork. In this chapter, I will explore how two aspects of sexuality, my intimate relationship with my best informant, whom I married, and the omnipresent threat of sexual violence in my fieldsite, influenced and informed my work on gender and sexuality in the West Indies. I am using the term 'sexual violence' to refer to violence and the threat of violence directed against women because of their gender or their participation in a sexual relationship; my discussion is limited to rape and sexual harassment, because of their personal applicability.

In choosing to write about both my love affair and sexual violence, I am attempting to explore what Carole Vance described as:

> The tension between sexual danger and sexual pleasure . . . Sexuality is simultaneously a domain of restriction, repression, and danger as well as a domain of exploration, pleasure, and agency. To focus only on pleasure and gratification ignores the patriarchal structure in which women act, yet to speak only of sexual violence and oppression ignores women's experience with sexual agency and choice.
>
> (1984: 1)

In this chapter, I hope to present a balanced picture that reflects my experience as a woman, and in addressing the issues of fear of sexual assault and sexual involvements in the field, I hope to help illuminate the patriarchal structures which operate in both the professional lives and the fieldsites of women anthropologists.

Going to the field

I lived in St. Vincent from 1983 until 1985, while doing research for my doctoral dissertation on women and migration (Gearing 1988). St. Vincent is a small island located in the lower Eastern Caribbean with a total population of about 100,000, of largely African and mixed African and European descent, with small groups of Amerindian, European, Asian, and Middle Eastern ethnics. There is a small but powerful upper class consisting of approximately 2 per cent of the population, a middle class comprising 10 per cent, and the lower class, the 88 per cent majority. The primary languages spoken are an English Creole and Standard West Indian English. St. Vincent became a British possession in the late eighteenth century, and enjoyed a brief heyday as a prosperous sugar colony socially structured by plantation slavery, until Emancipation in 1834 and the collapse of the West Indian sugar market in the 1850s. For the next 125 years, St. Vincent remained a British colony and associated state, a relatively quiet backwater of the empire, becoming an independent nation only in 1979. St. Vincent, like many other West Indian islands, is today an agrarian society heavily dependent on remittances sent home by migrants to sustain its economy.

I chose St. Vincent on the basis of historical and demographic criteria, and on the recommendation of several friends who had travelled or done work there. I had never visited the island, but took great comfort in my friends' comments that St. Vincent was beautiful and its inhabitants very friendly, especially toward Americans. Shortly before I left the United States, however, an older colleague of mine warned me to be careful about my personal safety, and told me that two Peace Corps Volunteers had been raped on St. Vincent within recent months. He cautioned me quite seriously that I would be especially vulnerable as a white American woman, because West Indian men perceived us as being the ultimate in sexual desirability and as sexually promiscuous.[4] Thus, even before entering the field, I was wary, frightened, and concerned. I wondered: did Vincentian women also fear sexual violence? What part did sexual violence play in the dynamics of female–male relationships in St. Vincent? How would Vincentians, men and women, regard me, as a white American woman, and how would their perceptions affect my fieldwork?

Almost immediately upon my arrival on the island, I was advised by one of my initial Vincentian contacts that the guest house I had planned to stay in while conducting preliminary research was unsafe: another female researcher staying there had been assaulted in her rooms. I relocated to a more expensive, but still moderately priced, hotel in the capital. Two days later, one of the customs officers from the airport, who had met me when I arrived in the country, called and asked me out on a date. While politely declining his invitation, I wondered if I would spend my entire field experience dodging the amorous or violent intentions of Vincentian men.

Largely because of concerns for my physical safety, I spent much of my first three months in St. Vincent in the company of Peace Corps (PC) and VSO (British) volunteers, and ended up living in a house in a middle-class suburb near the capital. From the PC and VSO volunteers I learned how to access the inner workings of the Vincentian government bureaucracy to locate documents and archival data. The Vincentians I met through PC volunteers were accustomed to Americans, and cognizant of the differences between Vincentian and American social norms. They patiently explained Vincentian etiquette to me as they had to their volunteer friends, and acted as self-appointed informants. With their help and my own efforts, my social network expanded and I began conducting interviews.

Early ethnography: gender and sexuality

My ethnographic efforts were greatly facilitated by the emphasis Vincentians place on talking and telling stories about their lives. Vincentians regard talk seriously; a person's verbal virtuosity is an important marker of social prestige (Abrahams 1983). Sexuality is a frequent topic of conversation; serious and joking talk about sexual behavior and sexual relationships pervades social interaction between acquaintances and friends. Vincentian discussions of sexuality are more open and more frequent than is normative in middle-class American society. My review of the extensive literature on the West Indian family, my experience teaching human sexuality, and my own liberal attitudes prepared me to participate in conversation without embarrassment or dismay. Many PC volunteers, particularly older ones, were quite taken aback and very critical of what they perceived as 'promiscuity' on the part of even 'respectable' middle-aged and middle-class Vincentians.

Vincentians strongly believe that sexual activity is pleasurable and good, and that adults of all ages need to be active sexually to maintain their physical and emotional health (cf. MacCormack and Draper 1987; Sobo 1993). Vincentians describe life as a struggle, filled with work and the likelihood of suffering. Sex provides a release from hardship and a source of pleasure, and is one of the most positive things life offers. Sexual relationships are valued in themselves and also because of the kinship ties created through the birth of children. Both men and women perceive women as wanting and enjoying sexual activity as much as or even more than men. There is no emphasis placed on female virginity, and a sexually experienced woman, even one with children, is considered a desirable sexual partner. Sexuality is a subtext to nearly all encounters between men and women, regardless of their relationship status (cf. Freilich 1971). Being in love does not preclude being sexually attracted to others and sexual fidelity does not automatically concur with any relationship. Vincentian men and women are constantly renegotiating sexual relationships; there are no categories of potential heterosexual partners who are 'off limits', except for persons defined as 'close kin'.[5] Vincentians recognize a variety of heterosexual relationships as socially acceptable, and do not expect couples to wait until marriage to begin having children.[6]

As my circle of Vincentian contacts grew, and I became a familiar and accepted presence around my neighborhood, I was included more frequently in both sexual joking and *commess*, or gossip (Abrahams 1983; Morth 1973). In *commess*, both men and women discuss the dynamics of relationships as well as their partners' physical appearance and sexual abilities in detail. My relationship status was a frequent question Vincentians, stranger and friend, men and women alike, asked me. First, they would ask if I was married. When I replied in the negative, they would ask if I had any children, since marriage and childbearing are not necessarily associated in Vincentian society. When I replied again in the negative, my by now very concerned Vincentian contacts would suggest that I find someone, and have a baby soon, before it was too late. As a childless (and manless) woman in my late twenties, I was an anomaly, one which Vincentian men I encountered frequently offered to remedy.

In many respects, Vincentian sexual attitudes are very positive for women. Women's sexuality is recognized and appreciated. Women do not associate their sexuality with innate depravity, shamefulness, or uncleanliness, and women in St. Vincent are freer than women in many other parts of the world to choose their sexual partners and terminate their relationships. However, as I was quick to learn, St. Vincent is not a woman's sexual paradise. There is a sexual double standard, under which the sexual conquest of multiple partners contributes significantly to a man's prestige, while women are expected to be faithful to one partner at a time (cf. Freilich 1971; MacCormack and Draper 1987).[7] Men use the cultural perception of women's strong sexuality as evidence of women's greater emotionality and physicality, and argue that this justifies male control over women. A well-elaborated concept of male superiority and dominance pervades Vincentian gender ideology. Women need 'a man's head' or 'a man's hand' to stay within the boundaries of social acceptability. Women are frequently referred to by the biblical allusion of 'the weaker vessel', despite daily evidence of their physical strength and intellectual capabilities. Women as well as men say 'The man should control the woman' and 'Woman should not be above man'. Lacking other forms of social control, such as a restrictive sexual ideology, men use threatened and actual violence to control women and restrict their social and spatial mobility.

Sexual violence in St. Vincent

Sexual violence, including sexual harassment, rape, and spousal battery, emerged as a frequent topic during my casual conversations and interviews with Vincentians, especially with Vincentian women. The early warnings I received, from American colleagues, PC volunteers, and Vincentian contacts, were often repeated. The longer I stayed, the more I learned about specific violent incidents and how very real the threat of sexual violence was for Vincentian women, tourists, volunteers, and myself.

Sexual harassment was the most frequent problem I encountered. Sexual harassment can be defined as unwelcome sexual verbal and physical advances, lewd remarks, jokes, and gestures, which create a hostile social atmosphere for women (and, less often, for men). Although associated in the United States with the workplace, sexual harassment can occur in schools, doctors' offices, stores, and on the street. Although not labeled as such, sexual harassment was widespread in St. Vincent. Vincentian women use phrases like 'he was botherin' she' to describe behavior Americans would call sexual harassment.

In public, I and other women faced harassment in the form of sexually explicit remarks or overtures when passing by men sitting in rum shops or loitering on the street corners. Rum shops are a neighborhood feature in every community in St. Vincent from the poorest to the wealthiest, where men gather, drink, play dominoes, listen to calypso, debate politics, and observe and discuss passers-by, especially women (cf. Brana-Shute 1979). Patronizing a rum shop is an expected part of adult male social life and does not reflect on a man's social standing in the community. Unless accompanied by a man, I avoided going into rum shops. I was told by my female neighbors that 'respectable' women did not drink in public, and that women who frequent the rum shops are assumed to be arranging assignations with their lovers.

It was much more difficult to avoid the young unemployed men who 'lime' or hang out on downtown street corners, hoping to be recruited for daily casual work. These 'rude boys' entertain themselves by cadging money from passers by, while ogling and making comments to women. Young Vincentian women deflect the rude boys' remarks with spirited rejoinders, usually debunking the young man's sexual prowess. For example, one evening, while waiting for a bus, I overheard a young man standing by the streetlamp greet a passing young woman and her female companion, who were about to turn down a dark alley. The young man then offered the young woman his 'long flashlight' to guide their way down that 'long dark hole'. She laughed, and said, no thanks, it looked more like a 'feeble little pen-light' to her. He laughed and shrugged.

The rude boys' shouted comments startled and frightened me. I lacked the fluency in the dialect to make the rapid repartee that Vincentian women used to defuse the situation. Instead, I learned to keep my eyes focused downward or into the distance, never to make eye contact, never to smile or even respond. (See also Morton's contribution to this volume.) During daylight, in downtown Kingstown, Vincentian women dismissed such encounters as 'foolishness', but after dark or in more isolated places these interactions could be anxiety-provoking.

While the rude boys could be dismissed as annoyances, and the men in the rum shops avoided, other types of sexual harassment were not so easy to evade. I learned from personal experience during meetings with some government officials that the rude boys' style could be dressed up in a suit and tie. I was told that information I needed would be more readily obtainable if I went out for 'dates'. Suggestive remarks and invitations to go out for drinks were more difficult to dismiss as mere annoyances when the power relations between us were reversed, and my research depended on gaining access to government records or getting permission to conduct interviews. After several unpleasant encounters, I learned to rely on my personal network and obtained information through indirect channels.

Lurking behind the atmosphere of sexual intimidation expressed in sexual harassment was the threat of rape, which affected Vincentian women of all classes, foreign volunteers, and this anthropologist. Rape in the Vincentian idiom refers to a violent sexual assault, occurring either between strangers or between men and women who are acquainted but not involved in an ongoing relationship with each other. During my field stay, several rapes occurred, which became public knowledge and the subject of much conversation. In public opinion, the number of sexual assaults was increasing in the early 1980s. These ongoing events stimulated discussion on the subject of rape in general and elicited accounts of previous similar events.[8] Since I had a contact in the police department, and an extensive network in the capital and in my own community, I learned the details of many sexual assaults, including several others which did not warrant much public commentary.

Vincentians often attributed rape to something the victim did to precipitate the attack, such as dressing or acting provocatively, letting the man believe she was willing to have sex and then refusing, or having broken off a relationship before the man was willing. Vincentians believed that a woman should know better than to encourage a man or accept anything from him if she does not want to have sex with him. Some rapes occurred when jilted men attacked partners who had left them for other men. Other rapes occurred when women ventured alone into places or situations which were deemed dangerous or inappropriate, a case of 'being in the wrong place at the wrong time'. These 'dangerous' places included almost anywhere outside after dark, and any isolated or infrequently travelled place at any time.

Vincentian women attempted to lessen the threat of rape by restricting their social and spatial mobility. Except in their immediate neighborhood or for daytime shopping trips downtown, women did not walk about alone but went out accompanied by other women or their children. Women curtailed their movements after dark, remaining at home. If they had to go out, they sought escorts, usually a male relative or partner. I received numerous cautions from Vincentians, men and women, concerned about my personal safety. More times than I can remember, friends and neighbors offered to walk with me as I went about the community, and they also stopped in to check on me in the evenings. I was very cautious going out after dark or even during the day, and maintained a constant vigilance around strange men. As an ethnographer, I felt constrained, limited in my access to social events that occurred at night, and always concerned, when meeting a man I had not met before, how the interaction would go, and how I would manage to turn down the nearly inevitable proposition gracefully.

Sex and tourism

As an American woman living in St. Vincent, I also became aware how the behavior of vacationing Euro-Americans had negatively affected Vincentians' perceptions of Euro-American women. Tourist women had a reputation for being sexually promiscuous, and their behavior contrasted dramatically with that of the PC or VSO volunteers. I had many opportunities to observe the interactions between tourists and Vincentians, since most of St. Vincent's tourist facilities and popular beaches were located near the suburban community where I lived. Late in the afternoon and on weekends, the small, cove-like beaches would be crowded with natives and visitors alike. Vincentian women usually wore modestly cut one- or two-piece bathing suits and put their pants or skirts back on before they left the sand. Tourist women, in contrast, wore very skimpy bikinis or high-cut and low-cut suits, and wore short shorts or miniskirts over them at best. The appearance of female tourists scantily clad in bathing attire and resort wear on the streets of the capital frequently provoked the hostile reaction of Vincentian women, who would furiously criticize the disrepect shown. Vincentian men also expressed disapproval for the tourists' flaunting of norms of public modesty, but they looked just the same.

Sitting on the beach with non-Vincentian female friends, I was frequently approached by young Vincentian men, who would stop and offer to sell us trinkets or *ganja* (marijuana), and flirt openly given the slightest encouragement. The beach boys were frequently successful in their efforts to strike up casual romances with female tourists. Many of the blond young Scandinavian women seemed particularly attracted to young Vincentian men, the darker-skinned the better. Much to their parents' dismay, many young Vincentian middle-class youths affected the Rastafarian dreadlock hairstyle and speech idiom, because these were known to increase their appeal to the tourists. In the evenings, Vincentian men and women frequented the tourist bars, picking up quite willing partners among the tourists, overseas medical students, and visiting development personnel.

Relationships between Euro-American women tourists and Vincentian men violated several key Vincentian components of sexual relationships. While sexuality may be central to male–female interaction in St. Vincent, all socially acceptable unions are accompanied by a mutual understanding of the obligations of each partner. Men in Vincentian relationships provide financial support to their partners in exchange for sexual and domestic services. Partners are expected to have feelings for each other, even love each other. All serious involvements, whether the partners are married or not, should lead to the birth of children and the extension of kinship ties. Men in the upper and middle classes enter into casual and extramarital liaisons with lower-class women, but upper- and middle-class women are not permitted relationships with men beneath their own class. Most tourist–Vincentian affairs were brief, centered exclusively on sex, had no emotional component, did not result in the birth of children, and reversed the normal balance of economic power and class relations.

While Vincentians who entered into relationships with tourists often profited in the short run when their lovers bought them meals, drinks, or presents, the men in particular did not categorize themselves as prostitutes. As men, they saw themselves as dominating the women with whom they had sex, and many thought it only fair that these rich (comparatively speaking) European and American women should pay their bills and buy them presents out of gratitude for the 'good loving' they were receiving (cf. Bowman 1989).[9] The actual power imbalances in these relationships may have stimulated the negative stereotyping of Euro-American women as 'promiscuous' by Vincentian men.

While many sexual relationships between tourists and Vincentians were consensual, they reinforced Vincentian men's attitudes that all female tourists were sexually available. Foreign women who innocently flirted with Vincentian men, accepted offers of drinks or went out dancing with the young men they met on the beach or in the bars, put themselves at risk of sexual assault. Vincentian men interpreted their actions as they would the actions of Vincentian women; by agreeing to a date and accepting drinks or dinner, they had agreed to sex. Since many foreign women did come to St. Vincent looking for sexual adventure, many Vincentian men assumed all foreign women were equally interested in a sexual escapade with them. As a result, the men did not take seriously tourist women's refusals of sexual contact, and this in turn led to several incidents of sexual assault (including one of the PC volunteers about whom I had been told before I arrived).

For many reasons, I tried to avoid being perceived as a tourist. I modeled my appearance and behavior on that of female PC and VSO volunteer teachers, who dressed modestly, did not flirt with Vincentian men casually, and avoided going to the tourist bars or restaurants unaccompanied by male volunteers. I also lived 'on the economy' and did not flaunt my comparative wealth by wearing expensive jewelry or clothing. When PC and VSO volunteers became romantically involved with Vincentians, which occurred from time to time, the relationships were serious and long-lasting, and several romances ended in marriage.[10] I learned from the volunteers, and from Vincentians' comments about them, that it was not sexual involvement *per se* that created Euro-American women's bad reputation, but their failure as tourists to observe Vincentian rules of conduct in their relationships. I was also able to learn much more about Vincentian relationships, as the next section describes, directly from my own experience of falling in love and becoming intimately involved with a Vincentian man.

Falling in love

During my first few months on the island, I socialized mostly with the PC and VSO volunteers and their circle of Vincentian friends and co-workers. Several PC volunteers had been friends with another American anthropologist who had completed her research just before I arrived. They were aware of the kinds of topic anthropologists studied, and asked me about my research. One of the PC volunteers offered to introduce me to a friend and neighbor of hers, a man she described as very well informed about Vincentian history and folklore, who enjoyed sharing his knowledge, and who might be a valuable research assistant. From her description of this sterling character, I had the mental impression of an older man, perhaps a former schoolteacher. After receiving a formal letter from this person, I decided to meet and interview him. I got my first opportunity at a PC party, held about two months after my arrival.

A week before the party, I attended a variety show performance accompanied by another female PC worker. I enjoyed the singers and dancers, but was most impressed by a young man who had done a stand-up comedy routine. Although most of his material was in Vincentian Creole, and my understanding was still limited, his timing, delivery, and mastery of the witty double-entrendre were very impressive. He was also handsome and had a charismatic charm that carried across the stage. To come to the point, the comedian and the knowledgeable friend turned out to be the same man, to whom I shall refer as 'E.C.'[11] As we talked at the party, an immediate attraction developed between us.

When I first met E.C., I felt as though I had stepped out onto a tightrope. How I navigated the crossing would affect my personal life and my research. I had been feeling very lonely. Several Vincentians I had met had offered to become my boyfriend, but I had not been attracted to them and had not felt that a relationship would work out between us. Until I met E.C., I had not considered the possibility that I might meet someone with whom I would actually fall in love. I was very concerned about how E.C. would react if we became sexually involved and how an involvement would be perceived by other Vincentians. I had tried very hard to create an image of a serious person, a 'quasi-volunteer', and did not want to slip into 'tourist' status.

I had heard such good things abut E.C. and his in-depth knowledge of Vincentian culture, and I was afraid that an attachment would destroy a valuable working relationship that I needed. I worried that if I got sexually involved with this very attractive man, I would become emotionally attached and lose my objectivity about the information I learned from him. As a woman, I was afraid of getting hurt; I felt lonely, isolated, and terribly vulnerable already, thousands of miles away from family and supportive friends. But also as a woman, I was aware of an immensely powerful sexual pull between us, which kept getting stronger the more time we spent together.

I would have been attracted to E.C. no matter where we met. He has the qualities I've always responded to emotionally and physically: he's tall, well built, handsome, intelligent, funny, charming, considerate, and affectionate. Our relationship began with E.C. acting as an informant. I did his geneaology, and interviewed him about his family and his life history. When we first met, E.C. was unemployed, and would come by to visit and talk in the late afternoons or early evenings, alone or with a friend or two. We spent many hours together during the next few weeks, decorously sitting on my front porch, in public view, respectably discussing the details of Vincentian kinship and of male–female relationships. E.C. was a terrific informant, a wonderful raconteur to whom I listened for hours, taking notes until I got cramps in my hand, only occasionally prompting him with a question or query. E.C. could move from Creole to standard English in the same sentence, and was very helpful in increasing my knowledge of idiomatic expressions.

In a multitude of ways, E.C. became an immensely important collaborator in my research efforts. I would often describe an incident

I had witnessed, or a conversation I had overheard or participated in that had left me feeling bewildered and confused, and E.C. would decode and 'translate' what had happened in terms that I could understand. He was invaluable as a way of cross-checking my interpretations of Vincentian concepts and behaviors, and helped me devise effective strategies and queries in obtaining information I needed. He also introduced me to friends, relatives, and acquaintances whom he thought would be good interview subjects, assisted in doing some interviews, helped with transcriptions, and provided me with indirect access to data when direct channels were impossible to negotiate.

E.C. presented himself as 'different' from most Vincentian men.[12] Although he was also intersted in me, and made his interest obvious, he was not aggressive, and accepted my initial demurrals. He was critical of the way many Vincentian men treated their partners, and of the underlying gender dynamics of his culture. While E.C. illustrated the male perspective on Vincentian gender dynamics with numerous anecdotes, he also expressed considerable disgust at the attitudes and behavior that most of his peers accepted without coment. Like many other key informants mentioned in the ethnographic literature, E.C. was very intelligent, cognizant of his cultural milieu, and aware that in many ways he did not conform to his own culture's norms. I thought at the time, and still do, that E.C. would make an excellent anthropologist himself.

As I got to know E.C. rather well through our intensive interviews and conversations, I also began to perceive him as 'different' and as special. For example, E.C. was the only Vincentian man I met, of his age and class background (upper-working-class), who had not had any children by any previous partner, and moreover had deliberately decided not to have children out of wedlock. As we spent more time together, discussing our respective family histories, I came to trust him and began to see him as a person I cared for deeply, as well as a person to whom I was strongly sexually attracted. I was also impressed by the sacrifices E.C. made to help me, and his refusal to take any money in return, even though I explained to him how valuable his help was to me. E.C. was always considerate, was concerned about my safety, and often brought me small gifts of food or flowers.

The combination of personal and professional attractions was incredibly appealing, and eventually impossible to resist. My intellectual excitement kept pace with my physical attraction as I learned more and more. Ironically, I had assumed before going to the Caribbean that I would be limited by my gender to accessing only women, whom I had intended to focus on, but I was concerned to give a balanced picture of Vincentian life. Now I had an incredible entrée into the male perspective on women, but I was very worried that if I explored this further, through the direct experience of having a Vincentian boyfriend, I would then lose credibility with the women I had come to study.

My next-door neighbor, another valuable informant, asked me indirectly about my new 'friend'. Feeling defensive, I told her that he was helping me with my work, that he was a friend of some PC workers. She pressed for more details about his background, and seemed curious and concerned. I was anxious not to divulge too much; one of the reasons my neighbor was such a valuable informant was because she loved to gossip. I knew I was already a topic of conversation in the neighborhood, but I did not wish to be a source of scandal and ruin the developing relationships with my neighbors. I expressed these concerns to E.C., who took them seriously. He introduced himself to my neighbor and her husband, properly identifying himself as to village origin and kin ties, and spent some time getting to know them and others in the neighborhood. St. Vincent is a very small island, and most people are able to establish some connection, through kinship, church, school, or neighborhood. In a matter of hours, E.C. was well linked to half a dozen people in my neighborhood.

Once E.C. became an accepted presence in the neighborhood, I felt more comfortable acknowledging to myself and to others that our relationship was developing beyond work. I publicly referred to him as my 'boyfriend' and we went out together in public. Community reaction to our relationship was either positive or neutral.[13] Contrary to my expectation that my relationship with my boyfriend would provoke comments about my 'loose morals', several of my female neighbors told me they were glad 'I had a man about the house', and that they had been concerned about my living alone. My previous 'standoffishness', demonstrated by living alone and not having a boyfriend, had been cause for worry and comment. My Vincentian neighbors let me know in subtle ways that by being in a sexual relationship I was finally acting like a normal adult.

Our developing relationship was socially acceptable because it paralleled a traditional Vincentian courtship. E.C.'s public visits and sitting on my porch conformed to courting behavior. E.C.'s introduction of himself around the neighborhood was a public pronouncement that he was a suitor with serious, rather than clandestine, attentions. Moreover, he was always neatly dressed, well spoken, and sober when he came by, and our conversations were usually conducted in the afternoon or early evening, accepted times for socializing. Perhaps most importantly, he was the only visitor I saw; I did not entertain a variety of men. My neighbors had gotten to know me, before the relationship began, as a polite and friendly person who attended local events, frequented merchants' shops, and maintained courteous relationships with my neighbors. Unlike tourists, I got to know people, and was interested in learning and following local customs.

My relationship with E.C. was also accepted because of the nature of the community in which I lived. My neighborhood was in a suburban community, a type of settlement that has developed in St. Vincent only in the past thirty years. The suburbs have emerged as population growth, expanded secondary education and government employment, universal adult suffrage, tourism, and extensive circular migration to metropolitan countries have created upward mobility and expanded membership in the middle class.[14] Color barriers to sexual and romantic relationships have become more permeable as class has become less dependent on inherited social position. My neighbors ranged from working-class to upper-middle-class, from all ethnic and racial groups. The majority of the community were rural–urban migrants who had either lived overseas or had close contact with migrant relatives. Their experiences overseas may have predisposed my neighbors to accept the possibility that an American woman and a Vincentian man could become involved romantically. Both men and women told me stories about their relationships with Europeans and Americans while living overseas, and some individuals had even brought back foreign spouses (cf. Lindsay 1986).

Two months after we began 'friending', as the Vincentians refer to a 'visiting relationship' (when a man sleeps over but is not co-resident), E.C. was offered a job with the government which necessitated his moving from his home on the outskirts of the capital to a place nearer the city. Since I lived near the capital, I offered to let him stay at my house while he looked for a place of his own. His new job took most of the time, but E.C. continued to assist me on my research for the remainder of my field stay. Living together created a strong emotional bond between us. About three months after moving in together, six months after our first meeting, the thought of separating, perhaps forever, when I returned to the U.S. to write my dissertation was extremely painful. We realized we loved each other, and that getting married was a statement of the way we felt and the only way for E.C. to accompany me back to the U.S. Almost exactly one year after we met, we married. I also got pregnant and gave birth to our son before we left St. Vincent, 22 months after I had first arrived on the island.

My Vincentian female friends and neighbors commented approvingly on our relationship because we 'lived loving', seldom arguing, and treating each other with respect and affection. They also approved of our being monogamous. They marvelled at the extent to which E.C. helped me with routine household chores, although privately they probably thought he did so because I was so obviously inept in my housewifely duties. They also viewed E.C. as 'different' from the typical Vincentian male, and expressed the wish that more men should be like him. Since they also perceived him as attractive and a socially desirable partner, they did not express much surprise that I had fallen in love with him and married him. I think I gained in stature by having attracted such a partner and by being able to negotiate our relationship successfully. My serious relationship, then marriage to E.C., demonstrated publicly that I viewed Vincentians as my equals in status, not mere 'research subjects', and also established me as a non-racist.

In addition to increasing my social acceptability and status, my relationship with E.C. also provided me with an intimate view of the erotic dimension of Vincentian life. As the sexual partner of a Vincentian man, I could and did ask him directly about sexual practices and beliefs. Vincentian women saw me as sharing a common life experience with them, and Vincentian men considered me more of a 'real woman', one who would not be offended by sexually explicit talk. Several Vincentians told me that they thought most Americans and Europeans were very prudish, easily offended by talk about sex, and so they avoided these topics when Euro-Americans were present. They told me that they felt comfortable around me and could act and speak more normally in my presence. As a result, I gained tremendous insight into Vincentian sexual behavior and ideology, which contributed to my understanding of Vincentian gender, kinship, and household, the substance of my dissertation. While this was important to me personally, my experiences are also relevant to a reflexive examination of anthropology, sexuality, and fieldwork.

The recent explosion of writings, from Said's *Orientalism* (1978) onward, that expose and castigate the way in which subjugated people are appropriated into Western discourses as erotically charged signs could easily result in individual anthropologists feeling dismayed by any desire that may arise within them in fieldwork settings. Awareness of these Western discourses of exploitation may cause some anthropologists to feel that sexual attraction to a person in the field represents some new form of colonialist exploitation. Although current critical exploration of the erotic gaze and its role in the construction of exotic peoples has yielded some fascinating insights into the psychosexual preoccupations of late nineteenth- and early twentieth-century colonial men, I'm not sure that this analysis can automatically be transferred to the anthropologist in the field today. The new, the novel, and, yes, the exotic have always had erotic appeal for humans and other primates. Feeling sexually attracted to the people we live among and study is a much more positive reaction then feeling repulsed by them. As long as we enter relationships honestly and considerately, and are observant of local norms, we should not reject our sexual feelings toward people with whom we work. In fact, at times, to consider them to be inappropriate sexual partners is itself a potentially racist and neocolonialist reaction.

I met several Vincentian men I considered extremely attractive and sexually appealing. I chose not to become involved with them for the same kinds of reason I have not pursued relationships in the U.S.; we lacked mutual interests and were temperamentally incompatible. I also did not become involved with other Vincentian men because I fell in love with one particular man, and chose to be exclusively with him, just as I have been in love with Euro-American men and chosen to be exclusively with them at other times in my life.

Reflections on relationships and fieldwork

Speaking as a woman, my relationship with E.C. in St. Vincent was wonderful, fulfilling emotionally, sexually, and intellectually. E.C. took care of me when I was sick, comforted me when I was lonely and homesick, and helped me keep my personal and research experiences in perspective. Ten years later, I still do not doubt that my relationship with E.C. immeasurably enriched both my life and my research. I did not then, nor do I now, perceive our relationship as exploitive or unethical. Although I had more formal education, in St. Vincent I was dependent upon E.C.'s expert knowledge of Vincentian culture. Ours was a mutual attraction whose consequences we considered and discussed before embarking on a relationship. E.C. was as free as I was to terminate the relationship at any time. When we first started seeing each other, I told E.C. that I was only going to be in St. Vincent for a year. When the relationship became serious, we married, and E.C. came back with me to the United States.

E.C. enjoyed telling me stories about his life and that of his friends and family, and he was able to explain in detail how Vincentians categorized certain types of relationship, what expectations of partners were, and how the broader community reacted. In the field, I rehearsed interview questions with him, and discovered the most appropriate way to learn the information I wanted. E.C. introduced me to his friends, co-workers, and acquaintances. He acted as an intermediary, arranging interviews and helping explain what I was doing. Without E.C., collecting data on men's perceptions of gender and sexuality would have been difficult, perhaps impossible. My relationship with E.C. identified me as a legitimate researcher when I interviewed other men, to whom I could then talk to about relationships with women without their interpreting my interest as a sexual overture. Accompanied by E.C., I was able to attend many evening events, such as political rallies, and visit places such as rum shops and nightclubs that would have been too dangerous for me to go to alone. While I did not become involved with E.C. because he could protect me, the personal safety his presence provided me was another advantage of our relationship that I greatly appreciated.

Fear did not propel me into my relationship with E.C. I did not choose to have a Vincentian boyfriend to avoid having to fend off other men. Although my relationship acted as a deterrent in my neighborhood, I was still perceived by strangers as a potential sexual partner, and I continued to receive propositions from Vincentian men until my seventh month of pregnancy! (Cf., again, Morton's contribution to this volume.) Although my ability to go to some events and places would have been severely circumscribed without E.C., I could still have collected valuable data by concentrating exclusively on women. Being involved with a Vincentian man helped me to keep some perspective and to appreciate that not all Vincentian men were sexual predators or potential rapists. Our relationship did make me feel safer, and arguably made me safer in reality as well. I felt loved, and I felt safe when I was with E.C. My relationship also helped me understand why some Vincentian women stayed in their relationships with their partners; safety was also highly prized by Vincentian women and being in a steady relationship was safer than being a woman alone.

For personal and professional reasons, I invested heavily in the success of our relationship. In retrospect I realize that I overlooked and minimized problems that caused us tremendous difficulties when we came to the United States. While in St. Vincent, I accommodated myself to E.C. and his culture. It was part of my training as an anthropologist, and as a woman, to fit into life in St. Vincent and to adapt myself to him. My desire to succeed as a fieldworker, and as E.C.'s lover, led me to make compromises because I thought they would help my research and my personal life function smoothly. E.C. had to accommodate himself to me, as well, and he did. He was already accustomed to Americans from his friendships with some of the PC volunteers, although he had never been romantically involved with any of them. But, while he had to learn my idiosyncrasies, we remained in his cultural milieu, surrounded by his friends and relatives. The emotional distance he had to travel was much less than that I covered. We were very compatible sexually, and in the throes of romantic passion, every obstacle, even culture, seems a minor impediment to true love. Although our relationship worked very well in St. Vincent, it did not 'survive the translation' to a new cultural context, and we separated two years after moving to the United States, eventually divorcing after several attempts at reconciliation. We remain cooperative co-parents and friends.

Although in St. Vincent I maintained my professional identity as an anthropologist, I also assumed the role of E.C.'s girlfriend, and when we were together in public, I acted appropriately by Vincentian norms. I let him take the lead in social interactions with people we encountered when we went out, he paid for meals and movie tickets, and he escorted me publicly to places such as rum shops that I did not go to without him. At social gatherings, I spoke and danced with other men, but always deferred to E.C. I did this out of courtesy and to signal to other men that I was not available. I did not flirt with other men, and frequently referred to E.C. in conversation. We entertained his relatives and friends at our house, and shared other resources with them.

When we were home alone, I asked E.C. detailed questions about interactions I had witnessed and conversations we had participated in. I gained many valuable insights during informal get-togethers, when E.C. and his friends would be at our house, just hanging out and discussing relationships, gender roles, and sexual behavior in context rather than as part of an interview. E.C.'s questions of me, and his reactions to my expectations and behavior, helped me identify the differences between Vincentian and Euro-American values and concepts.

My interactions with E.C. could be characterized as a critical dialogue, as described by Harrison (1991b: 101): 'not only a two-way flow of "raw data," but an exchange of information subjected to analysis and critique'. In some ways, my relationship with E.C. can be viewed as the ultimate in dialogic ethnography, although I did not plan it that way. I often felt my research was really a joint endeavor, and at the time and ever since have acknowledged the incredible debt I owe E.C. for helping me learn about Vincentian culture and society.

However, when I went to the field in 1983, I had never heard about 'dialogic ethnography', and instead carried with me the classic model of the detached, emotionally uninvolved, participant observer. Our relationship conflicted with this internalized image. Occasionally I questioned my objectivity, and that of E.C., and I sometimes wondered whether he was telling me only what he thought I wanted to hear, what would please me. While this is a worry many face in intimate relationships, I was also concerned about the validity of my data, about how representative this man's knowledge was in comparison to other Vincentian men. My emotional well-being and my intellectual responsibilities became intertwined.

I often felt that I wasn't getting enough real work done; was the time we were spending together 'work' or 'personal' time? I criticized myself for constantly following up E.C.'s comments with questions that were more about my research than about us. Although I interviewed many other Vincentians, whose perspective generally corroborated E.C.'s, and collected a vast amount of data from other sources, I often felt that I should be spending more time doing 'real' interviews, that is, with strangers. When I cross-checked information provided by E.C. with other sources, I felt like a better ethnographer, but I also felt disloyal to him. In retrospect, the relationship was a tremendous advantage, but as a neophyte anthropologist, it sometimes felt as though I was 'cheating', that I was taking a short cut through a personal relationship rather than demonstrating genuine skill as an ethnographer.

I think I was particularly troubled because 'going to the field' was supposed to demonstrate that I could do ethnographic research to my committee and graduate-school colleagues. I turned to anthropology after earning undergraduate and master's degrees in psychology, a discipline whose scientific methodology stresses the distance between the researcher and the 'subject'. I was attracted to anthropology because ethnographic research meant understanding people from their own perspective, getting to know them in the context of their own lives, and not in some artificial laboratory. While I enthusiastically absorbed the theory and ethnographic content taught in my courses, I remained uncertain about how one actually did ethnographic research, and whether it was something I could do. In graduate school, I felt inadequate when I compared myself to students who had undergraduate degrees in anthropology and had already done fieldwork. Many of my friends were PC veterans and had spent several years living in the 'Third World' as adults. While I grew up as a military dependent, wandering from place to place, never quite fitting in, I hadn't lived outside the U.S. since I was a small child. 'Going to the field' was a very important rite of passage for me, marking the transition between a 'wannabe' anthropologist and a 'real' one.

When I went to St. Vincent, I experienced culture-shock, but culture-shock was not new, and the lessons I learned in childhood and perfected in graduate school about relating to people across racial and cultural boundaries proved just as relevant as the anthropological theories I had absorbed.[15] As time has passed, and as reflexive anthropology has become more accepted, I have come to feel less defensive about falling in love with and marrying my 'best informant'.

Steps toward an emotionally aware ethnography[16]

I now firmly believe that successful ethnographic research is always a joint endeavor between anthropologists and informants, one that ultimately depends upon the quality of our personal relationships. Consultation with colleagues, and a review of the reflexive anthropology literature,[17] has lead me to conclude that as anthropologists we typically use very subjective emotional reactions, as well as so-called 'objective' intellectual criteria, to evaluate the success or failure of our research enquiries. Positive and negative emotional reactions to individuals or to situations guide what we pay attention to, and how we interpret the significance of our observations. As researchers, we must learn to take our emotions seriously, and not dismiss them as interfering with our objectivity (Delany 1989; Jaggar 1989; Johnson 1984; Newton 1993; Tedlock 1991; Vendler 1984; Wikan 1991).

In my case, the emotions that were particularly salient were fear, sexual attraction, and love. As detailed above, I was afraid of being victimized by sexual violence in St. Vincent. I learned from Vincentian women, as well as other American residents, that this was a realistic reaction to conditions women faced on the island. Recognizing my own fears helped me to understand how Vincentian women were also affected, and how the threat of sexual violence reinforced male dominance and female solidarity. Sexual violence was equally threatening to us all; it created a common emotional bond that helped me form close relationships with Vincentian women about whose lives I was learning.

My fieldwork fears were not unique; many women anthropologists who have worked in the Caribbean, in Latin America, in Asia, and in Europe have since admitted to me privately that they have been afraid of sexual violence in the field. They reported experiencing sexual harassment, exhibitionism, molestation, and attempted rape. Yet the threat of sexual violence is seldom discussed openly. Howell, in her recent book *Surviving Fieldwork* (1990: 93–4), writes:

> many women did not want to discuss the topic . . . Some of them are motivated by the fear that women who have been raped lose status and respect . . . Other women are more concerned about issues of employment and research opportunities that could be denied to them on the excuse (or perhaps the true motive) of wanting to protect women from the risk of rape in the field.[18]

Our professional silence about the dangers of fieldwork may also partly result from continued romanticization of the 'traditional' lifestyles of many of the groups studied by anthropologists, and, hence a resistance to discussing more 'modern' dimensions of life such as urban violence and crime.[19]

I would like to make it very plain, however, that I do not regard St. Vincent or any other 'Third World' site as any more violent or dangerous than the United States; both societies exhibit unacceptably high levels of sexual violence. Many American women I know who have never left the U.S. have been victimized by sexual harassment, spousal battery, incest, and rape. As a feminist, I feel a responsibility to speak out about sexual violence and its impact on women, and on the relations between women and men, whether the setting is the U.S. or St. Vincent. My Vincentian research has led me to a stronger commitment to work against conditions which oppress women, including sexual violence, wherever I encounter them.[20]

If fear alone had been my experience on St. Vincent, however, I would not have learned nearly so much about gender and sexuality, nor would I have come to appreciate how Vincentian women and men also become deeply emotionally attached to each other. I would not have realized what powerful attractions and pleasures there were for Vincentian women in relationships, as well as what dangers. Again, my involvement with a Vincentian man created a shared context of experience between myself and Vincentian women; they felt more open about discussing their relationships when I could exchange confidences and comments with them about 'my man'. I came to appreciate the favorable attitude and sense of entitlement that many Vincentian women expressed about women's sexuality. From knowing one Vincentian man very well, and by meeting others through him, I also learned about the wide diversity present among Vincentian men; again, as is true of men in the United States, not all Vincentian men are harassers, batterers, or rapists.

Conclusion: 'going too far' in the field

In conclusion, I wish to return to the issue raised in the first section: why do anthropologists avoid sexual and romantic relationships in the field? And, if they do get involved, why do they seldom talk (or write) about it? If sexual relationships are acknowledged at all in our profession, they are usually referred to derogatorily as 'going too far' and 'going native'. Sexual and romantic relationships dissolve the boundaries between 'us' and 'them' in a most intimate way, creating attachments that are incompatible with the detached, 'objective' participant observer (Delany 1988; Tedlock 1991). Many anthropologists seem to regard this emotional involvement with those with whom we work and study as jeopardizing our ability to analyze and describe dispassionately another people's way of life. I would agree with those who argue that this reflects the Eurocentric and androcentric philosophic biases of our discipline's epistemology, the concept of an unbreachable dichotomy between intellect and emotion that supposedly distinguishes 'science' from other ways of knowing (Jaggar 1989; Jaggar and Bordo 1989; Bordo 1990). I do not think effective ethnographic research can be done without emotional engagement, and the pursuit of a methodology that ignores what we learn from our emotions is undermining the validity of the resulting information. To quote Alison M. Jaggar (1989: 165):

> 'Emotions are neither more basic than observation, reason, or action in building theory, nor are they secondary to them. Each of these human faculties reflects an aspect of human knowing inseparable from the other aspects.'

In fieldwork as in all of life, sensation, emotion, and intellect operate simulataneously to structure and interpret our experience of the world. Our emotional reactions, and those with whom we interact, guide our analyses of life 'at home' as well as 'in the field'.

Ostensibly, then, the taboo against 'sex in the field' is held up as a way to protect our claim to scientific credibility, to our ideal of ethnographic research as unbiased participant observation guided by trustworthy intellect rather than troublesome emotions (Jaggar 1989; Newton 1993). However, a critical analysis of the contrasting emotional reactions of my Vincentian friends and those of my doctoral committee and graduate-school colleagues to my marriage announcement reveals the deeply held, if unspoken, elitist and colonialist biases that permeate anthropology (D'Amico-Samuels 1991). I believe these emotional reactions point to a deeper cultural rationale for the taboo on sex in the field.

Vincentians greeted my marriage announcement with pleasure, particularly when I also told them I was expecting a child. I was typically told that I was becoming a 'real Vinci'. My American colleagues reacted with shocked surprise, often masking their negativity with concerned enquiries such as 'Are you sure you're doing the right thing?' I was also frequently reminded that I might be jeopardizing my career.[21] I was surprised at their reaction, because several of my male graduate-school colleagues were in fact married to non-American women they had met while serving in the PC and two (one male, one female) of our faculty were married to non-Americans as well. Even now, when I tell new anthropological acquaintances that 'I married my key informant', I am often greeted with an uncomfortable pause, as many colleagues struggle to cover their initial dismay. Those who also brought back spouses from the field tend to respond with increased warmth during subsequent conversation, as if I had established membership in some shared secret society. Interestingly, these reactions vary not by gender but by having married someone from the fieldsite.

The lack of a neutral or noncommittal response reveals how embedded colonialist and elitist prejudices are in anthropology. Anthropologists are accustomed to emphasizing the differences between ourselves and those whom we study, and all too often the description of 'difference' disguises an implicit assumption of the subordinate status of those studied (Mascia-Lees *et al.* 1989). Although postmodernist anthropologists castigate themselves and other anthropologists for perpetuating colonialist discourse, they continue to distinguish them'Selves' from those 'Others'. As D'Amico-Samuels (1991: 75) writes so eloquently, 'the phrasing of the discourse of fieldwork in terms of Self and Other preserves distance, difference and distinction as the normal state of cross-cultural affairs.' Anthropologists pride themselves on living among the people they study, but they are always able to leave, to return to a wealthy society and often a privileged academic existence. 'Coming home' is contrasted with 'going to the field' in a way that clearly demarcates which arena is 'real life' (Harrison 1991a). Most practicing Euro-American anthropologists are imbued with elitist attitudes predicated on their status as members of a highly educated, mostly upper-middle-class cadre, whose professional existence is permeated by competitive, status-seeking, and status-guarding behavior that begins in graduate school (D'Amico-Samuels 1991; Delany 1988; Whitehead 1986).

When I married my best informant I crossed over the line between 'us' and 'them' in such a way as to negate the implicit assumption of Euro-American cultural superiority. The comments that my choice provoked, in contrast to the lack of comment my male colleagues' choices received, also demonstrates how deeply gender, class, and race hierarchies structure the American cultural perspective on sexuality and emotional attachment. Euro-American society restricts women more than men in their choice of sexual partners and mates. Women are expected to find partners within their own racial group and socioeconomic class; women in lower ranks economically are allowed to marry 'up' as well, as long as they maintain racial endogamy. Men are permitted to marry down – again, as long as they maintain racial endogamy. As Dubisch notes in this volume, many Americans tend to regard white Euro-American culture as dominating non-white, Third World cultures, and while American male anthropologists can have relationships with women in the field, their female counterparts who have sexual relationships with Third World men of color are contradicting the hierarchy of culture, race, class, and gender. Thus, as a white, American, middle-class woman, my marriage to a black, Vincentian, working-class man was greeted with dismay. Ironically, the reactions to my marriage also reinforced my research conclusions that the class/color line is less rigid in St. Vincent than it is in the supposedly 'advanced' United States.

The glorification of the ethnographic researcher as the detached, positivist, participant observer of yore, or as the free-floating, postmodern, dialogic anthropologist of today, is inimical to the creation of a non-sexist, non-racist, decolonized, praxis-oriented anthropology. If we are to have an anthropology that is relevant in a postcolonial world, then we are faced with the challenge not only of writing ethnography in a new way, but of doing research differently as well. We must transform our model of the dispassionate participant observer into an emotionally aware inter-actor engaged with other actors.

Notes

1 Although anthropology graduate students are increasingly focused on ethnic groups and other subcultures in the United States, they still rely on participant observation and qualitative interviews to examine domestic 'others'. I concur with D'Amico-Samuels' indictment of the term 'fieldwork' as fostering 'the illusion of separation between the fieldsites of anthropology, where data are gathered and emotional experiences had, and the rest of the world, where decisions are made, data interpreted, ethnographies written and racist stereotypes perpetuated' (1991: 68). I am retaining the term 'fieldwork' in this chapter because that is how I referred to what I was doing when I was in graduate school. (See also Andrew P. Killick's contribution to this volume.)

2 Contemporary anthropologists may claim allegiance to some, all, or none of these perspectives as I have chosen to label them in this chapter, even while espousing similar points of view. The paradigmatic turmoil currently ranging in the anthropological journals has not yet firmly congealed into clearly defined theoretical schools, and I apologize if any of the individuals cited resent my use of these labels to delineate their contributions to the ongoing reassessment of anthropological theory and practice. I would also like to emphasize that individuals may adopt more than one of these perspectives simultaneously in their critiques of anthropology.

3 I am using 'historic person' to mean an individual who is both the product of a unique personal history and acting during a particular historical period, the late twentieth century. Ethnographers bring both histories with them into the field, where they encounter 'others' who are similarly unique historic persons.

4 An Ecuadorian male friend with extensive Caribbean work experience echoed this warning about personal safety. He also made the salient point that our community of Gainesville, Florida, had a high sexual assault rate, too; if I maintained the same level of precautions in St. Vincent as I did at home, I would be reasonably safe. The realization that I had already learned to cope with the constant threat of sexual violence was bizarrely comforting, and I finished my trip preparations. Other than cautions about my personal safety, I received little direct advice from my committee about sexual behavior in the field. One woman professor diplomatically recommended leaving the island for 'recreation', so that my respectable image might be preserved and emotional entanglements avoided.

5 Close kin include full and half-siblings, parents, step-parents, aunts, uncles, nieces, nephews, grandparents, and first cousins. Cousins frequently grow up together in a shared grandparental household and regard each other almost as siblings.

6 Socially acceptable sexual relationships in St. Vincent conform to well-defined patterns which vary by class. Among the lower-class majority, the most common types of relationship are referred to as visiting or 'friending', 'keeping', cohabitation or 'common-law' marriage, and legal marriage. Relationships can be distinguished by the co-residence or not of the partners, legal or non-legal status, and the degree of support the woman

and the couple's children receive from the man. Among the middle and upper classes, women are expected to marry and remain faithful to their spouses, while men are expected to marry within their class and to maintain lower-class women as their girlfriends or 'keepers' (concubines), a widespread Caribbean pattern that R.T. Smith has labelled the 'dual marriage system' (1988): cf. Alexander (1984).

Illicit sexual relationships and activities occur as well. These include casual sexual encounters ('one-night stands', in American idiom), extramarital affairs, prostitution, homosexual relationships, bestiality, and incest. Most illicit sexual activities, especially homosexuality, incest, and bestiality, are regarded with disapproval and disgust.

7 Upper- and middle-class women lose social status if they are openly sexually promiscuous, while lower-class women maintain the appearance of fidelity to be able to establish paternity if they get pregnant. Unfaithful women of all classes are threatened with the loss of the relationship and of their partner's economic support, and in many cases are beaten by their men, referred to in St. Vincent as 'givin' she licks'.

8 My preferred data-gathering technique on these occasions was to sit back and listen, sometimes jogging the conversation with a comment of my own, a request for elaboration, or a related question such as 'Has anything like this ever happened before?' While this method does not yield incidence rates or other data amenable to statistical tests of generalizability or reliability, it did yield spontaneous information, presented in the ongoing flow of conversation. This allowed me to gauge Vincentians' perceptions, attitudes, and emotional reactions toward the topic, as well as understand better how the topic is framed conversationally. The drawback to this method of unobtrusive participation was my inability at the time to take notes, which would have transformed the interaction into an interview. My conclusions are based on dozens of different conversations with women and men.

While I did not collect statistical data on the incidence of reported rapes, I interviewed both of the PC women who had been raped, and I attended the Assizes (court hearings held at regular intervals throughout the Eastern Caribbean), and saw several cases featuring spousal battery. I interviewed three lawyers about the prosecution of sexual offenses as part of a longer interview about the legal status of women in St. Vincent. I also participated in group discussions of the topic of violence against women held during the 1984 meetings of CARIWA, the Caribbean Women's Association, and had informal conversations on the subject with members of St. Vincent's National Women's Council and other women's groups.

9 Other Vincentian men and women who became involved with Euro-American tourists had more romantic feelings about their relationships. One young man I met spoke with great affection for his short-term girlfriend, an American yachtie, and expressed the hope that she would come back and visit him on her next trip through the Grenadines. Several others I spoke to also entertained the hope that a true love affair might blossom, and they might then reap the great reward of marrying an American or Canadian and getting an emigration visa.

10 In addition to my own romance, there were also several long-term

relationships and two marriages between PC, VSO volunteers, and even USAID officials and young Vincentians while I was living in St. Vincent. Three young Scandinavian women were also living with and supporting their Vincentian lovers.

11 I am using initials to maintain my now ex-husband's privacy. I did not adopt his last name at marriage, which is not the Vincentian custom. Most of our friends and neighbors insisted on addressing me as 'Mistress C.' and I usually refrained from correcting them.

12 I would like to add that other Vincentian men who were my friends and informants were also 'different' from the stereotype. They too commented critically on the behavior and attitudes of the 'typical' Vincentian man, and adhered to a monogamous lifestyle. These same individuals were also quite willing to tell me that they were atypical, and that I should be very careful around men I did not know.

13 In contrast, our interracial romance was greeted with some uneasiness by some older PC volunteers. The younger PC and VSO volunteers were not so judgmental; several of them were also involved with Vincentians.

14 For a much longer discussion of the impact of migration on Vincentian society, especially on gender and household dynamics, see Gearing (1988). Although international migration has affected perceptions of class and color, gender dynamics seem more resistant to change.

15 I came of age in the early 1970s, strongly identifying with the civil rights, the anti-war, and the women's liberation movements, all of which were attacks on the establishment. In high school, college, and graduate school, I belonged to multiracial and multicultural groups. Perhaps because I grew up female in a lower-middle-class family and attended a non-elite state university, I have always identified more with the have-nots than the haves, and have always felt more like an 'Other'. Long before going to the Caribbean, I had had friendships and romantic relationships with people who were racially and culturally different.

16 My apologies to the memory of Gregory Bateson, whose title *Steps to an Ecology of Mind* (1972) I have unabashedly and admiringly stolen. As Laura Nader points out (1989), Bateson was an unheralded and underappreciated pioneer in reflexive, experimental ethnography.

17 Works that discuss the relationship between ethnographer and informant, in all its possibilities, include Cesara (1982); D'Amico-Samuels (1991); Delany (1988); DeVita (1990); Golde (1970); Johnson (1984); King (1987), quoted in Johannsen (1992); Murphy (1987); Myerhoff (1978); Newton (1993); Rosaldo (1989); Rose (1990); Ruby (1982); Shostak (1981); Stoller (1989); Tedlock (1991); Warren (1977), quoted in Newton (1993); Whitehead and Conaway (1986); Wikan (1991).

18 I believe another factor in woman anthropologists' silence may be lingering self-blame, a common reaction felt by female victims of sexual violence in Euro-American culture, a consequence of cultural 'rape myths' that hold the victim responsible for the abuse suffered.

19 My thanks to Don Kulick for this point and for his many helpful suggestions on the writing of this chapter.

20 While in St. Vincent, I was a supportive participant in the Vincentian National Women's Organization's efforts in raising awareness of sexual violence. As an intellectual worker, I do research which documents the

reality of sexual violence and its impact on women's lives, I write about it in my academic publications, I teach about it in my classroom, and I confront those who would minimize its effects with my own experience and with 'hard data'.

21 Some of my professors, and many colleagues, still believe that women who want careers should not get married and have children, that these roles are incompatible. Among the U.S. upper-middle-class, wives and mothers are an asset to professional men, while husbands and babies are a liability for professional women. This perspective, of course, is not unique to anthropology but widespread throughout academia and professional circles.

References

Abrahams, Roger D. (1983) *The Man-of-Words in the West Indies.* Baltimore, Md.: Johns Hopkins University Press.

Alexander, Jack (1984) 'Love, Race, Slavery, and Sexuality in Jamaican Images of the Family', in Raymond T. Smith (ed.) *Kinship Ideology and Practice in Latin America.* Chapel Hill, N.C.: University of North Carolina Press.

Bateson, Gregory (1972) *Steps to an Ecology of Mind.* New York: Ballantine Books.

Bordo, Susan (1990) 'Feminism, Postmodernism, and Gender-Scepticism', in Linda J. Nicholson (ed.) *Feminism and Postmodernism.* New York: Routledge.

Bourgois, Philippe (1991) 'Confronting the Ethics of Ethnography: Lessons from Fieldwork in Central America', in Faye V. Harrison (ed.) *Decolonizing Anthropology.* Washington, D.C.: American Anthropological Association.

Bowman, Glen (1988) 'Fucking Tourists: Sexual Relations and Tourism in Jerusalem's Old City'. *Critique of Anthropology.* Vol. 9, No. 2, pp. 77–93.

Brana-Shute, Gary (1979) *On the Corner.* Assen: Van Gorcum.

Cesara, Manda (1982) *Reflections of a Woman Anthropologist: No Hiding Place.* London and New York: Academic Press.

Clifford, James (1986) 'Introduction', in James Clifford and George E. Marcus (eds) *Writing Culture: The Poetics and Politics of Ethnography* Berkeley, Calif.: University of California Press.

——— and George E. Marcus (eds) (1986) *Writing Culture: The Poetics and Politics of Ethnography.* Berkeley, Calif.: University of California Press.

Crapanzano, Vincent (1980) *Tuhami, Portrait of a Moroccan.* Chicago: University of Chicago Press.

D'Amico-Samuels, Deborah (1991) 'Undoing Fieldwork: Personal, Political, Theoretical and Methodological Implications', in Faye V. Harrison (ed.) *Decolonizing Anthropology.* Washington, D.C.: American Anthropological Association.

Delany, Carol (1988) 'Participant-observation: The Razor's Edge'. *Dialectical Anthropology.* Vol. 13, pp. 291–300.

DeVita, P.R. (ed.) (1980) *The Humbled Anthropologist: Tales from the Pacific.* Belmont, Calif.: Wadsworth.

Dwyer, K. (1982) *Moroccan Dialogues: Anthropology in Question*. Baltimore, Md.: Johns Hopkins University Press.

Farganis, Sondra (1989) 'Feminism and the Reconstruction of Social Science', in Alison M. Jaggar and Susan R. Bordo (eds) *Gender/Body/Knowledge: Feminist Reconstructions of Being and Knowing*. New Brunswick, N.J.: Rutgers University Press.

Favret-Saada, J. (1980) *Deadly Words: Witchcraft in the Bocage*. Cambridge: Cambridge University Press.

Freilich, Morris (1971) 'Sex, Secrets and Systems', in Stanford N. Gerber (ed.) *The Family in the Caribbean*. Rio Piedras: Institute of Caribbean Studies.

Gearing, M. Jean (1988) 'The Reproduction of Labor in a Migration Society: Gender, Kinship, and Household in St. Vincent, West Indies'. Ph.D. dissertation, University of Florida.

Geertz, Clifford (1988) *Works and Lives: The Anthropologist as Author*. Stanford, Calif.: Stanford University Press.

Golde, Peggy (ed.) (1970) *Women in the Field: Anthropological Experiences*. Berkeley, Calif.: University of California Press.

Harding, S. (1987) *Feminism and Methodology: Social Science Issues*. Bloomington: Indiana University Press.

Harrison, Faye V. (1991a) 'Anthropology as an Agent of Transformation: Introductory Comments and Queries', in Faye V. Harrison (ed.) *Decolonizing Anthropology*. Washington, D.C.: American Anthropological Association.

——— (1991b) 'Ethnography as Politics', in Faye V. Harrison (ed.) *Decolonizing Anthropology*. Washington, D.C.: American Anthropological Association.

Howell, Nancy (1990) *Surviving Fieldwork*. Special Publication of the American Anthropological Association No. 26. Washington, D.C.: American Anthropological Association.

Jaggar, Alison M. (1989) 'Love and Knowledge: Emotion in Feminist Epistemology', in Alison M. Jaggar and Susan R. Bordo (eds) *Gender/Body/Knowledge: Feminist Reconstructions of Being and Knowing*. New Brunswick, N.J.: Rutgers University Press.

——— and Susan Bordo (1989) 'Introduction' in Alison M. Jaggar and Susan R. Bordo (eds) *Gender/Body/Knowledge: Feminist Reconstructions of Being and Knowing*. New Brunswick, N.J.: Rutgers University Press.

Johannsen, Agneta M. (1992) 'Applied Anthropology and Post-Modernist Ethnography'. *Human Organization*. Vol. 51, No. 1, pp. 71–81.

Johnson, Norris Brock (1984) 'Sex, Color, and Rites of Passage in Ethnographic Research'. *Human Organization*. Vol 43, No. 2, pp. 108–20.

King, Arden, (1987) 'Anthropologist as Human: The Ultimate Paradox'. *Anthropology and Humanism Quarterly*. Vol. 12, pp. 47–51.

Lindsay, Lydia (1986) 'Interracial Relationships: Jamaican Immigrant Women in Birmingham, England, 1951–1971'. *Journal of Caribbean Studies*. pp. 179–201.

MacCormack, Carol P. and Alizon Draper (1987) 'Social and Cognitive Aspects of Female Sexuality in Jamaica', in Pat Caplan (ed.) *The Cultural Construction of Sexuality*. New York: Tavistock.

Marcus, George and Dick Cushman (1982) 'Ethnographies as Texts'. *Annual Review of Anthropology*. Vol. 11, pp. 25–69.

——— and Michael Fischer (1986) *Anthropology as Cultural Critique*. Chicago: University of Chicago Press.

Mascia-Lees, Frances E., Patricia Sharpe, and Colleen Ballerino Cohen (1989) 'The Postmodernist Turn in Anthropology: Cautions from a Feminist Perspective'. *Signs: Journal of Women in Culture and Society*. Vol. 15, No. 1, pp. 7–33.

Morth, Grace E. (1973) 'Commess: Traditional and Official Forms of Social Control', in Thomas M. Fraser, Jr. (ed.) *Windward Road: Contributions to the Anthropology of St. Vincent*. Department of Anthropology Research Report No. 12. Amherst, Mass.: University of Massachusetts.

Murphy, Robert (1987) *The Body Silent*. New York: Henry Holt.

Myerhoff, Barbara (1978) *Number Our Days*. New York: Simon and Schuster.

Nader, Laura (1989) 'Post-interpretive Anthropology'. *Anthropology Quarterly*. Vol. 62, No. 3, pp. 149–59.

Newton, Esther (1993) 'My Best Informant's Dress: The Erotic Equation in Fieldwork'. *Cultural Anthropology*. Vol. 8, No. 1, pp. 3–23.

Rabinow, Paul (1977) *Reflections on Fieldwork in Morocco*. Berkeley, Calif.: University of California Press.

Rosaldo, Renato (1989) *Culture and Truth: The Remaking of Social Analysis*. Boston, Mass.: Beacon Press.

Rose, Dan (1990) *Living the Ethnographic Life*. Qualitative Research Methods, Vol. 23, Newbury Park, Calif.: Sage.

Ruby, Jay (ed.) (1982) *A Crack in the Mirror: Reflexive Perspectives in Anthropology*. Philadelphia: University of Pennsylvania Press.

Said, Edward (1978) *Orientalism*. New York: Vintage Books.

Shostak, Marjorie (1981) *Nisa: The Life and Words of a !Kung Woman*. Cambridge, Mass.: Harvard University Press.

Smith, R.T. (1988) *Kinship and Class in the West Indies*. Cambridge: Cambridge University Press.

Sobo, Elisa, J. (1993) 'Bodies, Kin, and Flow: Family Planning in Rural Jamaica'. *Medical Anthropology Quarterly*. Vol. 7, No. 1, pp. 50–73.

Spencer, Jonathan (1989) 'Anthropology as a Kind of Writing'. *Man*. Vol. 24, pp. 145–64.

Stoller, Paul (1989) *The Taste of Ethnographic Things*. Philadelphia: University of Pennsylvania Press.

Tedlock, Barbara (1991) 'From Participant Observation to the Observation of Participation: The Emergence of Narrative Ethnography'. *Journal of Anthropological Research*. Vol. 47, No. 1, pp. 69–94.

Vance, Carole S. (1984) 'Pleasure and Danger: Toward a Politics of Sexuality', in Carole S. Vance (ed.) *Pleasure and Danger: Exploring Female Sexuality*. Boston, Mass.: Routledge and Kegan Paul.

Vendler, Zeno (1984) 'Understanding People', in Richard A. Shweder and Robert Levine (eds) *Culture Theory: Essays on Mind, Self, and Emotion*. Cambridge: Cambridge University Press.

Warren, Carol A.B. (1977) 'Fieldwork in the Gay World: Issues in Phenomenological Research'. *Journal of Social Issues*. Vol. 33, No. 4, pp. 93–107.

Whitehead, Tony Larry (1986) 'Breakdown, Resolution, and Coherence: The Fieldwork Experience of a Big, Brown, Pretty-talking Man in a West Indian Community', in Tony Larry Whitehead and Mary Ellen Conaway (eds) *Self,*

Sex and Gender in Cross-cultural Fieldwork. Urbana and Chicago: University of Illinois Press.

——— Mary Ellen Conaway (1986) 'Introduction', in Tony Larry Whitehead and Mary Ellen Conaway (eds) *Self, Sex and Gender in Cross-cultural Fieldwork*. Urbana and Chicago: University of Illinois Press.

Wikan, Unni (1991) 'Toward an Experience-near Anthropology'. *Cultural Anthropology*. Vol. 6, No. 3, pp. 285–305.

Chapter 8

Rape in the field

Reflections from a survivor

*Eva Moreno**

> Through field work at the pleasure of the host culture one learns one's place there and that it is one's only vantage point for penetrating the culture. Mistakes and mishaps in the field are great lamps of illumination if one survives; friendships there are the only greater source, besides being a divine comfort.
>
> (Landes 1986: 139)

Aside from outright murder, rape is the ultimate sanction used by men to maintain the gender order.[1] Fear of rape forces women to abide by restrictions on physical movement and demeanor, and to conform to behavioral rules that govern most aspects of their entire lives.[2] That women are themselves to be blamed for rape is a prevalent notion in many societies, one that stems from the idea that it is the responsibility of women to make sure that they are not 'in the wrong place at the wrong time'. In other words, there are times, places, and situations out of bounds for women, which they traverse only at their own risk.

Rape and female anthropologists

Anthropologists who do fieldwork in foreign societies or among unfamiliar groups find themselves outside the bounds of their own gender order. They seldom conform completely to the gender conventions of the society in which they do fieldwork. An acute problem for female anthropologists, like myself, is that members of the host society may try to force us into a local gender order, in precisely the same way as local women, who wittingly or unwittingly provoke and challenge the

* The author's name and all other names in this chapter are pseudonyms.

existing order, are punished and brought into line. To some female anthropologists this can be a familiar situation, since we, in our home environment, may be perceived as recalcitrant rebels against a gendered order that does not easily allow independent, able women to rise above the prestige levels of our peers, and where sexual harassment is a standard measure taken by men to keep a male-dominated gender hierarchy intact. The potential for sexual violence against women, from harassment to rape-related murder, is present everywhere. In a field situation, the mere fact that one is a single female anthropologist doing her own thing may present an intolerable provocation to some individuals. Knowing that such risks face female fieldworkers, it is surprising that the anthropological literature is almost devoid of references to sexual violence to anthropologists.

There are many good reasons for this silence, some of them mentioned in other contributions to this volume. The element of blame that still attaches itself to the rape survivor means that women who have suffered sexual violence are afraid to damage their professional standing by talking about it. Among anthropologists, there is a tacit assumption often at work that a competent anthropologist would not place herself in a position where she could be raped in the first place (cf. Howell 1990: 93). There is also a predominant masculine view that equates vulnerability with weakness, which makes many women afraid to confront vulnerability for fear of being considered lesser anthropologists than our male colleagues. In the 'West', rape is still a stigmatized topic and victims often expect (and receive) little sympathy for their descriptions of assault. The recent reaction of some colleagues to reports of other kinds of personal violence against anthropologists in field situations, where the violence was seen as somehow the author's 'fault', suggests that the silence of rape victims is based on fairly accurate assumptions (Kulick 1994). The two instances of rape and attempted rape mentioned in Howell's book both led to the death of the victims, which may, sadly enough, be the reason why they are reported; since no further damage can be done to the professional lives of the victims, and they cannot themselves control what is written about them.

Besides concern about one's professional reputation, a further, major reason for the silence on rape and sexual assault is that those who have experienced such assault are very likely suffering from rape trauma syndrome. In describing the rape inflicted on her and her subsequent attempts to cope with it, Cathy Winkler observes that,

> Rapists overrule not only the words and actions of their victims but also attack victims' definition of their body and their sexual self. Rapists' threats extend beyond superficial retorts and mentally and psychologically invade victims' beings and self-definition.
>
> (1991: 12)

At the best of times, it takes a long time to overcome a rape trauma syndrome. Such an experience is devastating enough if it occurs in familiar surroundings. If it happens in a situation such as fieldwork, where one's sense of self is already under attack (Wengle 1988), many dimensions of the trauma, such as feelings of guilt, responsibility, and self-loathing, will be further aggravated. Unless the purpose of the writing is therapeutic or to provide legal testimony, it is almost impossible to write about the rape before the trauma is somehow brought under manageable control.

Then there is pure fear, a generalized fear by the survivor and an insidious relationship of fear between rapist and survivor that is likely to last until the death of either party. For the victim, this is fear of being raped again, or killed. Winkler writes that 'rapists bury land-mines in the bodies of their victims', land mines that explode in confusion, nausea, nightmares, tremors, depression, and shakiness (Winkler 1991). If the victim reports the crime, she fears retribution from the rapist. If the rapist should be brought to trial, not only does the survivor have to relive the experience publicly and see the assailant once again, but he may be acquitted of the crime, perhaps with a mind to seek revenge on her for turning him in. And even if the rapist is convicted, the survivor knows he will soon be out, perhaps ready to take revenge on his accuser.

Twenty years have passed since the events I am about to describe took place. After all that time it has still been difficult to write this piece. It is impossible to be a participant observer and eventual reporter in a situation where your life and self are at stake. Your emotions and fundamentally disturbed equilibrium are too private to be be traded in for anthropological credits.[3] Nevertheless, time does make a difference. I can look back on the young person who was me, with sadness and fear, but also tolerance and a profound gratitude to the people in the field who interfered and stood by me. I now feel that I owe it to that young woman who was me, and to many other fledgling anthropologists, to recount this story as I understand events after two decades of trying to come to grips with what happened and why.

A fieldwork experience

I first went to Ethiopia in 1964, on a five-week stay. I was 20 years old and propelled by an acute infatuation with an Ethiopian student in Sweden, my home country. A year later, I went back as a member of the Swedish Volunteer Service, to work for two years as a social scientist in a development-aid-funded technical organization. After those two years, I returned to Sweden to finish my undergraduate studies in sociology, but I was soon back in Ethiopia for several months in 1968 to do fieldwork for my final research paper.

When I returned to Ethiopia in February 1972 to do fieldwork for my doctoral dissertation, I had used the intervening years to delve into social anthropology for the Africanist knowledge I could not find in Swedish sociology. The goal of my research was to do an urban study, in the small southern town of Ketema, using both survey methods and life history interviews. To do this work, I needed an assistant to help me, preferably a person with a high level of education and a good command of English.

I would have preferred to work with a woman, and I spread that word through my contacts at the university and elsewhere. My networks came up with a couple of female candidates for the job; but in the end neither was interested in prolonged sojourns outside the capital. To most young, educated persons in Ethiopia, living outside the capital was extremely unappealing. If work 'in the provinces' was unattractive to young men, it was nearly impossible for young women. Educated girls, like all girls belonging to the upper echelon, were kept, as far as was possible, within their families until they were married. The few who were not under the guardianship of their families had other concerns that made them unwilling to leave the urban scene.

In the end, I had two young men to choose between, both of whom had been suggested by my university contacts. One was several years younger than myself, a sociology major with a high Afro hair-style, flared trousers, nervous at the interview: the very picture of a dandy from the city. The other – whom I will call Yonas – was a man my own age, unobtrusively dressed and coiffed, with previous experience as a fieldworker for one of the national government agencies. Yonas professed to be politically interested (which at that time meant that he was leftist) and did not seem nervous when we spoke. Both Yonas and my other prospective assistant had recently been thrown out of the university, the younger man for the first time, Yonas for the third.

Being expelled from the university was common in those days of political tension, as university students in Ethiopia took the lead in protesting against autocratic political regimes. To be expelled three times, however, was odd. At the time, though, I interpreted this as a sign that Yonas was possessed by a commendable zeal in the pursuit of truth and justice – an interpretation no doubt encouraged by Yonas himself. After some consideration of which of the two men to choose, I finally decided on Yonas, on the basis of this zeal, his experience, his apparent calmness, and his professed interest in the study.

From the very beginning of my relationship with Yonas, I had problems with authority. In my mind, and consequently in my behavior and talk, several conflicting conceptions of authority were superimposed. In my own society, differences of social and economic class certainly existed but were only subtly marked. In the 1940s and 1950s, the existence of class differences in Sweden had been ignored in official political rhetoric. This had changed drastically in the 1960s. Heightened awareness of class differences propelled attempts to eliminate the class markers and undermine the social and economic dynamics that reproduced class inequalities. This effort took many different forms, both officially and informally, from far-reaching reforms of the educational system, to an abolition of the formal, polite *vous* pronoun of address in speech.

In workplaces, this meant doing away with the markers of rank. One newly built university campus, for instance, had no separate dining or meeting spaces reserved for faculty; the same conditions were meant to apply to everyone. Although we never quite reached the point of addressing one another as 'comrade', titles were no longer used in face-to-face communication, and employees of all ranks within the same organization used first names to address one another.

But things were not really what they seemed to be. Beneath the professed equality we all knew perfectly well who the boss was and who the subordinate was; who decided and who was compelled to follow 'suggestions'. All we had done was set aside the more obvious markers of class and status. This worked, in an odd kind of way, because Swedes were a fairly homogeneous people with one religion, one language, and one race; descendants of the two-thirds that were left behind while the more daring lot disappeared to the United States at the turn of the century.

In addition to this confusing and contradictory stance toward authority that I brought with me from home, I also possessed a familiarity, mostly on a subconscious level, with the modern Ethiopian systems of stratification. Ethiopia was, and is, an extremely complex society where different kinds of hierarchies intersect, enforce, and contradict each other. In the 1960s, the most prominent of those hierarchies was the political ('feudal') hierarchy, with the Emperor at the apex. Relatives of the Emperor made up the upper segments of this hierarchy.[4] Other hierarchies were the ethnic ones, the religious ones, the one based on modern secular education, and the one based on wealth. Superimposed on all of these were the gender orders, which were distinct for each ethnic group, including a separate gender order for the urban, 'modern' sector of society in which I had planted my roots.

This intricate webwork of hierarchy permeated every aspect of social life. It was everywhere, and was continually reinforced by practices of deference and domination that were inescapable if you were part of Ethiopian society. To be sure, my Ethiopian cronies abroad and in the capital were appalled at the open and ruthless exploitation built into and sustained by the manifold hierarchies; nevertheless, they – and I along with them – were part of the system and we all acted our part in dealing with ministers, beggars, officials, bosses, servants, prostitutes, brokers, thieves, husbands, and wives.

Without being aware of it, I had adopted the same attitudes and behavior towards people around me as my Ethiopian middle-class friends and companions. Unthinkingly, I expected the same kind of response from subordinates as they would have expected and received. I did not realize that the status I had held while living in Ethiopia before had been status by association, derived from the organization I worked for and from the status of the Ethiopians I associated with. Initially, my interaction with others as a solitary foreign researcher, equipped with a car and official permits and certificates, appeared to make most people accept the status I claimed.

After three months in Ethiopia, and one month working with Yonas in the capital on some archives, all preparations were over and I finally moved on to Ketema, with Yonas in tow.

Ketema twenty years ago was a busy town, expanding almost as one stood watching. It had about 12,000 inhabitants, from all of the major ethnic groups in the country. Its structure was typical of African roadside towns; a narrow belt of one-story adobe buildings with tin roofs that clung to a one-kilometer strip of all-weather highway. Nowhere did the town extend more than 500 meters from the highway.

The inhabitants of Ketema earned their living through trade, communication, services, and administration. The town was a town of newcomers, divided along class, ethnic, religious, and neighborhood lines. It catered to travellers and traders; it was full of eating places, dormitories, 'nightclubs', and it hosted many one-room bars, run by single women who served local beer – and themselves – on demand. There were also a couple of banks, several gas pumps, two elementary schools and one junior high school, a police station, a sizeable daily market, and a very large weekly market. You could eat out in Ketema on anything from 5 US cents to 1.5 US dollars; you could spend the night in a dormitory for 10 cents or in a highly respectable hotel for 2 dollars.

When Yonas and I first arrived in Ketema, I decided to stay in the respectable hotel. I rented a room for Yonas in the same place, thus introducing a firm note of (assumed) equality into our relationship from the very start. Once we were established in the hotel, the first task that faced me was to find some place to live. I felt that as an anthropologist, I was expected either to live with a family or to have a household of my own. After all, who among us has not been appalled at backstage rumors of senior anthropologists working out of hotels? I realized later that in my situation in Ketema, the obvious thing would have been to set up permanent camp in one of the lesser hotels. But I had no eye for the obvious. I was set on doing things according to the book, and thus began house-hunting.

After having gone through the available dwellings in the town itself, I decided on a house a few hundred meters outside the town, even though it did not fit my idea of an ideal anthropological residence. The house was set apart from the town, and it was nice, spacious, and expensive. It was a stone construction, built by a minor official in a subdivision neighboring that of Ketema, for his eventual retirement. In the meantime, he wanted to rent out the house for a cost corresponding to that of his bank loan. With the house came the official's uncle and the uncle's wife, who lived in the servants' quarters in the back of the house and who looked after the house, when it was empty. On one side of the building was an unfinished hotel, on the other a plot of land used for growing potatoes.

The house was big enough for both me and my assistant, so I invited Yonas to have a room in the building. My rationale was that I could not afford to find him a reasonable place in town. In addition, however, I also felt that I might become very lonely in the evenings, so I wanted him around to have someone to talk to. I discussed the advisability of this arrangement with Yonas because I feared that living together might signal to the townspeople that the relationship between Yonas and myself was more than one of employer–employee. Yonas told me that people in town would assume that we had sexual relations regardless of whether he shared the house with me or not, and that I therefore should choose the arrangement that was most practical. My apprehension was eased by the reactions of the old uncle, Benjamin, who was the caretaker of the house. Benjamin obviously did not imagine that Yonas and I were a couple; instead it was clear that he perceived Yonas as a kind of combination bodyguard/staff member.

Ketema, being the transient roadside town that it was, had nearly all essentials for hire. Before long, I had set up office, bedrooms, and kitchen with the aid of the local rental agency and some strong-armed daily laborers.

Early on, I developed serious doubts about Yonas' suitability as a field assistant. He was brooding, moody, excessively flattering, and habitually bragging – often of how he had got the better of someone who had insulted him. This was uncomfortable at the time. In hindsight, it was ominous. But time was short and I felt that I had no real alternative with whom I could replace him. I simply hoped for the best, calmed by my previous positive experience of working relations with young men who seemed superficially similar to Yonas.

One of the first nights in Ketema, while we were still in the hotel, Yonas appeared in my room one evening, dressed only in his underwear. This was my first indication that his interpretation of our relationship was very different from my own. In his view, he explained, the time had come for me to become his lover. I did not take his advance seriously, and I fended him off easily by reiterating my position: I had a permanent partner at home and I had no intention of having other relations while in Ethiopia. He went back to his room with no further protestations.

In retrospect, it seems incredible that this instance did not make me react more definitely. Thinking back, I realize that as a young woman I was so accustomed to men making unwelcome advances toward me that I considered Yonas' proposition quite 'normal'. It never occurred to me that, as his employer, I was actually in a position to demand that he stop bothering me with requests for sex. In addition, part of my own cultural baggage was an astonishing lack of fear. My generation of young women in Scandinavia felt safe, and was safe,[5] in our own countries. We carried our insouciance with us from the Arctic circle to the Sahara, fearing nothing, and usually getting away with it. Maybe our very innocence protected us. In addition, I had received no relevant field training, nor did I have any senior colleague at home or in the field to whom I could turn for advice. And furthermore, I was also reassured by the chivalrous courtship I had experienced during my earlier years in Ethiopia. What I did not realize was that during those earlier years, I had seemed very young to my Ethiopian friends. They often thought me no more than a teenager – that is to say, inexperienced and in need of protection. Now, four years later, I was clearly a mature woman with no husband or male guardian present. Therefore, I appeared available.

At any rate, as far as Yonas was concerned, this was clearly the case, and soon his campaign was launched. For several weeks it consisted mainly of nagging – interminable 'why nots?' – and of not heeding my persistent refusals – refusals that became more determined, definite, and exasperated as time went on. I did not understand why he would not give up. He did not understand why I would not give in.

While all this was going on, data collection got under way. My aim in gathering data was to trace as many of the respondents as I could from a household survey that had been conducted several years previously by the national statistical agency. I wanted to check on the reliability of the survey technique in a setting such as Ketema, and to get an inkling of different kinds of change in the population.

To help with this work, I had employed a middle-aged messenger from the Community Development Center. He was the scout; he went around town with a list of the respondents, starting out by finding the ones he already knew, and then locating others in a snowball fashion. His work was absolutely crucial; not only did he find or get information on 80 per cent of the original respondents, he explained the study to the respondents, persuaded them to agree to a second interview, and set the time for that interview. The messenger, Yonas, and I would then interview the respondent with a modified version of the original questionnaire.

As time went by, I felt that my presence was not required during the interviews and I increasingly left Yonas and the messenger to carry them out on their own, while I devoted myself to checking and organizing the compiled data. I was gradually recovering the language skills I had possessed when I left Ethiopia in 1968, but I had not mastered the art of conducting a formal interview with strangers. In the unnatural situation of a formal interview, I realized that I was using Amharic as if it had been Swedish, in a manner as alien to Ethiopians as if I had in fact been speaking a foreign language. Furthermore, hardly any of the respondents had spoken to a foreigner before and the experience affected them greatly. Some simply did not hear me and merely stared, or mumbled that they did not speak English. After proddings from the people listening in on the interview (there were always people listening in) they would listen and respond, but the situation clearly made them feel uncomfortable. I could not have carried out this work on my own. Not that Yonas was much of an interviewer himself, being much too direct and brusque. Without the preparations done by the messenger we would probably have ended up with a large number of refusals. As an interviewer, I think Yonas was conditioned by his previous role as an official in interview situations where the respondents had no choice about whether they wanted to participate or not. At this point in the work, however, I was not yet aware of Yonas' faults as an interviewer. That insight came later, when I could compare his style with that of other persons working with me.

After weeks of daily nagging, Yonas quieted down, and for a while I thought he had given up the idea of sexual conquest. I later understood that he had merely changed his tactics. He now embarked on impressing on me how crucial his presence was to my work. In the picture he painted, the townspeople identified the study with him, not with me. He led me to believe that our industrious messenger would take orders only from him, and that I would have to start all over, from scratch, in another town, if he decided to quit and leave me.

What went on in the town I did not know. I was used to being stared at, to parents picking up their children to show them the *ferenji*, the foreigner. Ketema was not a friendly place. It was a town of strangers, with different languages and habits, full of prejudice and mutual suspicion. Although I was uneasy about the way the townspeople ignored me, I was not surprised. I blamed it on my own ineptness and inherent timidity. Increasingly I felt that I lived in a glass bowl, with people looking in on me and me I looking out at them, but with no real contact, no genuine communication.

By the time we had been at work in Ketema for two months, I was beginning to feel quite shaken. My uneasiness about my isolation was compounded by Yonas' broodiness, which seemed to grow by the day. He had frightening, screaming nightmares, easily audible in my room, which was next to his. When he went out at night, he had taken to carrying a gun. The gun worried me, even though I knew that Ethiopian men prided themselves on being armed, and I had often seen other educated men from the capital bringing hand-guns along when they went out of town. My concern was over what Yonas, in his agitated and surly frame of mind, might do with his gun.

Lacking effective authority, I tried to handle the situation with quasi-psychological techniques that were meaningless, inefficient, and condescending under the circumstances. For instance, thinking/hoping that showing trust would generate trustworthiness, I did not lock my bedroom door. Sure enough, I woke up one night to find Yonas in the middle of the room, furiously accusing me of sleeping with everybody else except him.

I do not remember how I repelled this particular advance, but Yonas left the room after a few minutes of loud complaining about my sexual discrimination against Ethiopian men. He believed me to be promiscuous: why, he demanded to know, would I not be promiscuous with him? Henceforth I locked my room carefully, with a bitter feeling of failure and guilt.

Then, one day, Yonas suddenly announced that he quit. The next day he left.

At first, his decision to leave the job made me frantic. His continual insistence that I was dependent on him had influenced me profoundly: I had no doubt that my work in Ketema was linked to his person and that I would have to start all over again in another town if he left. Months into fieldwork, I still seemed to be completely incapable of establishing rapport with anybody. The townspeople were distant; even though most respondents answered our questions, they did so with little enthusiasm and the interviews led to no further contact. At this point I believed that this was because the townspeople wanted nothing to do with me.

Besides Yonas, the only people in Ketema with whom I had any kind of social relationship were Benjamin, the old guard who had come attached to my house, so to speak, and his wife. Benjamin was a retired soldier in his late seventies who used to be in the Emperor's service. Upon retiring, he had been promised a piece of land near Ketema where he would be able to support himself farming. Once actually there, however, the local officials would not honor his claim and he was left without means of support. It was his firm opinion that 'if the king only knew' things would be put right. But he had no ways of reaching the king, and while waiting for imperial intercession, he had accepted the position of guard for his nephew's house. Not that he held a very high opinion of his nephew, whose apparent wealth implied advanced levels of corruption, but . . .

His wife Sofia was many years his junior. They had been living together for a year when we met. She had only one eye, and was energetic, industrious, and realistic. She saw the old man as a gullible dreamer but a good man, to be respected for his bravery and his old age. She told Yonas that she had had offers from wealthier, and therefore more attractive, men, but that she felt it her duty to stay by the old soldier, who, in her opinion, could not possibly manage on his own.

The two of them had an easy-going, friendly relationship. Sofia supplemented their income by going around baking in wealthier households several times a week. She also distilled spirits in an ingenious still, composed mainly of bamboo sticks, calabashes, and cow dung. The couple consumed much of what they produced themselves; they often called me in for a snort on my route to and from the latrine ('Good for the heart!'). What they did not drink themselves went to supply some of the simple drinking places in town. The old man, in addition, furthered their economy by renting a piece of land where he grew cereals for their own use and for the market.

Sofia helped me out with washing, cleaning, and shopping. She was very interested in the doings of other people, and was lively and talkative, making her a wonderful source of information about everyday life in Ketema. Through her I learnt many things, including some of the strategies the townspeople used to manage economically.

Benjamin took his guarding seriously. When I told him that Yonas was no longer going to work for me and had left the house, he made no comments. Yet the same night when it was time to go to bed, he came into the house, bringing his big coat and blanket (and a kitten for company), and proceeded to bed down in front of my bedroom door. I was touched, of course, but also deeply embarrassed. The guard did not budge; there was no other way to keep me safe at night, he explained: he could not hear me from his home should anything happen, and it was his responsibility to see that nothing did. In the morning he wrapped up his bedding and went home.

After a couple of days on my own, I was beginning to collect my wits again and, to my surprise, I actually began to feel relieved at Yonas' departure. It looked as if I was finally getting out of what had become an insufferable situation. Changing towns might not be such a bad idea. I was beginning to think that I could start anew with an assistant from whatever town I might choose to work in. A real worry, however, was the short time at my disposal for my fieldwork. My whole project had already been delayed substantially because of the Ethiopian government's reaction to some critical articles that my anthropology supervisor had published in Swedish newspapers. Because of those articles, my research visa had been put on ice, and I spent nine months at home, waiting for the visa and consequently using up my research grant money. Moving to a new town and starting over would mean risking running out of money. However, my plan was simply to be less ambitious, and to try to make as much use as possible out of the material that had already been gathered in Ketema.

At that point, as I was actually beginning to feel happy at the prospect of starting over again, Yonas came back. He returned nonchalantly, as if nothing had happened, to see if I had changed my mind. Of course, he told me, he never really intended to quit. He was just upset because I would not sleep with him. But now he was ready to get to work again.

In spite of my relief that Yonas had gone, I realized that to take him back would be the 'easy' way out. I was going to be leaving Ethiopia soon for a month-long vacation. Yonas and the messenger could wrap up the re-study phase on their own, I reasoned. In a month or so, the first phase of the investigation would be over. Some sort of study seemed possible even if I had completely abandoned the notion of doing fieldwork with the depth I had intended, or the way I assumed all other anthropologists did it. I acquiesced to Yonas' return.

I returned to Ethiopia a month later and found the situation in Ketema as I had left it. Yonas was, if possible, more aggravated than before, and he resumed his campaign of sexual conquest immediately. He began taking out his gun at home. Glowering, he would put it on the table, together with his stock of bullets – five or six – and polish them, trying at the same time to impress me with the potential danger of gun use. I hysterically refused to admit even to myself that this little arms demonstration in any way concerned me. Gradually my sense of reality was giving way until I became just as preoccupied with Yonas, his moods, threats, resignations, and pleadings, as he had become obsessed with me and my resistance to his desires.

Our situation resembled that of a battered wife and her assailant. Seen from the outside, I could have stepped out of the situation at any time. But inside the circle cast by our grotesque relations, I had no ability to defend myself against his manipulations. I could not understand what was going on, except that Yonas seemed to be in the grip of a neurotic, fixed idea and could not be reached by reason or argument. All I could hope for was that the first phase of the study would soon be completed, so that I would have an excuse to put an end somehow to my association with Yonas.

In trying to cope with the extreme stress I felt, I found pretenses to visit the capital. I also fled regularly into writing and reading, and I could bring myself to make no decisions about the next step in the investigation. Gloom.

Finally, one of my oldest Ethiopian friends managed to break through my inertia. I had dropped in at his office in the capital for a cup of coffee and a chat. Casually I told him, as a joke, no doubt, about the bullet-polishing sessions. My situation in Ketema was assuming an eerie quality of normality as my vision of anthropological fieldwork receded. My friend Michael's reaction was unequivocal: 'Get rid of the man at once! If you don't he is likely to kill you.' Michael offered to lend me a gun. In his view, the situation was too serious for me to be unarmed. I declined, but I returned to Ketema finally realizing that I was in danger.

Even now, though, I was not up to firing Yonas. The many months in Ketema had locked us in a ghastly struggle of wills over which of us would be the one to define our relations. This ongoing battle had left me with a sense of Yonas' inevitability. During the previous several months, however, I had made the acquaintance of two expatriate ladies living in the neighboring town of Woha, 20 kilometers away. They were seasoned in the service of British Overseas Aid and the World Health Organisation (WHO), and had worked for more than fifteen years in Asia and Africa. Seeking temporary escape from my glass bowl, I had taken to visiting them during weekends, in what provided a tremendous release from the pressures of 'home'. I had a car, and the younger of the two had a spare bedroom. Ketema was less than 20 minutes away by car. To break up our incongruous household, I decided to leave Ketema and accept the younger woman's standing offer of bed and breakfast, even if this act felt like the final betrayal of my own neurotic fixed idea – that of fieldwork 'according to the book'.

On the morning of 4 October, I told Yonas that I was dissolving the household. Furthermore, I would do it the next day. To my surprise, Yonas seemed to accept the new arrangement. But the same night I woke up. Someone was knocking at my door. I turned on the light and looked at my watch. It was one o'clock in the morning.

'What is it?'

'It is me, Yonas! I'm being eaten alive. Hand me the flea spray!'

The flea spray? Was it in my room? Why was it in my room?

I put on my dressing gown. Flea spray in hand, I unlocked and opened my door. Yonas pushed the door with all his strength and forced his entry into the room.

Time stopped. My room was fairly large and bare. My bed was in a corner. The window facing the front garden was shuttered from the inside. The guard Benjamin was sleeping in his own shuttered house, an unreachable 20 meters from where we were. My outer wall on the gable had no window. We were alone.

Yonas grabbed me, my gown, my hair. I was paralyzed. All I could bring myself to do was to retreat into the room, trying to loosen his hands from around my throat.

And then I screamed. Or rather, someone in me screamed. I heard myself screaming – an inarticulate scream, not calling for help, but shrill, loud, like a siren. My whole body seemed to have taken on a life of its own, refusing to move, to kick, to fight back – to do any of the things I knew that it could do. And that horrible scream. Even as I heard the screaming, though, I realized that there was nobody to hear me. There was a potato field just outside the house, but nobody was in that. Benjamin did not hear well, anyway there were three walls and many meters between us; his wife could not possibly hear me either. And what if someone did hear? Yonas had told me many times that people believed we were lovers anyway; men regularly beat their wives; they would side with Yonas, thinking that I had earned whatever was coming to me.

Yonas made no headway with me. We were the same height, he was no heavier than me and no stronger. My body was stiff as a tree trunk. It kept up its shrill, piercing screaming.

Cold sweat poured down Yonas' face and made his hands slippery. His eyes were huge, bulging, mad. He was beside himself with rage and determination. Unreachable.

He was wearing striped pyjamas with pockets. From one of those pockets, he now brought out his gun, almost reluctantly, making sure which way it pointed so as not to shoot himself accidentally. Backing up a few steps, he pointed the gun at me.

The screaming stopped; my mind and body reunited with the realization that my life was at stake, whether he shot me deliberately or not. If the gun went off accidentally, I might bleed to death.

As I looked at the mouth of the gun I had a vision of being directly beneath the black night and the cold, distant stars, cool, clear-headed, with death minutes, maybe seconds, away. And what for? A fixed idea, a manic determination not to give up, to uphold my definition of who I was at any cost?

Yonas began speaking. He told me that since I had decided to leave the house in Ketema he knew this was his last chance to have me. And he would have me now, whatever the cost to himself. He did not care any more if he lived or died as long as he finally had me. I replied, coldly and perfectly numb, that he could have anything he wanted, anything at all.

At precisely that moment, there was a tremendous pounding on the shutters. Loud voices, many voices, pummelling, shouting. Yonas momentarily lost his step. We were both astounded. Who could it be? Who? To me it was as if the black, void sky had opened and angels had descended to interfere. A fraction of a second passed. Then Yonas recovered and began shouting commands to the people outside. He was absolutely certain they would obey.

'Go back to your beds!', he ordered them, 'she only had a bad dream. She is alright. Go home!'

They did not oblige him at once. ' We can't hear her!', they shouted back, 'She is dead! You have killed her!'

Yonas grew more adamant, 'Go back to your beds! I am telling you, she is alright!'

The noise subsided. My hopes died. It was as I feared; the angels were of lesser rank than Yonas; they would have to obey. They would believe what he told them.

But then the voices came back, shouting, 'We can't hear her! We are going for the police!'

While this was going on, Yonas kept poking the gun at me, gesturing me toward the bed. His frenzy appeared to be fueled in part by the interference from outside. He let off a seemingly endless stream of words, accusations, explanations. Still beside himself, shaking, clammy, eyes popping, he told me his version of our fieldwork from the moment he had decided to apply for the job. He threw back at me words I had said to fend him off, and emphasize my determination not to have sex with him, but he twisted my words, interpreted them to mean the opposite of what I had intended. All I had said he understood against his image of me as an indiscriminate, promiscuous woman.

I moved toward the bed and sat down. He came toward me, holding me at gunpoint, and still talking, pausing in his tirade only long enough to fling occasional commands to the people outside, who had now gone back to pounding the shutters. He let his pyjama bottoms drop. I pulled up my nightgown and dressing gown. At the sight of my genitals his movements were arrested for a moment.

He fell on top of me but had problems with the gun. He tried to push the gun between our bodies to be sure of control while raping me.

But he had stretched his capacity to the limit. Keeping me subdued, telling his story, calming the people outside, and penetrating an unwilling woman – all at the same time – could not be done. The moment our genitals touched he ejaculated. I think. Perhaps his erection collapsed and all that wetness was my body's reaction to rape. I don't know.

And then Yonas' frenzy was over. His features returned to normal. His eyes became comprehending again. He was afraid. He wanted to be comforted, so he sat on my lap, with the gun still in his hand but no longer pointed at me. After a while he pulled up his pyjama pants, went to the front door, and unlocked it to let the people see for themselves that I was alive and 'alright'.

Yonas must have been a frightening sight, disheveled and pouring with sweat, with a gun in his hand. The people outside drew back. For all they knew he had a corpse inside.

Then Benjamin stepped forward, with all the authority of a royal soldier, erect and tall. 'Let me in to see her', he commanded.

And Yonas did. Then he turned on his heels and rushed away into his own room, locking the door behind him.

Benjamin entered my bedroom, and stretched out his arms towards me. 'My dear child', he cried, 'has he raped you?'

I fell into his arms, not weeping, but shaking uncontrollably. I wanted to get out of the house immediately. I dressed hurriedly, with difficulty.

Benjamin went past Yonas' room to get me a glass of water. As he returned from the kitchen, Yonas stormed out of his room, again frantic, prepared to shoot. The old man stepped between us, and told Yonas to return to his room. He did, and I went out to the car and drove the 20 minutes down to Woha where I found refuge with Sally, one of my two foreign friends.

I never saw Yonas again.

I later learnt that after I left, Yonas appeared from his room again and agreed to hand over his gun to the old man. Benjamin promptly carried the gun outside and buried it under the dirt floor of his own house. He then locked the doors to my room, the kitchen, and the office inside the house so that Yonas could not enter any room other than his own.

In the morning, Yonas asked to be let into the other rooms, claiming he had personal belongings in the office. The old man refused to let him in, saying that I had locked the doors and taken the keys with me when I left. He was afraid, as I was, that Yonas would destroy the material we had already collected. Yonas then took off for Woha himself, seeking shelter with some co-ethnic friends of his who were teachers and officials in that town.

Perspectives on the rape

Rape in any form is about power and male domination. From the literature, it appears that the most common form of rape is for a man to violate a woman he already knows. One frequent scenario is that of a man who considers himself entitled to sex with a woman who does not accept what he perceives as sexual obligation. These men's demands to have their expectations fulfilled fuel their sense that they have the right to obliterate the will of women under their domination (Brownmiller 1975). Seen in this light, what happened to me in Ketema differs little from what happens to thousands of women annually in every country in the world.

Nevertheless, Ketema is in Ethiopia, and an interpretation of the outrage must be peculiar to that country and the circles to which I and Yonas belonged. Having different Ethiopian interpretations spelled out for me immediately after the events helped me survive, cope, and eventually return to a 'normal' – but different – life as an anthropologist. The openness I encountered was triggered by the assault itself, then by my making the crisis public, by the genuine gratification people felt at pointing out what I ought to have done, and, I think, by the fact that Yonas had broken a series of taboos.

Yonas' justification of the rape

The following account of the way Yonas justified his act and intended to wreak revenge on me was given to me by Yonas himself during the rape, as described above. Although throughout the rape he appeared to be completely beside himself with fury and determination, he was absolutely lucid, clear, and comprehensible in his speech. He wanted to make certain that I understood exactly what he was saying. What he told me was burnt into my memory, because of the extreme situation, and because of the shock I experienced as he made me understand how I had been manipulated and maneuvered by him from the very beginning of our relationship.

Long afterwards, I wondered about Yonas' need to tell why he must rape me. Maybe it was not so remarkable. When rape is punishment, then surely it must be imperative for the assailant to assure himself that the object knows why she is being punished.[6] What follows is the essence of what Yonas said during the rape situation; this is his view as he stated it.

Yonas had taken the job as my field assistant and accepted the prospect of months of work in the provinces because he wanted to have a foreign lover. This was the premise on which he went to work for me. He did not say why he was so keen on having a foreign woman. I can only assume that he had accepted the imagery which circulated among some Ethiopian groups that foreign, uncircumcised, independent women were sexually adventurous and promiscuous. He wanted me to understand that there was no other reason why he had applied for the job as my field assistant.

From the beginning of our association I had, in his view, implied that a sexual relation was a real possibility; we only had to wait for the right time and place. He quoted verbatim my turns of phrase or choice of words that on numerous occasions had confirmed his belief that I did eventually intend to gratify his desire. His memory was astounding. I felt intense shame when I heard my own words accurately repeated but distorted to imply meanings that were never intended. He started looking for significance and collecting signs that I would relent on my position when we met, and had continued until he began to suspect that he was going to be 'cheated'.

Yonas firmly believed that a woman will never reveal her true intentions to a man; therefore everything I said he understood in every way except the literal. All his friends, and his girlfriend in the capital, believed that we were living together as lovers. His girlfriend had therefore left him. The world pointed fingers at him. He had felt deep humiliation and failure when he was assumed to be my lover. In his view, no one would have believed him if he had said that it was not true. (I doubt that he had done much to inform his acquaintances about the true state of affairs. Not being able to seduce such a sexually voracious person as he had convinced himself that I was would not have improved his image as a man.)

He was positive that I had had sex with multitudes of other men. He had spied on me in the capital, and other persons had helped him follow me around. He knew exactly who I had seen. I met many white men unchaperoned; this meant that I had to be sleeping with them.

It was at this point I discovered the source of my isolation from the townspeople. Yonas explained to me that he wanted to keep me dependent on him. Therefore, he had actively worked to keep me isolated in Ketema. With great relish he told me how people had sought him out many times because they were keen to get to know me and to find out what my work in Ketema was all about. He had told them that I was not interested in the townspeople, that I did not want to talk to them or have anything to do with them. He was explicit on this point, wanting me to know how clever he had been in keeping me to himself. He probably also found satisfaction in making me understand how completely I had been in his power. *He* could make or break my work.

He was deeply disappointed and bewildered when I did not live up to my 'promises' of sex. He had come to the conclusion that my people were prejudiced against men who were not white. Racial prejudice became the only possible explanation for why I consistently refused his sexual overtures. He concluded that Swedes were as prone to racial prejudice as Americans or Britons, from whom one could expect no better.[7]

Once he had understood that I was not going to fulfill what he saw as his legitimate demands, he had begun planning his revenge. He told me that he had been planning the assault for months. He actually explained his entire scheme before he had brought it to completion because he was so certain that I was in his power, that no one would believe me. I think he was afraid that I might not understand that these events had happened because he willed them and because he was in absolute control.

Yonas had not only manipulated the past, but intended to control the future as well. This is how he predicted the chain of events following the rape: I would fire him. Since we had an employment contract, he would then take me to court for breach of contract. He would dispute my right to fire him. I would then say that he had raped me. He would deny the accusation and no one would believe me. I would have to pay him heavy compensation for firing him unfairly and maybe be made to take him back. My humiliation at his hands would then be total.

About six weeks prior to the attack, he had asked me to make some changes in our contract. I did not understand the reason for this at the time, but saw later how those changes, which in effect made it more difficult for me to end his employment, had strengthened Yonas' plan. When I suddenly announced to him that I was dismantling the household, I had forced his hand. He would either have to carry out his plan that last night or lose the opportunity.

Yonas' story poured out of him as he was pacing the floor in front of the shuttered window, gesticulating with the pistol, and pausing every once in a while to order the people outside to go away. I was sitting on the edge of my bed, waiting for what was going to happen next. On some level, I do not think I really believed that Yonas would complete the rape within earshot of the people outside. At the same time, though, I was beyond caring. My entire concern was about getting out of the situation alive.

Once the fire had gone out of him and his senses returned to normal, Yonas stopped talking.

Benjamin's and Sofia's reactions to the rape

Benjamin and Sofia later told me that they had not heard my screams. But on the other side of the fence that separated my compound from the potato fields was a temporary camp of farm laborers, men who had been hired to pick potatoes. Benjamin had visited them when they first came, and had invited them into the compound.

It is very significant that neither Yonas nor myself 'remembered' these farm laborers. In Ethiopia, not everybody is a person, a somebody. Servants, paupers, beggars, people from low-status ethnic groups, and 'heathens' do not count. As I had understood it, persons below one in ethnic, economic, or occupational rank were not regarded as 'people', whereas those equal and above always were. If you were a 'nobody' you might as well be part of the furniture as far as your superiors were concerned. Yonas knew the potato pickers were there. Still, he clearly did not recognize them as people who might intervene, and therefore he went ahead with his plan as if the field had, in fact, been empty. He had simply forgotten all about them.

But the field was not empty, and the farm laborers had been aroused at once by my screams. From Benjamin, they knew very well who I was. They also knew that the old man considered himself my ultimate guardian. Therefore, they lost no time in forcing the fence and waking the old man from his sleep.

Benjamin was horrified at Yonas' assault. He had not for an instant believed that I had sexual relations with Yonas. After the rape, again and again, the old man complained bitterly of how Yonas had failed him. 'I trusted him as I trusted myself', he said, 'I was sure you were safe with Yonas in the house. How could I otherwise have allowed you two to be alone in there?'

Once the old guard was aroused, he lost no time in coming to my rescue. He said that he and the others were certain that I was dead, because of the way my screams rang out and then stopped completely. Still, they had all hesitated about bringing in the police until they knew for certain what had happened.

I was profoundly moved by Benjamin's reasoning and his unquestioning solidarity with me. I probably owed him my life,[8] and had myself seen him put his life at stake for me.

Men's reactions to the rape

As the rape became known in Ketema, I received a number of reactions from both men and women. How men reacted depended on how close they were to me and to the drama itself, and how they perceived Yonas.

Benjamin, as I have just noted, was shocked and prepared to act. He voiced no opinions about what I should do afterwards; as far as I understood him, he thought my own shock and near breakdown were correct and adequate reactions to what happened. He agreed that he had indeed saved my life and recognized the deep obligation I had incurred because of this.

The only person who insisted that I go to the police was a young man in town, a teenager whom I had supported since my volunteer days. This man became very upset when I chose not to report the rape to the police. There were several reasons behind my decision not to report to the police. At the time of the rape, in the middle of the night, the main reason was that the only other rape of a foreign woman that I had heard about until then had taken place in a police station, with the police as rapists. I was afraid that the local police would simply carry on where Yonas had left off. Later on, other reasons became more important, such as not wanting to be held up in Ethiopia for months, maybe years, waiting for an uncertain trial. My fear of what would happen if Yonas were acquitted was very strong. I felt that he would be quite likely to seek revenge if I tried to turn him in. Indeed, months later I received an anonymous note from Yonas, handed in at the post office in Ketema, containing the single line, 'Stop your slander, or else.'

Among other men in town, more distant, the consensus seemed to be that something like rape had been bound to happen. I remember one civil servant telling me that Yonas and myself were like a young bull and a heifer locked in a corral. When I asked why no one had warned me of what they saw as an inevitability, he replied,'You know us, you know our habits and our culture. We did not want to insult you by coming with advice.'

Once the rape had occurred, I noticed no change in the behavior of people I regularly dealt with, such as the old messenger, officials at the local bank, post office, etc. It turned out that Yonas was not at all liked.

His *hauteur* and successful attempts at keeping me isolated had earned him no friends.

The day after the assault, after I definitely decided I did not want to involve the police, a bank official in the nearby town of Woha agreed to act as go-between, to help me terminate my employer–employee relationship with Yonas. The reason why I needed to contact Yonas again was because his story about how he would sue me for compensation haunted me. Until our contractual relations were dissolved, I lived in absolute panic about what he might do next. Maybe he would still find a way of hauling me into court to claim the official compensation he had been dreaming about. Or maybe the fact that he had not been able to penetrate me during the rape had left him in a worse position than when he was merely rejected. Would he try again, then? Or would he kill me to make me shut up?

The banker met Yonas two days after the events. Yonas denied that anything untoward had happened; he told the banker that he could not understand why I did not want to continue working with him. He very much wanted to continue assisting me. Yonas appeared completely calm and reasonable, there was no indication that things were not as he presented them. The banker believed him.

The banker then escorted me back up to Ketema, to pick up some necessities and to find out what had happened after I left. The house was exactly in the same state as it had been when I rushed off in the middle of the night. Benjamin had not opened the doors to my bedroom and the office since then. When the banker saw the confusion in my room, tufts of hair lying about,[9] and the remains of my torn dressing gown, he apologized. And if he had still had any doubts about the veracity of my tale he would have been convinced by Benjamin, who was bursting to tell all. This was the first time I found out how my rescue had been organized.

The banker's reflections were then typical of what I was told by several other men. 'We Ethiopians only rape women we know', he explained. His advice was that I should not have remained in one place for as long as I had. I think the maximum 'rape-safe' time he mentioned was three weeks. In order to escape molestation, I should have moved between towns, doing as much work as I could in that limited time. He failed to see that I had come to no harm at the hands of the local men from Ketema. The fact was that Yonas was much more like the banker than he was like the locals. Listening to other accounts of threats and assaults among women anthropologists and volunteers in Ethiopia, it later became clear to me that the most serious danger has always come from officials, assistants, and boyfriends – persons belonging to the section of educated, 'modern' men whom foreign women are most likely to depend on and befriend.

When I protested at the banker's advice, saying that no serious fieldwork could be done hopping from one place to the other, he suggested that the only other alternative was to 'do what our women do'. To observe and adjust. To create a 'family' and stay within its confines, protected by kinsmen and servants. This was in effect what Benjamin had tried to do for me, as he attempted to create a protective group that ensured that no ill-intended men could reach me. In Benjamin's eyes, I did not blunder when I allowed Yonas a room in the house. It was instead Yonas who was to be blamed and punished for not living up to the protective role that he had been expected to fulfill.

Another clue to the complex of sexual conquest and male domination was given to me by an old acquaintance, who, lamenting the fact that he had not propositioned me when we had had official dealings with one another six years earlier, explained that he had not made clear his intentions then because he was not certain I would have accepted him. 'You see', he told me, 'we do not ask until we are certain of being accepted. It is difficult for an Ethiopian to face being turned down.'

One dimension of the rape that prompted men to heap scorn on Yonas was the fact that he had used a gun. Rape is one thing, I came to learn, using a gun to subdue a woman is quite another. That, for many men, was what made this rape particularly inexcusable and shameful. Men should master women with words and the *dula*, a big stick that is a common means of defense and attack, one that looks more like a baseball bat than anything else. Many times I had heard Ethiopian men quote the saying, 'With donkeys and women you talk with a *dula*.'[10]

It seems as though, for some men who commented on the rape, the very masculinity that was to be proven by the rape was put in question by the use of the gun. What sort of man was this, who could not make it without threatening a woman with a gun? On this count I had men's unquestionable sympathy. Guns spelled death, which was something quite different from proving your point to a reluctant woman.

On a visit to Ethiopia many years after the rape, I discovered that Ethiopian legal praxis does not recognize 'rape' as a crime against women unless the woman concerned is a proven virgin. This was true in the 1970s and it is still true today.

Women's reactions to the rape

The rape in Ketema altered my relations with women in Ethiopia completely. My introduction to Ethiopian society had been through men. During my early years in the country, working as a volunteer, all my workmates were men. When I gathered material for my final research paper, in 1968, all my contacts had been men. My original fascination with Ethiopia was powered by intense infatuation with an Ethiopian man. Men, men, men. Women in this world of men were secretaries, servants, relatives, – to me 'non-persons', in effect.[11]

All of this now changed. If the women in my immediate surroundings, with the exception of Benjamin's wife Sofia, had until now demurred, served, kept quiet, looked down, and been 'nice', they now stood erect, left the shadows, looked me straight in the eye, spoke up, and were furiously cynical.

What they said was simply that this is what we all suffer for being women. As long as we are women we are at the mercy of men. There was no need for me to feel ashamed or unhappy. What had happened to me was horrible and dreadful, but, unfortunately, normal. 'As long as we are women . . .'

After the rape, women told me many tales of sexual violence at the hands of men. Their lack of trust in men was absolute. For many women, the prospect of a happy life was the possibility of a life without permanent bonds to men. Economic independence, surrounded by a family of your own, lovers if you wanted them, but no men with rights through marriage or the like – this was their utopian goal.

I felt guilty and ashamed of having been taken in by the male vision of the world, and the picture of sexual warfare painted by the women to whom I spoke was strangely comforting. In my conversations with women, the focus was frequently off me and on the iniquitous sexual organization of female dependency, where sex and domestic services are exchanged for economic security, and where the dependent woman loses her self-determination when she submits to a bond to an individual man. The man, in this contract, loses nothing except maybe his peace of mind, since he continually fears being 'outbid' by wealthier, more powerful, and therefore more attractive men.

My own reactions to the rape

After the rape, I was overwhelmed by a flood of information on gender relations and sexuality, but I was in no position to record, understand, or utilize the material. I felt naked, a simple civilian, a deserter from the anthropological field. Any idea that I should put my situation to anthropological use felt blasphemic, a continuation of the rape situation. There was nothing professional in what I was going through. I could barely hold myself together. I was dependent on my surroundings for security and my mental health. The rape had reversed a hierarchy where until then I had held the dominant position as researcher, professional, and foreigner. Now I was just a woman, looking to other women around me for guidance, safety, and advice.

Immediately after the assault, I had two strands of feelings. One was a tremendous fury. If I had had the gun my friend Michael had wanted to lend me, I felt capable of shooting Yonas on the spot. This rage remained with me for years.

The other was immense fear. Part of it was irrational. I felt I would die if I ever laid eyes on Yonas again. I know now that this is a standard reaction among rape survivors. Part of the fear was probably well founded. Yonas had set out to punish me and had constructed an elaborate plan of how this would be done. His plan had failed. If he started out by being humiliated by my refusal to accept him sexually, he left with a humiliation increased manyfold. His social inferiors had intercepted him, disobeyed him, and refused to accept his definition of our relations. He had been disarmed by a servant. He had been tricked and fooled. He had failed sexually. And I knew all this and could easily reveal it.

Intuition told me that I was in much greater danger after the assault than before, and that I would continue to be in danger until I was out of the country, a continent away. Or until one of us was dead.

As mentioned above, I used the regional manager of one of the national banks as intermediary to establish contact first with Yonas' intermediaries and then with Yonas himself. Yonas finally agreed to sign a paper releasing me from all further obligations, but to do so, he demanded two months' pay and a letter of recommendation. I paid and wrote the recommendation. He even had the audacity to amend the letter.[12]

The days until these matters were settled were days of panic. I recall crouching in the locked bathroom in the house of my hostess for hours, not daring to be alone in the rest of the house for a minute. 'There are those who cope, and those who don't', she told me, recalling incidents from her fifteen years as headmistress in a school in Tanzania. I was not sure that I belonged among those who coped.

With the release paper signed, I felt free to leave. I returned the rented furniture and sold the remaining household utensils. The research material I stored with friends. I made an agreement with Benjamin to continue paying his salary, and turned over the house to his nephew. I then returned to my home country to recover.

I came back to Ethiopia two months later, my morale bolstered by the presence of my mother and my partner from home, who had long planned to visit me in the field anyway. For the duration of their month-long visit, I debated whether or not I could bear to pick up the threads and continue work in Ketema. In the end I decided to stay.

I finished a second survey phase in Ketema, which took another few months. Without Yonas to isolate me, I developed a great number of contacts in the town and could easily have gone on to more intensive work if my mental equilibrium had not been so precarious. It seemed that the rape drama had made me a real person in the eyes of the townspeople, who no doubt had debated events thoroughly in my absence. I sensed neither lack of respect nor moral judgment of me, which, of course, does not mean that negative opinions were absent. After four months my time was up and I left Ethiopia.

I managed quite well as long as I was in Ketema, which ironically became the only place in Ethiopia where I really felt safe, since I was convinced Yonas would not dare to appear in the town again. Once home in Sweden after fieldwork, however, I suffered a delayed reaction. In part, this was similar to what any rape survivor goes through. I had nightmares for years, and for many months I was unable to think about anything else. 'Normal' guilt feelings were exacerbated by my thinking that I had created the situation myself, that I had in fact set up Yonas in the rapist role. Emotionally, I somehow felt that Yonas had the right to be seeking revenge. In fact, it was only in the course of writing this chapter that it has finally dawned on me that it was *Yonas* who maneuvred the whole relationship from the moment he first heard of a foreign woman wanting an assistant. I have known this ever since hearing Yonas' tale on that fateful night. Somehow, however, I have not understood what it meant until now.

Discussion

Despite the twenty-odd years since the start of the second wave of feminist anthropology, and despite the fact that 'gender', as a consequence, has definitively been brought into much of anthropological understanding and analysis, anthropology has yet to come to terms with the fact that anthropologists are themselves gendered.[13] The demographic breakdown of social and cultural anthropology is similar to that of many other disciplines in the humanistics and social sciences: there is a majority of young women among students, but a gradually decreasing proportion of women as one approaches the apex of the academic hierarchy (Sanjek 1982). This kind of gendered pyramid structure ensures that female dominance in numbers does not translate into corresponding influence on the academic establishment.

Anthropologists 'at home', in universities and departments, and in our lives outside academic institutions, are part of gender orders specific to the times and societies we live in. A central aspect of academic life, however, is the denial of gender at work. That is to say, we are expected to study, administer, write, and teach as if gender did not matter. This fiction is an integral part of academic life, and it can be upheld because we only spend part of our lives at the university. We leave the supposedly 'gender-free' world of academia at the end of the day to go out and assume a multitude of gendered roles. Some go home to put their feet up, read the evening newspaper, and delve into the latest anthropological periodicals after dinner has been provided. Others go home to shop, cook, and do dishes, laundry, and whatever else is necessary for life to go on.[14]

For female anthropologists, one of the consequences of the fictitiously 'gender-free' life we lead at university is that, if we bring up issues that are specific to us as women in the academic context, we run the risk of doing damage to our identities as anthropologists. This is, of course, because the archetypal anthropologist is a man. Part of the hidden agenda for female anthropologists is, therefore, to avoid drawing attention to ourselves as women when we establish our professional identities. After all, who wants to be a *female* anthropologist when it seems possible to be a 'real' anthropologist?[15] As far as the danger of sexual violence is concerned, it may be part of a woman's daily life, but it is not seen to be relevant to the professional part of ourselves – the 'anthropologist' part. 'Anthropologists' don't get harassed or raped. Women do.

In the field, the false division of time and space between the 'professional' and the 'private' that underpins the supposedly gender-neutral identity of the anthropologist collapses completely. In the field, it is not possible to maintain a fiction of a genderless self. It is not possible to be an unmarked 'anthropologist'. In the field, one is marked. One is perceived to be, and one perceives oneself to be, a gendered anthropologist – a female anthropologist or a male anthropologist. And as gendered anthropologists, we cannot only be attractive to others and feel attraction ourselves – we can also be the target of sexual violence; violence that is directed, as it was in my case, as much at our 'professional' selves as it is at our 'private' selves (where, indeed, is the difference?).

The multidimensional meanings of sexual relations in the field can never be the same for female and male anthropologists. The thundering silence of heterosexual men on the subject is in itself ominously meaningful. Field accounts from women have frequently mentioned sexual aspects of the field situation, probably because in many fields the sexual problematic is forced on female anthropologists and shapes the kind of work we are able to do. The possibility of sexual violence, explicit or implied, is a means by which the movement and activities of women are restricted in many social contexts, and it is therefore an issue that most female anthropologists must deal with, where male anthropologists need not.[16] The question of whether to have sexual relations in the field is something that many female anthropologists have to deal with not occasionally, or once in a while, but more or less continuously, as males like Yonas ask, nag, and demand. All of this is different for men. Other sexual activities are different as well. Commercial sex, for example, might be available for men but never for women.

Rape is a vicious, murderous relation. Rape creates a chasm of mutual incomprehension between women and men. The will to rape is impossible to comprehend for women, and the consequences of rape for the victim-survivor may be equally difficult to understand and to empathize with for men. This being the case, maybe it is not strange that rape has remained a non-subject within our discipline, all other considerations apart. When I returned to my university department in Sweden after the assault in Ethiopia, I told my colleagues what had happened. My female colleagues all expressed shock, concern, and support. My two academic supervisors, on the other hand (both of whom were men), listened to me recount the tale of the attack, but offered little sympathy and never mentioned the topic of rape again. I later heard that one of them told a female graduate student that I must have acted like a fool in the field. Another senior male anthropologist, upon hearing about the rape, sighed that 'Such things happen to women in the field'.

When I set out to do fieldwork in the 1970s, I worked in Ethiopia with no understanding that my own gender might be an important factor in the fieldwork I did. All I had heard on the topic was my male supervisor telling me that female fieldworkers had advantages over male fieldworkers, because female anthropologists often had access to both female and male social circles. In actuality, the niches open to female fieldworkers vary from field to field, just as the backgrounds of anthropologists vary, and as the fit between the anthropologist and her or his field varies.

What does not vary is the fact that women must always, everywhere, deal with the spectre of sexual violence in a way that fundamentally differs from anything that our male colleagues have to contend with. This does not mean that sexual violence is, by definition, a 'woman's problem'. On the contrary, rape is most certainly part of a profoundly male problematic. And the point of this chapter is that, whatever else sexual violence against anthropologists may be, it is *by definition* an anthropological problem. It concerns all of us, women and men, and it warrants a strong place on the mainstream anthropological agenda.

Afterword

Well after this chapter was completed and sent into the publishers with the book manuscript, I was suddenly confronted with another, quite unanticipated reason why sexual violence in the field is so rarely discussed in the anthropological literature. Just before the proofs were about to be set, Routledge contacted me and suggested that my contribution be changed to make 'Yonas' even more impossible to identify. Calling him by a pseudonym, as I had done (and continue to do), was not considered sufficient to ward off a possible slander suit against Routledge from 'Yonas' – even though the events described in my contribution took place twenty years ago and in a country in which, as I have noted, legal praxis does not recognize rape as a crime against women who are not proven virgins. Instead of introducing fictional elements into the text that would have distorted the dynamics of the situation that ultimately led to the assault, I chose to publish the chapter using a pseudonym for myself. My use of a pseudonym is therefore not to protect my own identity but, rather (and I hope that the weighty irony here is not lost on anybody), to protect the identity of the rapist.

Acknowledgements

I would like to thank Margaret Willson and Don Kulick for the encouragement and collaboration they have offered in the writing of this chapter.

Notes

1 Rape always implies death. In this chapter I discuss rape as a means to punish, chastise, and reform individual women. Men and children are also raped, and rape is used on collectives of women in war, but these instances are beyond the reflections made here.
2 See, for instance, Gearing's contribution to this volume.
3 In her contribution to the groundbreaking anthology *Women in the Field*, Diane Freedman writes about how she returned to the field soon after the death of her husband, and how she was overwhelmed with information on death and mourning, as her informants tried to comfort her. She could take no notes and made no professional use of all this. It was real life, aimed at her, not coins for the anthropological market (Freedman 1986).
4 See, for instance, Markakis (1974) for an authoritative description of the Ethiopian polity prior to 1974, or Kapuscinski (1983) for a picture of the atmosphere surrounding the imperial palace.
5 I am not implying that there was *no* sexual violence against women in Scandinavia at this time, only that the incidence was low – very low compared to the United States, for instance.
6 The man who raped Winkler also spoke to her at length.
7 I have not encountered this kind of interpretation from other Ethiopian men. Ethiopians are very color conscious, but *white* is certainly not at the apex of the color hierarchy. When I worked as a volunteer for the Swedish volunteer service, a number of my Ethiopian workmates told me that their families were afraid they would marry a foreigner and thereby 'ruin the blood' of the family. In a similar vein, Ethiopians are fond of telling foreigners of how God, when creating humankind, cast aside the black and the white man alike, preferring the brown Ethiopian, who was created with exactly the 'right' color. Yonas' accusations of racism may have arisen from conversations with his friends who had experienced racial prejudice outside Africa.
8 No matter what Yonas' plans had been before the rape, I honestly believe that had we been alone he would not have been able to extricate himself from the situation without killing me.
9 I did not feel Yonas pulling my hair out while trying to subdue me with his hands.
10 This saying was part of the reason why I expected no help even if someone heard my screaming.
11 To be truthful, this was no great change from how I saw the world of meaning and consequence at home.
12 It never occurred to me that there was actually an alternative to resolving the situation in the very Ethiopian way that I opted for. I could have gone all foreign – involving the embassy and the university that sponsored my stay, invoking all those beautiful letters of permission and protection that had circulated in the bureaucratic structure prior to my arrival in Ketema. In fact, while I felt I was only floundering about in Ketema, miserably failing my anthropological mission, I had actually acquired a thorough knowledge of many salient aspects of Ethiopian urban life. Maybe participant observation is often like this. We have our minds set on the goals of research agendas, invested in long before we ever arrive in the field, and so we do not appreciate the knowledge and insights that are

thrust upon us, since it is the 'wrong' knowledge and insight, not primarily about the topics we had set our hearts on studying.

13 There are certainly many other important distinctions largely ignored or unrecognized.

14 Micaela di Leonardo writes in the acknowledgements of her 1991 anthology: 'Most of the contributors (and I) are women in "sandwich generation" positions: especially subject to medical and personal crises – and to those of kin and friends of both parents' and children's generations' (di Leonardo 1991: xi). It goes without saying that there is as yet no 'sandwich generation' of men.

15 Dorothy Smith has coined the phrase 'bifurcated consciousness' to describe how women in social science manage to take part in an academic enterprise that denies the validity of our life experience as women, and where we are brought to accept male definitions of academic standards in the theory and practice of our disciplines (Smith 1987: 6).

16 Unless they are accompanied by wives or daughters. But again, that is 'private', and they might not consider their safety to be part of the fieldwork.

References

Brownmiller, Susan (1975) *Against Our Will: Men, Women and Rape*. New York: Simon and Schuster.

di Leonardo, Micaela (1991) 'Introduction', in *Gender at the Crossroads of Knowledge: Feminist Anthropology in the Postmodern Era*. Berkeley, Calif.: University of California Press.

Freedman, Diane (1986) 'Wife, Widow, Woman: Roles of an Anthropologist in a Transsylvanian Village', in Peggy Golde (ed.) *Women in the Field: Anthropological Experiences*. Berkeley, Calif.: University of California Press.

Howell, Nancy (1990) *Surviving Fieldwork: A Report of the Advisory Panel on Health and Safety in Fieldwork*. Special Publication of the American Anthropological Association No. 26. Washington, D.C.: American Anthropological Association.

Kapuscinski, Ryszard (1983) *The Emperor: The Downfall of an Autocrat*. New York: Harcourt Brace Jovanovich.

Kulick, Don (1994) 'Response to David Lipset's letter to *Anthropology Today*, December 1993'. *Anthropology Today*. Vol. 10, No. 1, p. 13.

Landes, Ruth (1986) 'A Woman Anthropologist in Brazil', in Peggy Golde (ed.) *Women in the Field: Anthropological Experiences*. Berkeley, Calif.: University of California Press.

Markakis, John (1974) *Ethiopia: The Anatomy of a Traditional Polity*. London: Oxford University Press.

Sanjek, Roger (1982) 'The AAA Resolution on the Employment of Women: Genesis, Implementation, Disavowal and Resurrection'. *Signs: Journal of Women in Culture and Society*. Vol. 7, No. 4, pp. 845–68.

Smith, Dorothy E. (1987) *The Everyday World as Problematic: A Feminist Sociology*. Milton Keyes: Open University Press.

Wengle, John L. (1988) *Ethnographers in the Field: The Psychology of Research*. Tuscaloosa, Ala.: University of Alabama Press.

Winkler, Cathy (1991) 'Rape as Social Murder'. *Anthropology Today*. Vol. 7, No. 3, pp. 12–14.

Afterword
Perspective and difference: sexualization, the field, and the ethnographer

Margaret Willson

The field of sexuality; sexuality in the field: I offer here an analysis of the discussions in this volume. As editors, Don Kulick and I did not dictate or even suggest what areas of sexuality in anthropological fieldwork our contributors might wish to discuss, but they produced a surprisingly integrated group of articles. Each one reflects and adds to the insights of the others – an Escher effect of argument – to create a prism of refracted ideas and possibilities. In this afterword, I shall have space to explore only a few of these.

The ideas in the chapters seemed to connect as concentric circles. I arrange my analysis starting from the larger circle – a consideration of sexuality as it exists in the concept of the field itself and the sexualized relationship between the theoretical 'ethnographer' and the 'field'. In the second section, I discuss the ethnographer's position – and how the ethnographer is positioned – as a sexualized subject *within* the field. In the final section, in this ever decreasing series of concentric rings, I explore the notion of a sexual identity within the ethnographer, of the parts of body and parts of identity that communicate, and miscommunicate, the intentions of a sexual whole.

Perspectives and penetration: sexing the field

Potash's statement that 'we cannot describe institutions as if they were gender neutral when they are not' (cited in del Valle 1993: 4) is applicable to two central institutions of anthropology: the ethnographer and the field. In recent reflexive writing on the relationship of the role of ethnographer and his or her interpretation of cultures, Crapanzano compares the ethnographer to the phallic god Hermes, who sets the boundaries of culture through interpretation (1986: 52). Considering this and other reflexive writing (e.g. Stoller 1989), two of our contributors, Andrew P. Killick and Kate Altork, have explored the structural power of the sexualizing imaging that anthropologists implicitly give to the notions of both the field and the ethnographer. They took our directive to write about 'sex in the field' literally to mean the relationship of sexuality and the field, in addition to considerations of sex with people who inhabit 'the field.' In so doing, they have taken differing stances: Killick problematizes the widely accepted construction of a heterosexual masculine subject position that controls the representation of the feminized field. Altork argues for a place for changing the relationship and the gendering of the roles, allowing possibilities for a more 'sensual' and 'sensory' exchange. Altork writes about penetration *of* the anthropologist *by* the field and Killick about penetration *by* the anthropologist *of* the field. Their arguments lead us to question the role that the metaphorical image of the field plays in the maintenance of a hierarchical relationship between the anthropological enterprise and the world from which it derives its knowledge, as well as how this imaging influences the kind of information ethnographers consider worthy of anthropological interest.

Killick's critique of the white, straight male subject position argues that this position 'is required by the narrative structure of fieldwork accounts', and 'that the unequal relationships implicit in the concept of "the field", though rooted in anthropology's colonial and patriarchal traditions, will apply regardless of the identity of the ethnographer' (Chapter 3, p. 77). He images the fieldwork experience within a plot structure in which the field becomes a feminized, immobile plot-space and the ethnographer a male, mobile traveler who can move across the boundaries of the plot-space. He cites Crapanzano (1986) on the 'phallic' position of the ethnographer and quotes Teresa de Lauretis to establish that, regardless of morphology, the hero must be male and the obstacle female. The argument is that white straight male identity is not 'given and self-evident, but [is] achieved and ascribed through narratively structured experience, including that of the anthropologist's legitimizing myth: fieldwork' (p. 77). Ultimately, says Killick, the field 'serves mainly to enable the narcissistic project of the ethnographer's encounter with himself, *his* renewal of *him*self through penetration of feminized, other space' (p. 102, emphasis in original).

Altork's chapter focuses on 'the sensual nature of that reality [the field], along with an exploration of the erotic component in the fieldwork enterprise' (Chapter 4, p. 109). Thus her major concern is an encompassing sensuality of the field, and particularly how that sensuality affects what we learn and how we represent that experience. In her section entitled 'Places penetrating people', Altork writes of the seduction of the field (a phrase also used by Bolton and Morton), that if anthropologists are able to open themselves to the sensory impact of the field, if they use both the mind and the heart, then they will become aware of how the field enters them, and implants them with insight. Altork describes the fieldsite in which she worked, a temporary camp for fighting a forest fire, as a vibrant situation where it would have missed the point to filter out the total sensory immersion that she experienced: the smells of the fire, the excitement of the danger, the taste of starlit nights, the sensuality of the collective endeavor. Her ethnographic understanding came from 'feeling the field' (p. 126) – from moving within the experience and allowing it to permeate her. She argues that anthropologists, by allowing themselves to be seduced by the field, gain greater ethnographic knowledge and produce more readable and living texts. Her discussion challenges the rational and objectivist (and, as Killick discusses, masculine) emphasis in traditional ethnography and urges anthropologists to allow the sensory and the erotic to become valid fieldwork data and an acceptable part of the fieldwork narrative.

Both Altork and Killick position their field sexually: Altork, a heterosexual woman, presents her field as androgynous but full of sensual masculine imagery; Killick, a heterosexual male, examines his position within the more dominant imaging of the field as female. Their positioning of and within the field has two levels: a personal one and a metaphorical one, each influencing the other. On the personal level, Killick relates the space of Korea to Western ideals of Asian femininity, while Altork writes of the intense sexual energy she felt in the 'place' (the fire camp) itself. On a metaphorical level, their differing sexual perspectives give shape to the way they image their encounter with the field.

Such differing sexualized perspectives of 'the field' influence the kind of relationship that the ethnographer has with the field and this, in turn, affects interpretation. In criticizing predominant concepts of the field, Killick calls it a negative space, by definition that space which is not ours. Yet through writing about, representing and interpreting that space, the ethnographer can see himself or herself – and be seen – as metaphorically 'possessing' it. Some sort of relationship with one's fieldsite is almost unavoidable – it is not by accident that anthropologists have habitually (if, these days, somewhat more self-consciously) spoken of 'my' people or 'my' fieldsite. Such statements have understandably been read as the anthropologist's possession of the public representation of her or his fieldsite. Yet the 'possession' of the field experience is also bound up in its connection to the ethnographer's professional identity. The field area creates a category that professionally places the anthropologist (she is Melanesianist, he is a Brazilianist) and influences which departments will find them interesting, which specialty conferences they will attend, even which people will become their colleagues and friends. The relationship of ethnographer to the field is like a contract (comparable perhaps to a marriage contract, one that can of course be broken), and it is not surprising that anthropologists try to represent (to themselves as much as to others) a fictive kinship with 'their' field. The language of possession is double-edged: it can be taken as a symbolic conquest of that which is 'not ours', as Killick outlines, or, as Altork suggests, it can be a 'language of passionate attachment . . . [and a] . . . commitment to the work [we] are doing' (pp. 124–5). Altork images the field here as an experience that she does not possess, but which she takes into a part of herself. It is an experience that seduces and enfolds her. Thus in their discussions, both chapters present the experience and space of the field as something we could represent ourselves as possessing, but which could also possess us. When the firemen in Altork's chapter speak of 'my' fire, the question arises over who is, in fact, possessing whom. 'My field', 'my people', 'my village', 'my informants' may equally signify 'that which encompasses and binds me'. As Altork's firefighters are continually reminded, possession also entails the risk of engulfment.

Altork, Killick, and Bolton describe their experiences of the field in terms of sensual immediacy; Altork goes so far as to liken fieldwork to an erotic exchange between lovers. In their accounts, all these authors acknowledge the need – the pressure even – always to observe, to make continual notes on what is seen, to look continually for meaning in what people say and do. Such a heightened state of awareness is not a normal mode of existence for most people and is one dimension of what distinguishes the field from other life spaces. This is one reason why time in the field can be so exhausting, why most ethnographers rely so much upon the novels they bring, and why time away from the field to 'relax' becomes so important. These are the moments when the ethnographer escapes the intensity of enforced engagement with the present. This 'present' has a possessiveness of its own. As Hastrup (1992: 127) has written, 'the field-world has neither a firm past nor a distinct future because its reality is intersubjectively constructed and depends upon the ethnographer's presence in the field.' When the ethnographer leaves the field she or he carries this immediacy with her or him, it becomes a special and temporal capsule from which she or he derives anthropological meaning. The sensual immediacy lives on in a loosely defined 'ethnographic present', an experience to which the ethnographer returns many times through her or his fieldnotes and through the acquired identity she or he has gained. The 'ethnographic present' has no validity or relevance to the places or people that anthropologists visit. It is, instead, a floating space of immediacy in the individual pasts of ethnographers, a spatial time related to the ethnographer herself or himself.

Herein lies a conflict inherent to anthropology: our methods of gathering our data (which hinge on personal engagement and sensual immediacy) are at odds with the expectations we have that the data we collect and the writing we produce will conform to 'scientific' and 'analytical' standards. Altork decries this as an 'objective straitjacket' that theoretically forces anthropologists to confine their engagement of the field to the cerebral. Because the published end product is supposed to be 'objective' (whatever that might mean), the ethnographer is also presumed to uphold an 'objective' stance in the field. She or he is expected to stand back, be detached, make observations unencumbered by emotional influence. Above all, she or he is supposed to be in control of herself or himself, to act ultimately in a 'professional' and 'appropriate' manner. This creates a situation where the ethnographer is expected to be simultaneously detached and intensely engaged, not to express uncontrolled emotion, yet to live with people who become, for a short time, surrogate parents, surrogate siblings – and sometimes real lovers. Where is the living, breathing human here?

Many anthropologists use what might be called protective devices in trying to maintain a balance between the confusion they encounter in the field and the professional expectations of 'objectivity'. Killick found it necessary to close off receptivity to sensory impressions in order to cope with the cacophony of Seoul life, while Morton remained distant to protect herself from Tonga's 'seduction'. Anthropologists try to choose the areas – generally those related directly to the research – where they will concentrate their sensual exposure: Killick on Korean musical culture, Morton on the women who became her friends, Altork on the totalizing sensuality of a place.

The anthropological fiction of the ethnographer's objectivity is a cherished one and has indeed been a defining trait of the traditional fieldwork experience. The rational and positivist personal control inherent in this construction has, as Killick has explored, been implicitly imaged as male, with the ethnographer as a masculine controlling principle. Yet, ironically, the field is in reality a place and time where most anthropologists find personal control a continual challenge, and where they spend a great deal of effort grappling with new and conflicting sensibilities. As Altork so graphically states, we are all metaphorically 'naked' in the field: sometimes our pretenses to objectivity are the only clothing we have.

The 'schizophrenic' tension between the sensual immediacy of fieldwork and the professional expectations of the discipline has encouraged anthropologists to set up distinct boundaries around their 'public' and 'private' relationship to the fieldwork experience. The 'reality' of the field is generally imaged as private (in field journals), the 'data' of the field as public. The messy, partially understood, sometimes traumatic private memories are transformed into an 'objective', constructed image that will live immortal in the public realm of academe. Bolton recognizes the problems of the public/private dichotomy and consciously tries to defuse them when he asserts that in his fieldnotes he could never divide the data from the personal and that his text is a very personal one. Despite this stance, it is still true that he, like all anthropologists, chooses what he will reveal and what he omits.

These divided realms of public and private do not start or end with the ethnographic text. In the field, ethnographers try to negotiate a balance between the self-representation they feel they need to present and the people they think they are. Nearly all the contributors to this volume struggled with the dilemma of how to maintain a relatively honest relationship with their informants and the need, for various reasons, to keep details of their own agenda and their 'other' life private in the field. The resulting balance between 'knower' and 'known' is a delicate one, as expressed by Dubisch when, through a surprise visit made to her by an informant, she comes to recognize the subtle screen of hierarchy that she had placed between them. Blackwood is confronted with her assumptions about 'their' knowledge of cultural difference when her adoptive mother surprises her with her almost complacent reaction to Blackwood's revelation that she is lesbian. A similar dilemma occurs at home, where most ethnographers try to keep intimate details of their actual life and emotional involvement in the field private. At 'home', most ethnographers have many pages of their personal field journals – musings, recordings of events and interactions that they would prefer others 'at home' not to know about, as they have the potential of rendering the ethnographers' public image uncontrollable. But the 'ethnographically relevant' details become part of a personal public image. In other words, 'here' colleagues don't know what really happened 'there'; 'there' informants don't know what really happens 'here'. Bolton calls this conflict as regards sexual revelations one that 'perpetuates sexual hypocrisy' (Chapter 5, p. 161) but the issues are more complex and relate as well to the anthropologist's construction (and protection) of a public and private self. There is much invested (consciously or unconsciously) by the ethnographer in keeping these categories balanced and separate.

These conflicts between knower/known, there/here, public/private are most acutely expressed by Blackwood, who, in trying to find a (private) space in the field where she could express her lesbian identity, attempted to refashion part of the field from an alien space into a home. Within the realm that allowed her lesbian identity expression, she dissolved the metaphoric plot space of the field, making it, not a place to be entered (as discussed by Killick), but a place that meshed with her notion of 'home'. Because she, like Bolton, consciously identifies her home space with a marginalized status (gayness) rather than a country, alien space is, for her, not only a foreign country but the heterosexual world in general. Unlike Altork and Killick, she consciously divides the field into a public space that remains alien, and a private one which (despite her continual confrontation with difference which she tries valiantly to ignore) she images as familiar, marginal, and lesbian.

The problem of how one can maintain control over one's public image and over one's representation of personal relationships is indeed one reason why 'sex in the field' is such a tabooed topic: it is, in part, because of repressive morality (as Bolton notes), as well as an unspoken acceptance of the power structures that permit (hetero)sexual activity by male researchers, but also because it makes an object of analysis out of what we often experience as our own vulnerability. An analytical focus on sex in the field threatens to parade our most intimate moments before the critical noses of our peers (who indeed would want their private fieldnotes – uncensored – splashed around the world à la Malinowski?). Yet analysis of fieldwork sexuality does not need to become an academic encounter group. Instead we can look at the relationships between our sexual actions and the way we think about experience. In doing so we challenge ourselves to reconsider our perspectives, how we construct both the field itself and the written products that emerge from the field. In her final statement, Altork suggests that 'by acknowledging our own feelings and desires, we might actually look at other people and places more objectively by being able to ferret out our own biases and distortions as we do our work' (p. 132). The objectivity that Altork clearly has in mind is very different from the rationalist perspective considered earlier: it is a call for ethnographers to entertain simultaneous perspectives and to 'be open to interpreting from a more centered, stable vantage point' (p. 132). She consciously tries to refashion the relationship of the ethnographer and the field by visualizing the boundary between them as fluid. Killick describes a traditional perspective, that of the mobile masculine intruder who imposes upon an immobile feminine plot-space. Bolton images the field as a place he leaps into phallus first, all nerve endings open, allowing himself to be buffeted by the turmoils of love and trying to understand the insights he gains along the way. His is a gay field that he images as interactive with himself as ethnographer. Blackwood shows another perspective in her division of the field into spaces that include or exclude her lesbian identity. Her misgivings about the standard construction of the field as alien other and one's own country as a familiar home express themselves as she tries, in her relationship with Dayan, to balance her need for similarity against her realization of difference. Because Blackwood feels alien in the heterosexual world as a whole, she cannot accept the metaphorical divisions of a heterosexually structured anthropology. Her conception of the field shifts as she tries to reconcile her self and her experience with what a heterosexual anthropology has instructed her to believe.

Such conflicts – and the resolutions that emerge – affect the information the ethnographer gathers and the kinds of analysis she or he produces. Contributors to this volume (and others) speak of the relationship of ethnographer and field as an interaction belonging to both cultures, each one giving knowledge and taking it from the other. All these differing perspectives illustrate one reason why no ethnography can be definitive: each text is merely one perspective (cf. Pratt 1986) by one anthropologist on one specific fieldsite during one space of time – nothing more, and in its uniqueness, nothing less.

Do these explorations into perspective offer us new possibilities?[1] Altork, Bolton, Blackwood, and Killick all reveal explicitly that while the concepts and relationship of the field and the ethnographer are often gendered as metaphorically female and male, the complexity of a sexualized field is many-sided. What happens if we encourage the sexual nature of the fieldwork experience – both within the fieldwork relationship and in the texts that are produced from it – to reveal itself in a wider spectrum of dimensions? Would we then truly confront the 'anthropological perspective'? Through combining the insights of such discussions as these, perhaps we can evolve a multi-dimensional perspective that allows for the exploration of sexuality, equality, and difference.

Sexual perspectives within the field: positioning the subject

Anthropologists are generally now different in attitude, politics, and approach to Malinowski and other anthropologists of his time. Likewise, the world they encounter, including the field, has changed. The 'ethnographic dialogue' is now recognized by many as being truly dialogical rather than one-sided, and 'they' are not as likely to be viewed as powerless or passive in their relations to 'us'. However, as contributors to this volume considered how the field, and the people who inhabit a fieldsite, affected them as sexual subjects, they found themselves confronting issues not included in the general anthropological discourses on fieldwork. These issues revolved around the sexual position of the ethnographer within the field rather than the sexualization of the field itself. Jill Dubisch's central theme is her 'reactions . . . to being a foreign woman' in Greece that led her 'to reflect on the female anthropologist as both sexual actor and sexual object in the context of doing anthropology in Europe' (Chapter 1, p. 30). Jean Gearing's chapter explores 'how two aspects of sexuality, . . . [her] intimate relationship with [her] best informant, whom [she] married, and the omnipresent threat of sexual violence in [her] fieldsite, influenced and informed [her] work on gender and sexuality' (Chapter 7, p. 188). Her hope is that her discussions 'may help illuminate the patriarchal structures which operate in both the professional lives and fieldsites of women anthropologists' (p. 189). Morton's chapter focuses on how she, as a sexualized subject, had to continually negotiate her position – as anthropologist, as mother, as wife, as desirable foreign woman – in Tonga.

What becomes quickly apparent in these and the chapters of other contributors is that ethnographers' sexuality and sexual relations affect the kinds of boundary they place around what anthropology classes as 'the field'. Morton, Bolton, Moreno, and Killick all chose their fieldsites in part because of previous sexual, emotional, and individualized involvements. Killick's interest in Korean music and language developed alongside his relationship with a Korean American woman musician in the United States. Much of Morton's adult development, before she began her fieldwork project, was inexorably tied to Tonga:

through youthful exploration, through marriage, motherhood, divorce, and her experience as a single mother in Australia. Bolton and Moreno were drawn to their fieldsites through earlier infatuations. For these people, the 'field' was a point in a continuum – not a dive into a mystical, unknown other. Gearing began fieldwork with no previous connections, but when she married a local man and bore a child in the field, she established relationships that didn't stop when she (and they) returned to the United States. Such relationships with people in the field can influence, or in some cases even define, one's interest in that field. Both Morton and Killick had to contend with the realization that although a positive love affair could enhance a cultural involvement, an upsetting involvement could negate it. Esther Newton (1993: 15) writes that 'The most intense attractions have generated the most creative energy, as if the work were a form of courting and seduction.'[2] But she also relates that her fieldwork seemed finished when a woman she loved died. Thus for these writers, 'the field' developed into an ongoing relationship where boundaries become increasingly blurred through kin ties and through long-term connections.

Such relationships diffuse the boundaries between the peoples of one society and another, and in the process diffuse the boundaries of the 'field'. Sometimes the boundaries are consciously mitigated, as when Killick found a Korean lover in the hope that an essence of the field would remain with him, or when Morton literally brought a part of her home to the field with her through a fetus in her womb. Altork states that the sensual nature of the field so touched her that some of the best lovemaking she's had with her husband took place during her fieldwork period. Moreno's suffering from the trauma she experienced in the field did not stop – indeed it intensified in certain respects – once she returned home.

Because of the kinds of relationship these people developed with people in their fieldsites, they could no longer regard the field as 'elsewhere', as Other and marginal to 'home' life; relationships with individuals of the fieldsite became central to these anthropologists' lives. Such relations make it difficult to accept the homogeneous mask that anthropology, through constructing difference generally as the boundary between sites of sameness, has traditionally placed on a studied society, or on categories within that society. The temptation here is to reduce difference to dichotomies of self/other, but as Henrietta Moore has noted, these categories are 'a feature of anthropological discourse rather than the social or symbolic systems of the societies studied by the anthropologists' (1993: 193). Gearing relates that her fiancé E.C. was 'different' from other men in St. Vincent and that because of their relationship it was impossible for her to accept any encompassing generalization that 'St. Vincent men are . . .' Dubisch reflects that Nikos, a Greek man with whom she had a brief affair, was similar to but also different from the 'usual' *kamaki*; thus her personalized knowledge of him disallowed her from generalizing about even that category of a male 'type'. Evelyn Blackwood discovered, in looking for 'sameness' in another lesbian, that she was continually confronted with 'difference' that made her reconsider implicit assumptions she had made about this category that included herself.

When the anthropologist's engagement with the people of a society is conceived as individualized interactions that include sexualized relationships (intimate or otherwise), the anthropologist's control of her or his subject position becomes an even more difficult fiction to maintain. This is particularly true for women. The passive 'feminine' metaphor for the field that Killick critiques has been convenient because the power to position is balanced in favor of the (implicitly male) ethnographer. Such a construction does, however, not always reflect the gendered reality of the relationship of sexuality and dominance between ethnographer and the people in the field with whom they work closely. When Peter Wade (1993) and a female research assistant became lovers, the power balance, as he notes, was clearly established in his favor and reflected the traditionally male dominant role. However, Morton – and other female anthropologists – have noted how they were sexually positioned during interviews or in other ways not taken 'seriously' by male informants: Gearing was only taken seriously by male informants when she was accompanied by her husband. In these interactions, sexuality and dominance became issues whether the women wanted them to or not. The importance of this gendered dynamic is most graphically expressed in Eva Moreno's revelation that her rapist was her field assistant.

In all of these encounters and relationships, the anthropologist is not acting as an isolated agent. Fieldwork relationships involve at least two points of view: that of the ethnographer and that of the individuals who inhabit the area being researched. What is their reaction to the anthropologist? The concept of the untouched 'tribe' that has no knowledge of the West still holds power as an image, but has little relevance to current fieldsites. When anthropologists come to a fieldsite, particularly in recent years, the society they encounter typically has a preconceived image of *them*, as people returning to home communities for fieldwork (cf. Altork and El-Solh 1988) or as foreigners, the latter being the situation of this volume's contributors. The Westerner is often perceived by people in a non-Western host society as a commodity for future wealth and prestige – a mirror reflection of the view taken by anthropologists, who have implicitly conceived of the field as a commodity that they trade for future academic prestige. Approaches by locals that the anthropologist interprets as being directed at her or him as an individual may actually be directed to an almost indiscriminate representative of an already established group. This happened to Morton with her first – of many – marriage proposals. Killick notes that many Korean women who date foreign men decide they want to marry a foreigner before they ever meet a specific person.

Thus it would appear that anthropologists who are Westerners in non-Western fieldsites can represent for the people they meet both the wealth of the West and the West's power to exploit. This dual perception in turn affects how anthropologists may try to, or may be forced to, negotiate how they reconstruct their genders and sexuality. In a city where the general assumption among Koreans was that Western men exploited Korean women, Killick realizes that he was at first seen by the Koreans as an uncouth American and then, when people knew his nationality, as an English gentleman. As Koreans formed an impression of his social standing, he became a prospective husband, valuable because of his overseas connections and particularly because he would possibly accept Korean women that Korean men had rejected because of age, physical height, or high level of education. As for Blackwood, she recognizes how the complications of her role as a Westerner created difficulties in her relationship with her lover Dayan, when she records that Dayan once asked if she was only being 'used' as an informant. Dayan is thus questioning the sincerity of Blackwood's affection for her, an insecurity embedded in almost unavoidable discourses of exploitation. Morton, Gearing, and Dubisch all had to contend in their fieldsite encounters with a prevailing stereotype that Western women were desirable and promiscuous. Morton relates that Western women represented, particularly to the young Tongan men, a desirable culture and a potential ticket overseas.

These prevailing images are in part a result of the kinds of interaction that have taken place previously between the indigenous population and 'outsiders'. Killick relates that in Seoul, the predominant image was created by American servicemen and businessmen. The sexual image of Asians in the West has focused on Asian women as sexually desirable, but has not generally portrayed Asian men in this way. These images, and the subsequent attitudes of a majority of Euro-American men in Korea, were major factors in the kind of image Killick had to contend with during his visit to Korea. The prevalent attitudes that Morton, Gearing, Moreno, and Dubisch encountered were considerably different. All but Moreno did fieldwork in areas where the local men – Polynesians, Caribbeans, and Greeks – are promoted in the West as sexually attractive. Thus a significant number of Euro-American single female tourists visiting these areas came looking for (or were certainly open to) sexual liaisons. This situation combined with local attitudes about gendered status, possession, and power to create the prevalent assumption that Western women were 'loose'. Dubisch even goes so far as to state that where she was working in Greece 'loose' and 'foreign' were nearly synonymous (p. 31). As Gearing notes, this image is particularly threatening to patriarchal and economically impoverished societies because it reverses 'the normal balance of economic power and class relations' (Chapter 7, p. 196). The image can also be a symbol of conquest over the Western exploiter and work 'as a means of expressing and challenging economic and political inequalities' (Bowman 1988: 77). Or, as both Morton and Moreno point out, 'loose' is the signifier of lack of authorial control and is also a connection with an adventure with the other, of which a foreign woman – replete with explicitly sexual media representation – is a potent metaphor.

I would suggest that nearly any woman outsider who cannot be controlled by the norms of the dominant society is typecast as loose: loose because she is truly independent, and because she is not corralled by the male-ordered society. Dubisch is talking about a power differential when she notes that when a Western woman – who is the Other in her own culture and has lived with the attendant subordinate role – moves into a Southern European or Third World patriarchy, her status as subordinate becomes balanced by her increased status as a Euro-American. This difference gives women the potential for temporary freedom in other cultures that they seldom know in their own. In some ways it is harder to confront sexism in one's own society because one is intrinsically within the system it dominates. In another culture, a woman can move outside its rules, can use marginal status as a refusal to accept the cultural standards. She is in a position to *choose* which norms she wants to comply with and which ones she may want to ignore, depending upon how 'respectable' or 'deviant' (cf. Lederman 1970) she wants to be in the society at large. In a foreign culture, it is sometimes far easier to have the freedom to be 'loose', as Morton found during her youthful visit to Tonga.

Anthropologists, however, have a stake in being 'accepted' by the society in which they research: they need to *live* there, so they must counteract negative stereotypic images as much as possible. Morton, Gearing, and Dubisch all state that they had to present themselves as consistent with the prevailing image of respectable womanhood. The combination of gendered subject positioning and prevalent attitudes in patriarchal societies means that the woman anthropologist often has to negotiate (and is expected to refuse) continual amorous advances, while the man is often expected to make them (cf. Whitehead and Conaway 1986). Killick writes of a potential suitor being discreetly presented to him, but this was not a direct sexual advance by the woman. Implicit in the encounter is that the man, unlike women, is allowed to take control of the situation. The woman's choice is to accept the male advances or try to deflect them. Thus, as Dubisch notes, the woman ethnographer could find that a sexual encounter in the field is a 'threat to [her] 'privileged' position as an anthropologist' (p. 39), a threat that, as she also wryly suggests, may be perceived more strongly by the anthropologist herself than by her male informants, who never acknowledged her 'privileged' position from the outset. A woman who tries to represent herself as being in control of her own sexuality can run the risk of violent attack to 'correct' the power balance – an important dimension of the assault on Moreno. This is not the kind of censorship a male anthropologist faces. Any woman, foreign or otherwise, who takes control can become perceived as a threat to the order of a patriarchal society.

In this discussion of gendered censorship and patriarchal society let us not neglect to include the dictates of the society which the anthropologist calls 'home'. Dubisch writes that the concept of the field has 'implicit hierarchies of dominance which govern its conduct . . . The Other is more forbidden to the Western woman than to the Western man' (p. 34). She cites Newton (1993: 15) as pointing out that a 'veil of professional silence covers the face of indulgence toward men's casual sex with women in the field'. 'Female anthropologists', Dubisch writes, 'have not been granted such professional indulgence, whether their sexual encounters occur in their own society or in the field' (p. 34). By including the sexual mores of the ethnographer's society in their discussion as well as those of the informants, she and Bolton describe how Western cultural norms of 'respectability' and 'appropriate behavior' affect an author's credibility. Such norms have been explicitly deployed in attempts to discredit anthropologists, particularly women. Perhaps the most recent example of this is Derek Freeman's continuing attacks on Margaret Mead.

In a recent instalment of this 'debate', in which Samoans are merely a backdrop to a controversy that centers on Western textual authority and power (cf. Foerstel and Gilliam 1992), Freeman has insinuated that Mead's personal sexuality, in the United States and in Samoa, discredits her abilities as an ethnographer (Freeman 1991).[3] In an article published in *Visual Anthropology Review*, Freeman mentions affairs that Mead may have had with Ruth Benedict and Edward Sapir. He also discusses an affair she may have had in the field with a Samoan man. He claims that this alleged affair, affronting as it did the ceremonial status she had been given as a *taupou* (ceremonial virgin), was a major reason her female informants lied to her.[4]

It is not surprising that this target of public sexual gossip is a woman. As Ruth Landes has written,

> Though the woman field worker might be considered an honorific man by title, she was appraised and censored as a *private* woman-person by the patriarchal cultures she studied as well as by most of her male colleagues . . . A competing male Negro, Latin, Oriental is attacked for his scorned minority rank; a male Jew, Catholic, or Jehovah's Witness is belittled for his low-ranked or embattled religion; until recently male homosexuality constituted egregious vulnerability for a professional person . . . With a woman for a rival, many men and women have no need to seek her secondary traits of race, religion or national origin; her sex alone will suffice.
> (1970: 124, emphasis in original)

Landes' perception of the place of women in academic life arose in part from her own experience of having a rival Afro-Brazilianist scholar (Artur Ramos) make a series of accusations about her lack of scholarship and insinuations about her 'erotic' behavior (Landes 1970).

Such attacks against professional women can take many forms, of which fiction and the mass media – because of the large audiences they command – are among the most powerful. As Landes notes, these attacks 'cast the women's ways in an unfavorable light, making them appear ludicrous, suggesting that they are also astray socially' (1970: 124). A recent example of such characterizations is the role of 'Lucinda', an anthropology professor, in the American television series *Beverly Hills 90210*. 'Lucinda' is a worldly white woman with ethnic jewelry, unruly hair, and feminist sympathies. Her lectures are confined to racy topics like 'the yoke of monogamy' or female fecundity. When not sitting on the floor informing her (seemingly exclusively) female students about exotic sexual customs, 'Lucinda' actively pursues handsome male undergraduates (in a pointed reversal of the overwhelmingly more common situation of a male professor seducing his female students). In virtually every scene in which 'Lucinda' appears, she is either highlighted as destructive and vaguely evil, or she is openly humiliated, usually by the male undergraduates she spends so much of her time attempting to seduce.[5]

These kinds of portrayal of female anthropologists draw on and promote a value system in which a woman with authority is a threat to a male established order; a threat that can be diffused by displacing authority with sex. Those who use these representations have been able to utilize this moral standard, set particularly for women, as a weapon in the war of professional competition. It would appear that the woman Altork mentions who was afraid that revelation of a sexual involvement in the field would discredit her (p. 120) was reacting to cultural norms she knew only too well. A man who has an affair in the field may be in danger of being labeled in certain circles with the stereotype of the male explorer-exploiter (cf. Killick), while in other circles he might meet with approval or encouragement. In either case, his actions do not threaten the assumed hierarchy of superior-active-male-First-World-ethnographer complex, while a woman who has affairs or in other ways states explicitly her independence does.

Given such a prevailing acceptance of female censorship, it is intriguing but not surprising that the reality of sexual harassment and sexual assault is almost never mentioned in field manuals, even recently published ones. Nor, as Gearing notes, is it a topic discussed in fieldwork preparation courses. Nor, in my personal experience, do many female anthropologists discuss it openly either before they leave for the field or after they return. Yet, as illustrated by Morton, Gearing, and Moreno (and Howell 1990), it clearly exists. Euro-American society has begun to acknowledge the daily threat for women of sexual violence in its own backyard (particularly high in the United States), but within the anthropological community, while we now discuss academic harassment, sexual violence in the field is, if possible, an even more taboo topic than sex itself.

It seems amazing that the threat of sexual violence has not entered anthropological discourse; yet the reasons are obvious. First of all, since the victims are overwhelmingly women, it has been possible for men to avoid discussing it and not to take it seriously. Secondly, to contend with the realities of sexual violence and its relationship to male dominance – which extends into the academic world – men would have to contend with the entire realm of sexual harassment, an issue that is only being marginally accepted as relevant right now. In addition, the traditional role of fieldwork as a probation period of initiation, of macho conquest and ordeal, has made women students loath to mention the subject. After all, the men in power could tell us that therefore we shouldn't be considering fieldwork in the first place, or, equally insidious, they could censor women's access to fieldsites, pushing us toward the safer, 'softer' sites and reserving the adventurous ones as the terrain for men only. Isn't this what Boas did to Margaret Mead when he tried to prevent her from going to Samoa? Also, as Gearing notes, the role of the woman in sexual intimidation and assault is still ambiguous in Western society; a female anthropologist may feel, justifiably, that she will be 'blamed' for enticing such violent attention and, by speaking out, damage (or compromise) her professional status.

Sexual violence, both physical and emotional, was a prominent aspect of the fieldwork experience for Gearing, Morton, and Moreno. During much of my own doctoral fieldwork experience in urban Papua New Guinea, the threat of sexual violence was so high that I continually carried, and slept with, an illegal bottle of mace that had been given to me by a female anthropologist who was then working in Papua New Guinea's major city. This bottle was one of two that passed woman to woman as one researcher left and another arrived. Gearing notes that a major emotion she felt in the field was fear of sexual violence and that this strongly affected the subject position she assumed. Gearing and others feel they have to present themselves as sexually unavailable not just to be respectable, but in order to stave off possible assault. Gearing writes that because of these fears, her movements and friendships were curtailed. Although she became engaged to her primary informant for other reasons, she found in him reassurance and protection against possible sexual attack, reflecting the fact that a woman, to be 'safe' from male assaults, is often expected to place herself under the protection of a man (cf. Golde 1986; Landes 1970). Morton was continually intimidated by sexualized acts of dominance, which she, because of her differing cultural background and lack of fluency in the language, was unable to diffuse. Morton, Gearing, and Dubisch took pains to behave modestly and to separate themselves as much as possible from the tourist image. Yet Morton and Gearing note that for both of them the sexual harassment didn't stop until they were each in the advanced months of pregnancy, when their connection to a man was physically obvious. Moreno's account shows graphically how, piece by piece, her sense of self-determination was eroded. She was under constant threat of sexual violence, made worse by the fact that the very person who was threatening her was also in a position to make her dependent on him. The more she tried to correct the situation, the worse it got.

Relationships that include sexual domination and control can become volatile quickly – in the field and in the home countries of the ethnographers. Sexual violence is of course a problem that simultaneously includes and extends beyond the realms of women and anthropology. That the existence of sexual violence toward the ethnographer in the field has been virtually ignored in the anthropological literature speaks volumes about how even 'reflexivity' has only confronted issues that hold little threat for those who control the pen.

Personal perspectives: a sexual self within the subject

Henrietta Moore, in writing about similarities and difference 'within categories and entities' (1993: 202), notes that 'In spite of ethnographic data to the contrary, much anthropological writing on the self still proceeds on the implicit assumption that the physically discrete nature of the body is somehow evidence for the unity of the person' (1993: 203). In this, she has tied together not only the Western notions of the self as independent and free-acting, but also the concept that self-identity is somehow enclosed within an indivisible body. Many ethnographers go to the field with the illusion that their identity, like their body, is discrete and impenetrable, that although their public persona is controllable and flexible, they have an inner identity, a kind of holy ground, like a silent pool of water, that nothing will touch.

Their identity is, of course, touchable, and is embedded in not just how a person conceives of herself or himself but also how others react to her or him, to the gendered body – and to *parts* of that body. Contributors to this volume have noted how the symbolism and use of one part of the body, such as the eye, can define how a person is perceived and can reflect her or his status. The eye is considered in many cultures an entrance into the inner self. People from the United States are widely recognized by their direct gaze, which North Americans tend to associate with honesty. Chinese friends have told me they consider such a gaze an intrusion of privacy, while Brazilians associate it with sexual flirtation. Csordas writes that 'We less often conceptualize visual attention as a "turning toward" than as a disembodied, beam-like "gaze." We tend to think of it as a cognitive function rather than a bodily engagement' (1993: 138). This gaze is well symbolized in feminist literature as possession; the mesmerizing hold of the snake is its eyes; the power of the eye to hold sexually or otherwise is the stuff of myth and literature. Kate Altork states that she found eye contact useful in opening sensual and communicative doors with firefighters in the United States, but the communication in her case came in part because both she and these men were North American and white. Had they been from differing ethnic backgrounds, the gaze of either party could have been misinterpreted. Mutual projections such as this can easily lead to communicative – and sexual – misunderstanding.

Visual attention is not just a bodily engagement, it is a powerful symbol of dominance. Thus Gearing, when confronted by the 'rude boys' on the streets in St. Vincent, avoided eye contact and assumed the inferior role by casting her eyes to the ground. Here her eyes had no power and did not challenge the 'rude boys' to a contest of dominance, as would have been inevitable if she had glanced at them. Her only way to counter the eye challenge was in the 'talk': clever sexualized repartee that took contextual knowledge and language skills she had not yet mastered. Morton, in similar situations, was told by her Tongan friends to respond to the men's harassment by shoving her buttocks in their direction, implying (among other things) that their challenge was not worth engaging with her eyes but only with her backside. In all of these cases, the use of one body part (the eye) held power and meaning as a specific agent within the body whole; the relevance of similarity and difference was a division not just between bodies, but between contextualized parts of bodies, each of which could help maintain or decenter the stability of the ethnographer's identity.

Another aspect of embodiment that concerned several contributors was contextualized concepts of 'attractiveness' and how these representations of physicality contained evaluations of hierarchy and cultural difference. Several contributors became aware that their 'attractiveness' to others was defined by different standards in the field and at home. Bolton speculates that he was more popular in the field because he was 'more fully alive' (p. 150). Dubisch comments that the modest clothing she wore out of deference to the religious pilgrims who were the center of her research set her apart from the tourists in the area. When a *kamaki* does approach her, she notes with humor that it was at the end of the season when fewer female tourists were available for attention. Killick tries to examine why Korean American women were attracted to him when he was – as he describes himself – a nerdy bookworm type, and not the macho masculine type favored by most Korean women. He found that in Hawaii his interest in Korea set him off from most other non-Korean men, increasing his attractiveness to Korean-descent woman and making him less foreign. He likewise found that the women to whom he was initially attracted were Korean Americans (as distinct from Koreans), in part because he felt that their expectations of the relationship would be more similar to his and because with them he didn't feel he was slipping into the 'white guy exploiting Asian women' mold. Blackwood became confused about which parts of her were valued as 'attractive' by Dayan, as Dayan continuously signaled that she was attracted to Blackwood's *feminine* image and role, not the *feminist* ones that Blackwood herself valued. Morton notes that on her first visit to Tonga, she was charmed by all the attention she received from these men who were, in her eyes, extremely attractive. This attention made her feel more attractive herself. Then later, when she returned to the field as a woman attached to a male outsider, she realized another dimension of attractiveness: now in a non-competing realm, as regards male attention, Morton and her potential to attract (attached) men became less threatening to other women (and they likewise to her). It would appear that the meanings of 'attractiveness', being contextual, are one aspect of how an anthropologist negotiates her or his self-presentation.

Ethnographers who have written reflexively about themselves as sexual beings in the field have often noted how they felt obliged in their self-presentation to take a specific sexual and personal identity: as asexual, naive, chaste, non-threatening, or as supposedly sexually active (cf. Landes 1970; Whitehead and Conaway 1986). Such conflicts of self-representation are clear in the chapters by Dubisch, Morton, Blackwood, and Gearing when they describe how they manipulate their field personae, weaving and exchanging one presented identity for another, changing with context as a chameleon changes. This self-representation is perceived as a public persona in contrast to a stable, unchanging, interior self. Yet both Gearing and Morton, who married men from their field areas and who both tried to adapt to their husbands' lifestyle and world view as a way of life, found that they began to create fictional identities that grew and grew until, after returning to their homes with their husbands, these became a burden they could no longer carry. Their relationships with their husbands were at first contained and structured by the societies that were their husbands' homes. When the women returned with their husbands to their own home countries, where the societies were constituted differently, the measure of difference became acute and, in both cases, ended in separation.

What then is the relationship between self-representation, identity, similarity, and difference? What happens when the ethnographer's 'holy ground' of self-identity is challenged? Evelyn Blackwood writes about her struggles to keep her lesbian identity intact in an exclusively heterosexual field environment, and Eva Moreno writes about how the man who later raped her gradually eroded her identity and self-determination. Blackwood became involved in a sexual relationship in part for exactly the same reasons that Wengle (1988) believes cause anthropologists to remain celibate: namely, identity maintenance. She found in her relationship with Dayan a reaffirmation of identity and connectedness to 'home'. While working in Indonesia, she 'missed everything that was part of the self [she'd] left behind. [She] was tired of being someone for somebody else' (p. 60). Indeed, the need to have her lesbian identity recognized became so strong that first she told her Indonesian 'mother', an act that could have threatened her entire research, and later made concerted efforts to find another lesbian. When she did meet Dayan and became her lover, she clung to her own identity of 'lesbian', applying this to Dayan despite continual confusion over their differences. They each, of necessity, reconstructed the other to be a reflection of their own self-identity. In this way Blackwood protected her own identity through her misconception of sameness with another lesbian as much as through the actual involvement itself. Because she had a marginal status as a lesbian in her home society, she had developed an identity related to that marginality rather than trusting her identity to the society at large. Thus, as noted earlier, her reaffirmation of self came through a connection to others of that marginal category rather than to any specific place or society. That the lesbian reflection she thought she saw in Dayan was illuminated largely by her own cultural biases was an insight she only gained through time, consideration, and distance from the context of the involvement.

Blackwood's search for similarity and equality led to an uneasy reaffirmation of identity; Moreno's led to an assault on her identity, to collapse and reconstruction. For Moreno, the aspects of her identity connected to the influences of culture, such as ethnicity, profession, and gender, began to disintegrate when faced with the continual, undermining threat of sexual violence. She relates vividly how her cultural standards of ethnic and professional equality backfired as she tried to adapt them to Ethiopian class hierarchy. Her desire to find a research assistant who would be similar to her – in education and world outlook

– allowed her to overlook differences and made her less alert to the dangers of manipulation. The tortuous process of becoming increasingly dependent upon a man who continually sexually harassed her began gradually to dismantle her connections to herself, piece by piece. She found herself in a seemingly inescapable vortex where her ability to resolve the situation decreased while, at the same time, his threats to her became increasingly violent. Her self-assurance and connection to reality continued to disintegrate as everything she did and said was 'misunderstood' by her assistant. And finally came his rape of her and his insidious monologue, through which she began to understand that their entire interaction – indeed her interaction with the whole town – was being effectively manipulated by her assistant. Her stability of identity was replaced by fear; her identity lay in pieces around her, to be collected only after many years.

Much to her surprise, after the rape, it was her experience of sexual assault that bridged the differences between herself and the women of her research area, because she was suddenly someone who was 'similar' to them through her violent experience with her assistant. Through this deconstruction and reconstruction of her self, Moreno was forced to confront how aspects of difference and similarity, when they explode into sexual violence, reveal how fragile identity is, both for the person who holds it and for those one encounters.

The identity of self is not a constant, nor is the landscape of the Other: each affects the other and changes through time. Morton, through literally changing her body by coming to Tonga pregnant, thus changed her sexual engagement with the Tongan landscape. The two are inexorably connected. Likewise, in relation to continued field visits over many years, she, Killick, and Dubisch all recognize that their own maturation in body and perspective affects their self-identity and their relationship to the field. They have changed, and the areas which they had visited previously have changed as well. And their sexuality was integral to that change. Until anthropologists admit to being sexual beings, and admit that the sexuality of those with whom they work affects them, the discipline is in danger of continuing to ignore several vital issues. The censorship here could be compared to problems some groups have in dealing with the AIDS epidemic: in order to explore the possibilities of safer sex, the realities of sexual practice have first to be acknowledged publicly. Likewise, in anthropology, only by acknowledging our sexuality can we begin to deal effectively with sexual violence, sexual ethics in the field ('don't do it' doesn't work), and other issues – such as the unresolved relationship of sexual immediacy in the field and the unrelenting professional focus on rationalist objectivity – that indicate an inherent weakness in the fundamentals of anthropological theory. Toward this endeavor for exploration this volume offers a beginning.

Acknowledgements

I wish to thank Don Kulick, friend and colleague, not only for his insightful contributions to this afterword (which were considerable) but also for his humor and collaboration during the entire endeavour, from its conception as we discussed the idea over lunch at the Australia National University, through our growing excitement over the breadth of what we'd set ourselves to explore. This kind of partnership is rare and my appreciation of it is enormous. I also wish to thank others for their contributions to earlier versions of this afterword, particularly the anonymous reader at Routledge, Evelyn Blackwood, Kate Altork, Andrew P. Killick, Jonathan Benthall, and Michael Young. In addition, I am grateful to our contributors for their unflagging commitment through all rewrites, our editor at Routledge, Heather Gibson, for her support and humor, and Shelley Carberry for word processing and patience. The Research School for Pacific Studies Anthropology Department at the Australian National University and the Anthropology Department at Western Washington University both provided much appreciated support during various phases of the project.

Notes

1 See Wade 1993 for a related discussion.
2 It should be noted that in her situation, the power differential was relatively equal, her reputation in the field was not in question, the parameters of the relationship seemed clearly defined, and issues of danger were not a central concern.
3 Marshall (1993) has analyzed Freeman's word usage to show how he validates his own authority and undermines Mead's. Throughout the article of Freeman's considered here, he does a similar thing, using word and paragraph placement to develop innuendo that Mead was unprofessional in her sexual behavior, that it influenced others' opinion of her, and that she was neurotic. These insinuations lead directly to his conclusion that she was an inadequate ethnographer. His own sexual behavior and its relation to his own ethnographic authority are, of course, never mentioned.
4 A primary informant, Fa' apua'a, was also a *taupou* in the same polity as Mead, making Mead, according to Freeman, her potential rival, a rival who in Fa' apua'a's eyes was unqualified to be a *taupou*. Samoan friends at

the Australian National University, who often argued between themselves about anthropological representations of Samoans, told me that Fa' apua'a was unlikely to consider Mead a rival because both the statuses accorded to Mead as *taupou*, and to Freeman as a ceremonial chief, were gestures of public hospitality given to high-ranking outsiders. They were thus accorded the status of these roles but not the authority. In addition, according to these same Samoan friends, the public naming of the Samoan man in the alleged affair, who is still alive, brought the man, and his wife, unfortunate and unnecessary shame and embarrassment. In Freeman's gossip about Mead's relationships, the wishes of the Samoan man involved were never considered; he was simply an Other for whom the ramifications of this article were never apparently considered by Freeman.

5 Thanks to Barbara Miller for first pointing out the existence of *Beverly Hills 90210* and 'Lucinda' to Don Kulick (and he to me), to Kristen Elmquist for supplying us with videotapes of the relevant episodes, and to Shelley Carbery for her insights on the series.

References

Altorki, Soraya and Camillia Fawzi El-Solh (eds) (1988) *Arab Women in the Field: Studying Your Own Society*. Syracuse, N.Y.: Syracuse University Press.

Bowman, Glen (1989) 'Fucking Tourists: Sexual Relations and Tourism in Jerusalem's Old City'. *Critique of Anthropology*. Vol. 9, pp. 77–93.

Crapanzano, Vincent (1986) 'Hermes' Dilemma: The Making of Subversion in Ethnographic Description', in James Clifford and George E. Marcus (eds) *Writing Culture*. Berkeley, Calif.: Univerisity of California Press.

Csordas, Thomas (1993) 'Somic Modes of Attention'. *Cultural Anthropology*. Vol. 8, No. 2, pp. 135–56.

del Valle, Teresa (ed.) (1993) *Gendered Anthropology*. London: Routledge.

Foerstel, Lenara and Angela Gilliam (eds) (1992) *Confronting the Margaret Mead Legacy: Scholarship, Empire and the South Pacific*. Philadelphia: Temple University Press.

Freeman, Derek (1991) 'There's Tricks i' th' World: An Historical Analysis of the Samoan Researches of Margaret Mead'. *Visual Anthropology Review*. Vol. 7, No. 1, pp. 103–28.

Golde, Peggy (ed) (1986) *Women in the Field: Anthropological Experiences*. Berkeley, Calif.: University of California Press.

Hastrup, Kirsten (1992) 'Writing Ethnography: The State of the Art', in Judith Okely and Helen Callaway (eds) *Anthropology and Autobiography*. London and New York: Routledge.

Howell, Nancy (1990) *Survey Fieldwork: A Report of the Advisory Panel on Health and Safety in Fieldwork*. Special Publication of the American Anthropological Association 26. Washington, D.C.: American Anthropological Association.

Landes, Ruth (1970) 'A Woman Anthropologist in Brazil', in Peggy Golde (ed.) *Women in the Field*. Berkeley, Calif.: University of California Press.

Lederman, Rena (1970) 'The Return of Red Woman: Fieldwork in Highland New Guinea', in Peggy Golde (ed.) *Women in the Field*. Berkeley, Calif.: University of California Press.

Marshall, Mac (1993) 'The Wizard of Oz Meets the Wicked Witch of the East:

Freeman, Mead and Ethnographic Authority'. *American Ethnologist*, Vol. 20, No. 3, pp. 604–17.

Moore, Henrietta (1993) 'The Difference Within and the Difference Between', in Diane Bell, Pat Caplan, and Wazir Jahan Karim (eds) in *Gendered Fields: Women, Men and Ethnography*. London and New York: Routledge.

Newton, Esther (1993) 'My Best Informant's Dress: The Erotic Equation in Fieldwork'. *Cultural Anthropology*. Vol. 8, No. 1, pp. 3–23.

Pratt, Mary Louise (1986) 'Fieldwork in Common Places', in James Clifford and George E. Marcus (eds) *Writing Culture*. Berkeley, Calif.: University of California Press.

Stoller, Paul (1989) *The Taste of Ethnographic Things: The Senses in Anthropology*. Philadelphia: University of Pennylvania Press.

Wade, Peter (1993) 'Sexuality and Masculinity among Columbian Blacks', in Diane Bell, Pat Caplan, and Wazir Jahan Karim (eds) *Gendered Fields: Women, Men and Ethnography*. London and New York: Routledge.

Wengle, John L. (1988) *Ethnographers in the Field: The Psychology of Research*. Tuscaloosa, Ala.: University of Alabama Press.

Whitehead, Tony Larry and Mary Ellen Conaway (eds) (1986) *Self, Sex and Gender in Cross-cultural Fieldwork*. Urbana and Chicago: University of Illinois Press.

Index